Believers in Business

LAURA L. NASH, Ph.D.

THOMAS NELSON PUBLISHERS
Nashville • Atlanta • London • Vancouver

Published in Nashville, Tennessee, by Thomas Nelson, Inc., Publishers, and distributed in Canada by Word Communications, Ltd., Richmond, British Columbia, and in the United Kingdom by Word (UK), Ltd., Milton Keynes, England.

Unless otherwise noted, Scripture quotations are from the NEW KING JAMES VERSION of the Bible. Copyright © 1979, 1980, 1982, Thomas Nelson, Inc., Publishers.

Scripture quotations noted NIV are taken from the HOLY BIBLE, NEW INTERNATIONAL VERSION ®. Copyright © 1973, 1978, 1984 by International Bible Society. Used by permission of Zondervan Bible Publishing House. All rights reserved.

The "NIV" and "New International Version" trademarks are registered in the United States Patent and Trademark Office by International Bible Society. Use of either trademark requires the permission of International Bible Society.

Library of Congress Cataloging-in-Publication Data

Nash, Laura L.
    Believers in business / Laura L. Nash.
        p. cm.
    Includes bibliographical references.
    ISBN 0-7852-8181-9
    1. Executives—United States—Religious life. 2. Executives—United States—Conduct of life. 3. Evangelicalism—United States. 4. Business ethics—United States. I. Title.
BV4596.E93N37 1994
261.8'5'0973—dc20
                                                                94-25706
                                                                CIP

Printed in the United States of America

1 2 3 4 5 6 7 - 00 99 98 97 96 95 94

Acknowledgments

F or one who is not a professional theologian or sociologist of religion, it is hard to talk about God in diagnostic terms. Even when the topic is other people's relation to their God, one's own religious experience intrudes, or retreats into a corner in the search for objectivity. Which is worse?

This book became more difficult to write as time went on, and there are several people whose encouragement and advice must be acknowledged gratefully. Peter L. Berger first proposed the idea and as director of Boston University's Institute for the Study of Economic Culture, granted funds from ISEC for the research and writing. Special gratitude is due the Sarah Scaife Foundation and the Lynde and Harry Bradley Foundation. Berger's unflagging support and interest, even to the point of attending some of the interviews, was of invaluable help. The fact that he nearly got us arrested by walking into a restricted prayer room at the First Methodist Church in Dallas is beside the point. He still deserves thanks for his help. His own writings in this area, as well as his recent Noble Lectures at Harvard[1], were an invaluable influence on this book. Any shortcomings here, however, are my own.

Several theologians and clergy offered help at the outset. Professors Harvey Cox, Ralph Potter, and Dean Ronald Thiemann at Harvard University School of Divinity sent me prodigious reading lists. They later contributed invaluable feedback at a session of the joint Harvard Divinity and Business School luncheons on business ethics, as did Kenneth Andrews and the rest of the participants, including my colleagues from Boston University School of Theology. The Rev. Paul Toms at Park Street Church, Rev. Howard Clark at Grace Chapel in Lexington, Massachusetts (formerly of Northwest Bible Church in Dallas), and President Robert Cooley of Gordon Conwell Seminary provided invaluable insight into the issues to be confronted, as well as help in identifying interviewees. Thanks also are due to professors Stan Gaede and David Wells at Gordon College, President J. Richard Chase and Professor Paul DeVrie at Wheaton College (Illinois), Prof. James Hunter (Univ. of Virginia), and Prof. Stephen Mott (Gordon Conwell Seminary). Os Guinness (The Trinity Forum), Senator William L. Armstrong, Ted DeMoss of Christian Business Men's Committee of USA, Ambassador Doug Holladay (One-on-One), Jerry White of the Navigators, and Jarrell McCracken provided further advice and contacts. Their generosity and help truly made the project possible.

Many of the CEOs who were interviewed offered special help in the way of further contacts and support: Tom Phillips, Elmer Johnson, Robert Buford, Jack Feldballe, Allen Morris, and Charles Olcott particularly so. Howard Butt and the Laity Lodge Leadership Forum were a constant source of ideas and information, as well as friendship. Harry Rosenberg literally made the downtown Chicago interviews happen.

All of the executives who agreed to be interviewed deserve particular acknowledgement for their essential contribution to this book. A good number wish to remain anonymous. Others would not be strictly called evangelicals, and would not wish to be so called. But each made available their thoughts and experiences with business and the evangelical community. Those whose names I have permission to print are in the following list. Their position at the time of our interview is listed first, and their current position, if changed, is listed in parenthesis:

Charles I. Babco, Jr., Chairman, King Charter Company

Arnold B. Bandstra, Chicago Metro Director, Christian Business Men's Committee of USA

James Batten, Chairman and CEO, Knight-Ridder, Inc.

James F. Beré, Chairman and CEO, Borg-Warner Corporation (deceased)

Robert P. Buford, Chairman of the Board and CEO, Buford Television, Inc.

Philip Caldwell, Chairman of the Board and CEO (retired), Ford Motor Company

Richard G. Capen, Jr., Publisher, *The Miami Herald* (Ambassador and consultant)

James C. Caraher, President, The Caraher Corporation

James H. Carreker, President and CEO, Wyndham Hotels & Resorts (President, Trammell Crow and Wyndham Hotels & Resorts)

Alvah H. Chapman, Jr., Chairman of the Board, Knight-Ridder, Inc. (Director and Chairman of the Executive Committee, Knight-Ridder, Inc.)

Richard Crowell, The Boston Company (President, PanAgora Asset Management)

Jerry E. Dempsey, Chairman, Chemical Waste Management (Chairman and CEO, PPG Industries, Inc.)

Robert H. Denckhoff, Jr., President, Ga-Vehren Engineering

Max De Pree, Chairman of the Board of Directors, Herman Miller, Inc.

Edward A. Elliott, President, Domain Audio Services

Allan C. Emery, Jr., Director, The ServiceMaster Company

Jack Feldballe, CEO, Renaissance Video

Alberto Fernandez Gr., Executive Director, PYOSA

Thomas G. Gerendas, President, Temptronic Corporation

Gary D. Ginter, Executive Vice-President, CRT (Managing Director, Globex Corporation)

William R. Haljun, Leo Burnett, Inc. (Managing Partner, The Neighbor Group)

Herbert C. Hansen, Sawyer, Michigan (retired)

Vester T. Hughes, Jr., Dallas, Texas

Elmer W. Johnson, Partner, Kirkland & Ellis

Thomas O. Jones, formerly President & CEO, Epsilon, Inc.

George Kohl, Fifield Reality (Senior Vice President, Frain, Camins & Swartchild)

James Kubik, Executive President and Principal, Griffin, Kubik, Stephens, & Thompson

George M. Kubricht, President, ComCorp & Energes Inc.

Paul Kuck, Chairman and CEO, Regal Marine Industries

Steve Letson, Director of Operations, Dallas Mavericks

Mrs. Colman Mockler (Joanna)

Patrick M. Morley, President and CEO, Morley Properties (Patrick Morley Ministries)

W. Allen Morris, President and CEO, The Allen Morris Company

Charles Olcott, Chief Operating Officer, AquaFuture, Inc.

Thomas L. Phillips, Chairman & CEO, Raytheon Company (retired)

William H. Rentschler, President and CEO, The Medart Company (President and CEO, First American Private Counselors)

Frederick E. Roach, President & CEO, Centennial Homes, Inc. (President, The Leadership Center, Baylor Health Care System)

Jeff Semenchuk, ComCorp, Inc. (Director, VIA International Ltd.)

James M. Seneff, Jr., Orlando, Florida
Dennis W. Sheehan, Chairman, President, and CEO, AXIA, Inc.
Fred Smith, Dallas, Texas
John C. Snyder, Chairman, Snyder Oil Corporation
Norm Sonju, Chief Operating Officer and General Manager, Dallas Mavericks
Jack Turpin, Founder & Chairman, Hall-Mark Electronics Corp. (Chairman, Hall-Mark Energy, Inc.)
Frederick G. Wacker, Chairman of the Board, Liquid Controls Corporation
Stephen J. Waters, Jr., President, Miami Savings Bank (deceased)
Kenneth Wessner, Chairman, The ServiceMaster Company (deceased)
Ed Williamson, President, Williamson Cadillac Company
Jack Willome, President, Rayco Ltd.
Edmund R. Yates, President, Highland Park Cafeterias, Inc.
Zig Ziglar, President, The Zig Ziglar Corporation

And thanks to all those who, though they wished to remain anonymous, also contributed their time and wisdom. As the reader will imagine, it took a certain degree of trust, perhaps even faith, to consent to an interview with a total stranger concerning such personal and important matters. My very deep thanks to all who took that leap.

L.L.N.
Cambridge, Massachusetts

Contents

Preface

I t is said that the Reverend Norman Vincent Peale and Kenneth Blanchard, while writing *The Power of Ethical Management,* agreed on the advice of their business editors to delete "prayer" as the final ethical principle listed in their book. They replaced it with "perspective."[1]

In my own experience, the issue of personal religion has appeared to be essentially a self-imposed taboo among the business ethics and management community. As a result, both the clergy and businesspeople have lost the opportunity to explore and understand the role of faith and prayer in people's working lives.

So when noted sociologist Peter L. Berger suggested I do a study of evangelical CEOs, I was immediately intrigued. It disturbed me to see the bias against discussing personal religious values exhibited by my former colleagues at Harvard Business School and elsewhere. I was also keenly aware of the religion gap within my own work. For example, I had conducted a detailed study of Johnson & Johnson's wonderful Credo and their corporate culture for the Business Roundtable's Task Force on Corporate Ethics.[2] It had struck me at the time that then-chairman Jim Burke's Roman Catholic background and Holy Cross undergraduate training had much to do with the ethical leadership of Johnson & Johnson. Yet nowhere did I or anyone else venture to probe further. It was the self-imposed taboo.

Most discussions of business ethics ignore personal religious belief as it relates to individual decision making. Instead, the discussions focus on these issues:

- The "proper values" for business, as theorized by economist Milton Friedman or sociologist Amitai Etzioni
- Impersonal systems analysis of compliance programs, such as stud-

ies of corporate ethics codes and training programs, or sociological analyses of corporate crime
- Specific events that raise important ethical dilemmas, from business school case studies to extremely perceptive dissections of corporate scandals in the business press

Like so many other aspects of business, this extreme secularity of corporate culture and its analysts reflect some larger trends in our society. Writer Garry Wills noted the same taboo on religion in the media coverage of the 1988 presidential campaign.[3] The personal religion of the candidates, said Wills, was really an odd factoid among other lifestyle details. It was something the public and the press never really understood, appreciated, or even acknowledged. Newspaper editors sent no experts on religion to cover the presidential campaigns. The Reverend Jesse Jackson was described by *Time* magazine as a "civil rights leader" rather than as a minister. Pat Robertson, also a minister, preferred to refer to himself as a CEO of a broadcasting station in the early days of his campaign.

So this book began with an urgency, not about understanding evangelicals, but about acknowledging the role of religion in business leadership. In fact, I knew next to nothing about evangelicals at the time. Reared in a Protestant Congregational tradition (and now attending Harvard University's Memorial Church), I was accustomed to very private, austere, New England-type expressions of religious faith. Public displays of personal affection for Jesus were not in my social vocabulary.

It's important to keep in mind that the questions that initially led me to do a study of evangelicals were much larger than evangelicalism itself. I was hoping to gain insight into how people who were completely committed to living a Christian life and who were successful in business approached their responsibility at work, whatever their denomination. Were they different? Did their religious commitments have any discernible effect on their behavior? How did they organize their companies? Did their Christian faith help them to answer the questions about business ethics that plague most businesspeople? How does a religious ethic based on love and service fit into a business ethic of competition and opportunism? What *is* the relationship between faith and economics?

Such questions are important to every Christian in business. But several factors make them particularly urgent for the evangelical, which is why this study is potentially so powerful. First of all, I had expected to find extreme differences between an evangelical's religious culture and his or her business life. Evangelicals are self-alleged "full-time Christians" in very overt and immediate ways. They use the Bible to regulate every aspect of their lives. They see themselves in a "personal relationship with Jesus," and they bear a responsibility to spread the "good news" about their faith.

None of these commitments seems to fit with the world of balance sheets, special-interest groups, material success, or pluralistic social groups such as the corporation. Can a person really be wildly successful at making money, keep that money, and still go to heaven? How do evangelicals personally deal with business problems? How do they make it to the top? Are they carefully concealing bloodstained hands, or has the "invisible hand" of free-market enterprise placed a recognizably religious grip on business? What is "the truth" behind a Max De Pree, renowned chairman of the board of Herman Miller Corporation, or a Tom Phillips of Raytheon?

Questions like these are not mere curiosities. They represent a door-way into one of the least understood and fastest growing subcultures in America and in American leadership. Despite the strong strain of conservative Protestantism in the political leadership of both the United States and (until recently) Great Britain, the general public is as unabashedly ignorant as I was about evangelicalism, and especially about the business practices of evangelicals. Surprisingly, even many evangelicals are unaware of what their brethren think about business issues.

Evangelicals are generally portrayed as either saints or demons. Such views are highly distorted—especially when they are applied to the ways that evangelicals handle business responsibility. I find that the skeptics tend to confuse all evangelical businesspeople with Jim and Tammy Bakker and other televangelists who misappropriated millions in the name of the Church. Equally naive, however, are the many believers who exhibit an almost infinite capacity for tolerating even the most flagrant moral lapses in financial stewardship by the self-proclaimed brethren. As one woman who gave her entire life savings to the PTL said with a mild shrug:

> It wasn't my money anyway. It was God's money, and He must have wanted it to go to that purpose.

Given this general state of uncritical acceptance or intolerance about conservative Christian business leaders among both the skeptics and the believers, and because I believe that prejudice in any form is morally abhorrent and socially destructive, I undertook this project. Boston University's Institute for the Study of Economic Culture gave me the needed financial support and the freedom to form my own conclusions about the data I gathered.

My purpose is simple: *to explore and explain how successful evangelical CEOs understand business responsibility from the standpoint of being personally committed to Jesus.*

In exploring this issue, a number of familiar moral questions about business arise:

- Can a person morally—as a Christian or simply as a humanist—seek a profit in a capitalistic system?
- Is there a just limit to profit seeking?
- What role does personal compassion play when the reality of scarce resources and multiple stakeholders guarantees that someone will be a loser?
- What is a person's individual responsibility when his or her moral power is curtailed by outside constraints?

The interviews—conducted with over eighty-five evangelical CEOs and a number of top executives from the next management tier—provide some rich and intimate insights into these questions. The fact that most of the interviewees have been outstanding economic performers also caused me to speculate on whether, and in what ways, the evangelical viewpoint has made these people better managers. A number of possible connections between business success and the evangelical worldview are evident throughout this book.

Keep in mind as you read this book that the interviewees are not fundamentalists—that is, people who take biblical passages more or less at face value. A fundamentalist would interpret "seven days" in Genesis to literally mean 168 hours. An evangelical might interpret it as a period of time divided into seven parts. Although they do not interpret every word in the Bible literally, the interviewees here are committed Christians with a robust sense that *believing* is an active verb—a full-time process of interacting with God—rather than a passive label to be displayed and forgotten. (A detailed definition of evangelicalism as represented among my interviewees appears in Chapter 1.)

All the executive interviewees were men, though I tried without success to interview women CEOs as well. For this reason I have used the masculine pronoun to refer to the interviewees throughout the book, even though it sounds hopelessly chauvinistic and biased at times. I suspect my difficulty in locating evangelical women who were CEOs was in part because they are underrepresented in the general population of business CEOs but also because I was relying on a men's network to locate other CEOS who were a) admired as being faithful Christians, b) had achieved success in their businesses, and c) were willing to talk with me. Most of these networks did not include women CEOs. The few women CEOs I did locate (two) were extremely afraid of being misrepresented, and preferred not to talk with me. I suspect they already have to deal with credibility problems in the workplace and did not want to run the risk of being perceived as a "religious freak." (This fear also held for many men who refused my request to be interviewed, especially in the Boston area where an unflattering article on evangelicals had just appeared in a local business magazine.)

Although there were notable exceptions, those I interviewed mentioned with remarkable regularity certain critical conflicts between business culture and their faith. For the purposes of analysis, I have divided these conflicts into seven "tensions," and have devoted one chapter to each tension. Any businessperson with an ounce of humanity will be familiar with most of these tensions. The other tensions, such as the degree to which one overtly discusses a religious element of his thinking, are particularly intense for the evangelical.

Briefly, I suggest that we can find among these evangelicals three basic personal responses to the traditional moral conflicts of business. The first two types of evangelicals, whom I call the *generalists* and the *justifiers,* are characterized by their denial of conflicting impulses. These two groups either ignore or rationalize potential discrepancies between "business as usual" and Christian ethics.

The third type of evangelical, whom I call the *seeker,* has a more complicated response. Rather than seeing business and Christianity as automatically compatible, the seekers find that faith does two things simultaneously: *It demands an awareness* of conflicting values, while it also *becomes the mediating factor* in the ongoing tensions between the musts of religion and the musts of business. This is a way of thinking that is best described as a creative paradox: The seekers reject the idea of business success as an ultimate value, and yet they are extraordinarily able to manage their business activities so that the result is economic success. Their faith and their managerial effectiveness are strengthened, rather than diminished, because they confront these tensions. (The generalists, justifiers, and seekers are discussed in detail in Chapter 3.)

Consequently, this book is a portrait of a spiritual struggle—a struggle by individuals to understand and act as Christians in the marketplace.

Contrary to the blithe claims of some, not all Christians or even all evangelicals agree about what is the right thing to do. And yet I discovered that many businesspeople are reluctant to discuss the problematic spiritual issues that they encounter at work, for fear of being labeled unfaithful. Furthermore, they have often found that the clergy is intolerant or disdainful of their role as *businesspeople*. Discussions with spouses tend to stress family matters. And so their dialogue and opportunity for prayer and fellowship in this area have been mainly among other like-minded businesspeople—who are sometimes difficult to find.

Some of the most admired and economically successful Christians described in this book would be the first to acknowledge that knowing God's will is difficult and that doing it is even harder, no matter how good one's intentions, how strong one's faith, or how disciplined one's life.

Here is a simple case in point. A struggling arts center has always contracted its printing jobs with Company X, which is run by an evangelical. Company X does conscientious, fine work, and its prices are fair. The arts center's next performance features a gay chorus, with proceeds to benefit a new hospice shelter for AIDS patients. The arts center leaves an order for two thousand advertising notices with the print shop. Someone at the print shop who is also an evangelical happens to notice the content of the ad twenty-four hours before it is to be picked up. The CEO of the print shop is informed, and he has a problem. He does not support the promotion of homosexuality, on religious grounds. What does he do?

Two reactions to this scenario actually came to my attention during the course of interviewing. One was reported by a marketer for an arts group in New York, who had experienced an almost identical situation. When she went to pick up her order, she was told by the evangelical printer that he had refused to print it, on religious grounds. It was too late to take the printing job elsewhere, and the arts group lost its chance to circulate enough ads to make the performance a success. In fact, they lost money, and there was no surplus to contribute to the AIDS hospice that they wanted to support.

The arts center manager puzzled over the printer's response. Where was Christian compassion for the sick? What kind of ethic failed to keep promises and cost loyal customers money? The printer, however, was convinced that not only had he done the right thing but that his reasoning was easy to see. The whole issue was homosexuality and nothing else. He had struck a blow for Jesus against the deviltry in today's society.

Another evangelical whom I interviewed had a very different reaction when he encountered almost precisely the same scenario in his own printing business. He, too, feels that the promotion of homosexuality is a sin. However, he also has other values as a Christian. For him, promise keeping and honoring one's word are important obligations. This printing ad scenario put him on the line, because it posed a trade-off of commitments. Instead of quickly dismissing the problem, he prayed about it. Either way he went, he could not find a solution that would perfectly satisfy all the biblical perspectives that he wanted to uphold. He concluded that he must honor the agreement to print the notice but that he could not in good conscience make a profit off that job. He did not charge the customer, and he informed her that they would not in the future print any notices about performances celebrating homosexual groups.

Three aspects of this CEO's solution are notable. First, his faith was strengthened by his willingness to confront a potentially damning ethical dilemma. Second, his faith motivated him to pray, and through prayer he found a solution. Third, the solution itself was economically creative—he kept his customer—but his Christian values also caused him to take a financial hit in the short run. For this man, financial success is not tainted. He can be a millionaire and still go to heaven, as it were, *but doing so is not easy.*

The seekers in this book are sophisticated and devout evangelicals who recognize that it is hard for imperfect humans to "read God's handwriting," especially in a business environment. Fundamentally, they are struggling to know God's way and to keep their faith distinctive and alive within a culture that does not readily accept the trappings, language, and rituals of that faith. They pray about and study this problem daily.

Ultimately, the ability of seekers to draw on their faith so that they can creatively withstand the moral tensions posed by work appears to have four important outcomes:

- At the societal level, it can often keep at bay the more predatory aspects of advanced capitalism.
- At the economic level, it stimulates value creation.
- At the company level it stimulates commitment to high ethical standards and humane employee policies.
- At the individual level, it transforms economic activity into a meaningful experience, both personally and socially.

Such a portrait is especially relevant today. It identifies some of the most common and important moral issues confronting every business manager. It places the revelations of the Bible in a contemporary social context. It challenges the complacent Christian and agnostic alike to think again.

These findings can also create a map for organized religious leaders and fellowship groups who want to embark on a meaningful journey through the hazards of business leadership. As former U.S. Senator William Armstrong suggested after studying the themes of this book, the seven creative tensions provide a useful format for Bible-study groups to examine their own faith at work and at home. Evangelicalism and business do have something to say to each other, and so I have provided a Study Guide, containing some discussion questions for each chapter, at the back of this book.

Most important, the portrait created here begins to redefine the kind of leadership that is needed for responsible enterprise. As Western economies struggle with the prospect of decline on both the financial and moral fronts, the health of business becomes an increasingly pressing issue. The thoughts of the people in this book strike to the heart of these problems.

1

Who Are the Evangelicals?

To some persons the word "church" suggests so much hypocrisy and tyranny and meanness and tenacity of superstition that in a wholesale undiscerning way they glory in saying that they are "down" on religion altogether. Even we who belong to churches do not exempt other churches than our own from the general condemnation.
—William James[1]

W hen Jimmy Carter, a born-again Christian, ran for the United States presidency in 1976, the national press didn't know what to make of him. Liberal pundits from the Northeast and the West Coast were bewildered by the character of the man and his religion. Unfamiliar with Southern Baptist culture, suspicious that they were being had, and uncomfortable with past evangelical alliances such as the one between Billy Graham and Richard Nixon during the Vietnam war, the press struggled hard to find the false bottom in Carter's grinning bag of virtuous statements.

Many journalists, especially the honest ones, came away ambivalent. Take Robert Scheer, an antiestablishment writer for *Playboy* and the *Los Angeles Times* and once an outspoken critic of American policy in Vietnam. Following Carter around Plains, Georgia, during the primary days, Scheer described the candidate as someone waiting for Norman Rockwell to appear:

> On one level, the man is simply preposterous. On another, he seems reasonable, sincere, and eminently sensible. . . . My editor [from *Playboy*] tells me, "Hey, I really like this guy." Then, not thirty seconds later, he wonders aloud if we've been had.[2]

Evangelical practices tend to invite the kind of reaction Scheer had. Evangelicals pray a lot. Outsiders wonder whether they are devout or just trying to cut an inside deal with God. They try to share

1

the good news with a friend: Are they well-minded or just being manipulative of a friendship? They smile beatifically even in moments of crisis: Are they showing some special strength that comes from above or are they just in a state of psychological denial? Opinions and interpretations obviously vary, but no simpleminded stereotype (pro or con) can capture the complex, multifaceted characteristics of the evangelical movement.

Who are the evangelicals, anyway? And how many are there? There are several problems in seeking an exact number, primarily because evangelicalism reaches far beyond the traditional evangelical denominations. Moreover, not even all members of evangelical churches report having had a "born-again" or some other special experience that would definitively identify who the evangelicals are.[3] Nevertheless, it is clear from what data we have that evangelicalism is a significant and growing movement in America.

A 1976 Gallup Poll revealed that 34 percent of the respondents claimed to have had a "born-again" experience. This figure, along with other data, implied a population of nearly fifty million evangelicals in the United States, in some broad sense of the word. By 1988 that estimate had nearly doubled: 66 percent of the Americans surveyed said they had "made a commitment to Christ."[4] Since 1965 there has been a steady drop in membership in liberal Protestant denominations, while evangelical denominations have increased their membership at an average of 8 percent every five years.[5] A 1990 survey commissioned by the Graduate School of the City University of New York (using a larger database than most Gallup Polls) identified Baptists as representing 19 percent of the total U.S. population and United Methodists representing 8 percent. By contrast, Roman Catholics represented 26 percent and Jews 2 percent.[6]

In the past twenty years, nondenominational evangelical churches have been among the fastest growing congregations in the United States.[7]

There is clearly great latitude in such categorizations. Evangelicalism is not confined to one Christian denomination. Many so-called mainstream Protestant and Catholic churches now have an evangelical subgroup of members who are exerting increasing influence on the liturgy and social programs of their religious institutions.

While evangelical Protestant churches have traditionally been associated with such groups as Baptist, Assemblies of God, Seventh-day Adventists, and Church of the Nazarene, there have long been evangelical arms of mainline Protestantism such as those among the Episcopal, Presbyterian, and United Methodist groups. Even the Church of England, which is the nominal head of the most mainline American church of all, the Episcopal diocese, has in recent years installed an evangelical as the Archbishop of Canterbury. There are now evangelical Catholics, evangelical charismatics, and even self-defined evangelical Jews.

None of these groups shares a common doctrinal basis. Even the most traditional denominations such as the Southern Baptists have had profound internal disputes over doctrine, most notably over Bible inerrancy (fundamentalist interpretations of the Bible), in the last decade. Not all Baptists are fundamentalists, and not all conservative Protestants are Baptist.

Nor do evangelicals share a common social or ethnic heritage. While evangelical groups have been predominantly white Anglo-Saxon, there is a very strong African-American evangelical population as well as many central European offshoots, such as the German Pietists. While many evangelicals have strong denominational affiliations with traditional Protestant sects such as Baptists, Methodists, Presbyterians, or even Episcopalians, they also identify with and participate strongly in cross-denominational efforts such as the Billy Graham Evangelistic Association, state and national prayer breakfasts, and organized retreats. Many evangelicals express stronger ties to these groups than to their own churches.

What I Mean by *Evangelicalism*

When I began my research, I talked with several theologians at leading divinity schools and several pastors of large evangelical churches in an attempt to arrive at a general definition of evangelicalism. I wanted a definition that would be broad enough to encompass such diverse groups as the supporters of Billy Graham, but one that would still be in line with the beliefs of the congregations that those supporters represent. The theologians and pastors all agreed that there was no single, authoritative doctrinal definition of evan-gelicalism that would fill the bill. Professor David Martin describes evangelicalism as a "biblically based, personally appropriated faith."[8] Professor George Marsden notes that evangelicalism is distinctive not because of any one doctrine, but because its believers have certain shared concepts about the nature of Christian faith and the way it should be practiced in everyday life.[9]

For my own part, I identified three distinctive assumptions that seemed to reflect the various general definitions of evangelicalism offered by theologians and sociologists. These may not be full enough to meet academic standards, but they were important in providing an understandable basis for selecting potential interview-ees.

Among those I interviewed, if an executive called himself or herself an evangelical, a born-again Christian, or a conservative Protestant, and strongly identified with the general content of the three assumptions, then for the purposes of the study, that executive would fall into the evangelical category.

The three assumptions are these:

1. *A felt sense of sin and redemption that has resulted in an ongoing personal relationship with Jesus Christ.* Some, but not all, evangelicals describe this as a born-again experience in that their awareness of this relationship occurred as the result of a specific commitment or recommitment to Jesus—in other words, a second birth. The theo-logical assumption underlying this view is that Christ's resurrection was a real, historical, and saving event. While all forms of Christianity subscribe to the historical reality of the resurrection, in evangelical-ism salvation occurs mainly through personal commitment to Christ rather than through the mysteries of the liturgy, church rituals, mysticism, or death.

2. *An obligation to bear witness to Christ's love and to the divine nature of the Trinity.* The Greek root of the English word evangelize literally means "to announce the good news." Evangelicals bear this respon-sibility, which is usually called "witnessing" or "bearing witness." The ways in which witnessing is conducted, however, vary tremen-dously. The evangelical mission may be as concrete as presenting a verbal gospel message, one on one, that concludes with an invitation

to "receive Christ." This method of evangelism is used especially by Campus Crusade for Christ. But an evangelical's chosen form of witnessing may instead be as indirect as simply being a good Christian and hoping that others will be brought to Christ by his or her own good example. In the latter case, however, it is imperative for the evangelical to assume responsibility for helping any seeker in that journey.

3. *A belief that all aspects of life are subject to scriptural authority.* For the evangelical there is no such thing as a secular, as opposed to a sacred, context. In the evangelical worldview, postmodernist concepts such as the large corporation, though absent from the Bible, are nonetheless part of scriptural domain. Many of those whom I interviewed were puzzled when I suggested that it was important to discuss how they were making their way in the secular environment of business. As one CEO explained to me simply, "There is no secular aspect to my world. God is in everything."

These three assumptions characterize the main religious beliefs of evangelicals. They describe a "this-world" religion in which God's hand is constantly receiving tangible witness. Unlike a Lutheran emphasis on other-worldly truths, or, say, Martin Buber's intense, unsustainable existential experiences of the divine, the evangelical understands even the smallest details of life—say a good meeting or a new friendship—to be a direct expression of God's love or, at times, God's censure. A good example is the title of a book by Allan Emery, a Boston businessman and past treasurer of the Billy Graham Evangelical Association: *A Turtle on a Fencepost: Little Lessons of Large Importance* (Waco, Texas: Word, 1979).

This directness and personalization of religious belief has historically made the evangelical seemingly anti-intellectual, and suspicious of social doctrinism and fancy theologies that might remove the participant from the immediate experience of the Bible's authority. Evangelicalism does not focus mainly on reformist calls about current social ills—wealth, poverty, gender bias, racism, or the environment. For this reason, evangelicals are often accused of not caring about the problems of the underclass, despite their substantial mission work among the poor. Evangelicalism also draws no sharp line between phenomena that are capable of scientific, rational description and nonrational, spiritual phenomena.

Note that none of the preceding characteristics can be applied exclusively to evangelicalism. The devout nonevangelical Protestant and Catholic alike would not deny the possibility of the sacred in daily affairs, nor the importance of prayer and the Bible. But there are strong differences of emphasis. Mainline Protestantism has been, for the most part, a personally quieter and publicly more formalized faith. Evangelicalism, however, is at heart distinguished by its real-world, "lay" orientation and by its dependence on lay participation and authority over religious life. In other words, faith is experienced—and one's ultimate relationship with God is expressed—in the here and now and in a personalized way, rather than through other-world orientations such as life after death or mysticism.

Most of the men who were interviewed for this book professed, with slight exceptions to some detail or wording, to the three religious concepts I have described. Three other descriptive categories that encompass personal and community aspects of their faith are equally important perspectives to help fill out the conceptual agreements, the social networks, and the personality traits of the evangelicals in this study.

The Importance of Relations

The evangelicals I interviewed shared a number of social values and community rituals that are not as typical of mainstream Protestants. I discovered that many evangelical CEOs have formed networks of prayer groups or charitable foundations that bring them together as a religious community—a community that is much larger than any one church or geographical region. Doug Coe's National Prayer Breakfast, in Washington, D.C.; the Association of Christian Businessmen, in Atlanta; Os Guinness's Williamsburg Charter project and Trinity Forum; Boston's First Tuesday breakfast group of CEOs; and many other such organizations offer evangelical businesspeople a community of like-minded leaders with whom they can share their spiritual and career journeys—even if not all members are strictly speaking evangelicals.

Some of these networks are worldwide. One prayer group, for example, consisted of CEOs from three continents, who met through telephone conference calls several times a month. There is a White House prayer group, a New York group of CEOs from the investment world who meet at a well-heeled luncheon club for prayer and counseling, and a Capitol Hill prayer group that has quietly held sessions in a senator's office for years.

The community spirit of these networks is high. In some cases members call each other "brothers," and many speak of their personal "spiritual counselors." This spirit extended to most of their interpretations of religious meaning: a good prayer breakfast and friendship were worth far more than an abstract theological argument in terms of religious power.

While not unanimous, the interviewees certainly were slanted as a group toward social conservativism. Many cited their own opposition to abortion and divorce as chief examples of how their faith made an impact on their lives. Many spent personal time at religious retreats, in nice but not wildly lavish surroundings, such as the Navigators' Glen Eryie in Colorado Springs or the Butt Foundation's Laity Lodge in Kerrville, Texas.

I found, however, that there was no lack of enthusiasm for consumer goods such as fast cars, yachts, or summer homes. The most prominent CEOs in the group were clearly used to moving among the diamond-studded lifestyles of their fellow Fortune 500 CEOs, and yet they did not assume the flashy cosmopolitanism of, say, a Malcolm Forbes or a John Delorean. Nor did they go in for the ostentatious lifestyle of the televangelists. (Former U.S. Senator William Armstrong, an evangelical, was notorious in Capitol Hill circles for driving a frugal 1978 Pontiac.) It's important to note that other conservative social values associated with *fundamentalist* evangelicalism, such as no dancing or drinking caffeine, were not generally evidenced among my group.

One other element makes evangelicalism distinctive—and without it, this general portrait would be unrecognizable. That element is style. Evangelicals are indeed "different" in some basic way that goes beyond their conceptual, social, and institutional affinities.

From the first moment that I began contacting potential interviewees, I became aware that, however well-known these CEOs were in mainstream business circles, they were operating in a world with very different reference points and cultural norms from those of the standard executive. Naturally, the mental reference points of the evangelical CEO would color his or her basic styles of social interaction and interpretation of everyday events.

A Prayerful Life

First and foremost, references to religious phenomena were definitely *not* taboo among these evangelical CEOs. Many modern Americans avoid discussions of personal religion even with or espe-cially with their closest friends because of a fear of ruining a friend-ship. But many of the evangelicals I interviewed wouldn't hesitate to ask me about the state of my own spiritual health—even though I may have felt that such questions were an invasion of privacy. Many of them tended to include everyone in their own religious world-view, coming out with "Praise God!" for something you did, like making a timely phone call, that in your terms may have had no particular religious impulse at all. In short, there is a stylistic religi-osity to their speech and thinking that contrasts sharply with the studied secularism of most modern social interactions. Instead of impersonal, hyper-rational language, there is emotionalism.

All of these tendencies came out in my interviews. Within the first two minutes of each contact, it was clear to me that this was not going to be a typical business dialogue. Nearly every executive began our discussion with personal questions about my own religious background. During the interviews there were several occasions when participants cried openly. Many shared intimacies about their private lives and invoked the name of the Lord in connection with our own discussion. Many began the meeting with a prayer, espe-cially if we met as a small group.

Some of the participants could be described as being on the fringe of the business culture. One, for example, asserted in the first five minutes of our conversation that he could not wait to die so that he could meet Abraham Lincoln. Several carried the evangelical's general sexual conservatism so far as to insist that we not lunch alone together, even at a public restaurant, in order to avoid temptation and the appearance of wrongdoing, which would darken the reputation of evangelicals in general. Others, however, were clearly assimilated into the modern corporate culture, however high powered or "sophisticated" and intellectualized the setting. They themselves were disturbed by some of the more "peculiar" forms of theology and lifestyle that some of their fellow believers professed, such as never using a credit card or looking at a lingerie ad.

Such social behaviors and questions of style cannot be taken at face value if we are to understand the mind-set of the evangelical business leader. Many of the more sexist or naive statements can be attributed to regional language differences between the South and the North. When a Southern Baptist businessman talks of "pagans" (by which he may mean any atheist or agnostic, however cultured, or even a professed Christian who, say, supports premarital sex) or the "sacred role of mother," he may be no more naive or sexist than the northern liberal academic who scornfully ridicules conservative economics and the social standards of the establishment but who tolerates participating in a male-dominated department thirty years after the passage of equal-opportunity legislation.

The Intensity of Evangelicals

Noted sociologist Max Weber characterized conservative Protestants as sober, hard-working, and frugal. But none of the qualities I've just described are normally included in Weber's characterizations.[10] Yet these other, more emotional and relational sides to the evangelical personality demand acknowledgment, especially when contrasted to the emotional barrenness which is often associated with the so-called modern mind. So, in addition to the conceptual, social, and prayerful aspects, I would add a fourth aspect of the evangelical character: *intensity*. More than a question of personal style, evangelicalism is an intensifying experience from the standpoint of emotions, social behavior, and doctrinal belief.

This intensification factor is significant in understanding the evangelical and in distinguishing him or her from other Protestants. Not only is this religion "full time" and infused throughout daily activities, but it can also be quite emotionally engaging. The sources of this intensity are many:

- the personalization of belief
- the direct, relationship-oriented view of humankind and God
- strong social networks
- a direct acknowledgment of the concept of evil
- a holistic worldview that tends to magnify the meaning of even the most commonplace activity

The intense style and worldview of the evangelical is a product of history as well. American evangelicalism has always been characterized by its emotion and its intensity. From the fire-and-brimstone sermons of the Calvinists to the Great Awakenings, believers have never been short on feeling. For example, the so-called Second Great Awakening at the beginning of the nineteenth century saw previously indifferent crowds of Americans engaged in massive outdoor religious gatherings that lasted days. These gatherings were replete with emotional shouting, singing, shrieking, and fainting in the revival of religious spirit and conversion.[11]

The great evangelical Samuel John Mills (1783–1818), founding father of organized mission activity in America whose reports on the American frontier led to the founding of the American Bible Society, was described as a paragon of intensity. Historian Daniel Boorstin wrote the following about Mills:

> Even his friends described him as having "an awkward figure and ungainly manners and an unelastic and croaking sort of voice." But he had an intensity of purpose, a grandeur of vision, and a restless energy that made him an American prodigy in his brief thirty-five years of life.[12]

Among the group that I interviewed, the same kind of intensity and energy were not forgotten; there were regular instances of tears, intimate disclosures, joyful exclamations of "Praise the Lord!" and a staggering amount of energy for hard work.

Translated into the everyday manifestations of belief, evangelicalism is generally a more "enthusiastic" and emotional faith. This is not a shy religion, or one that is limited to the private meditations between an individual and his or her Maker. Given the invitation, evangelicals will talk about their faith at the drop of a hat. They refer frequently to God's role in everyday occurrences, and their religious conversation is not unlike the casual intimacies of a good friendship. They may, for example, speak of having "a date with Jesus."

Such talk can be uncomfortable to outsiders. Believers are suspected of merely trying to "sell" others, and even themselves, on the authenticity of their faith. They seem to exploit the privileges of friendship when they attempt to "introduce" a friend to Jesus. In a world where the ground rules on religion are that if you have to talk about it, it must not be authentic, the evangelical is doomed to be misunderstood and rejected.

These ground rules are, of course, precisely what most bothers the evangelical. By keeping religion private and separate from daily public interchanges, society submits to a secular monster, ungrounded in any moral certainty besides the chaotic and godless belief that humankind is the center of all things. The phrase I heard most frequently for describing this breakdown was "secular humanism," which to many evangelicals is best typified by the people in eastern liberal educational establishments or the predators on Wall Street as characterized in such books as *Liar's Poker, Bonfire of the Vanities,* and *Barbarians at the Gate.*

A Faith Portrait of the Evangelical CEO

Keeping in mind these many different aspects of evangelicalism, I've tried to create in this book a kind of life portrait of the evangelical CEO's faith, which rises above regional, educational, and income differences to capture what is most distinctive about evangelicalism today. Figure 1.1 summarizes its main features.

Figure 1.1 schematizes the characteristics that typify the evangelicals I interviewed. The evangelical faith is prayerful, it is personally experienced and expressed, and religious experience is found more in terms of real relations (with God, spouse, friends, etc.) than through a specific charitable act or abstract rule. Overlaying all three aspects are certain intensifying forces. These include a belief in the absolute authority of God, fortified by biblical authority and a rejection of secular humanism, and emotional involvement in both the sacred and the profane, expressed through feelings of ecstasy and fear. Keeping somewhat separate from some aspects of modern society also intensifies the evangelical's spiritual awareness. At the same time the evangelical has an understanding that all things are in God's divine order—an understanding that can elevate the human experience to one of divine significance.

In seeing God's hand very directly involved in the world's workings, the evangelical has a strong sense of order and harmony about the world. His or her strong sense of selfhood, the knowledge that humans are inherently sinful and yet redeemable by God's love, invites an inner confidence, calmness, and seriousness about the tasks that he or she performs.[13] Other socially responsible character traits seem to result from that perspective: sobriety, self-discipline, a sense of responsibility, attention to detail, and hard work.

These character traits can be both good and bad from an outsider's point of view. If unclouded by psychological repressions, they suggest a life of fulfillment, meaning, and harmony with the universe. In the extreme, they could be indications of compulsive-obsessive behavior or even hysteria. In some instances the self-control and sexual conservatism of the evangelical may be a fearful denial of the so-called darker side of the personality, as well as a frantic attempt to suppress it through intense pietism.

Extremes and stereotypes aside, the similarities among these evangelicals suggest a powerful commonality based on their religious perspective. The evangelical perspective stands in obvious contrast to the so-called secular humanist, not only for its orientation on God's authority, but also for its relational, holistic bias. Even though interviewees came from four different cities with very different regional cultures, were leaders in industries with quite different business norms, and had parents who were not all from the same economic class, they shared an outlook that colored all aspects of their life.

Figure 1.1
A Faith Portrait: the Evangelical CEO

Prayerful Aspects
- Submits to God's will, because of a sense of divine order in this world
- Directs his or her life according to biblical principles
- Leads an active devotional life
- Makes mention of religion or uses religious language in everyday speech

Personal Aspects
- Has experienced Jesus personally
- Eagerly converses about religion
- Considers personal witnessing important
- Believes that everyday events of personal life have sacred significance

Relational Aspects
- Has a "personal relationship" with Jesus
- Considers family harmony important
- Friendships and other interpersonal relationships are an important vehicle for living one's faith
- Forms social networks from prayer groups, mission work, and other activities
- Gives spiritual counsel and/or has a spiritual counselor
- Considers personal mission work (as opposed to simply giving money) important

Intensifying Factors
- Makes no distinction between the secular and the sacred
- Has a holistic approach to solving problems and to ordering and interpreting events
- Resists social values or intellectual viewpoints that might "dilute" the intensity of the Christian experience
- Has an emotional, supercharged spiritual life

The core traits which have been outlined here serve as a jumping off point for understanding how evangelical CEOs determine what is right from a Christian perspective. However, as I discussed various business situations with interviewees, I quickly found that evangelicalism, despite its coherent worldview, does not offer its believers an automatic solution to the many dilemmas attached to business necessities. Though evangelicalism provided interviewees with a strong core of values, it does not provide an unambiguous blueprint for life.

2

What the Believers
Say about Business

I would tell more minis-
ters to get out of the
ministry than I would tell
businessmen to get out
of business.
—An evangelical CEO
from Chicago

I t is said that the Reverend Billy Graham made a quiet visit to
Moscow just before the Soviet initiation of perestroika. Graham is said to have requested a private meeting with Gorbachev,
strictly off the record, to discuss Soviet problems of alcoholism and
the nonproductivity of workers. Graham argued that bringing the
Soviets to Jesus would have constructive results in overcoming and
inspiring a disciplined work ethic.

During that visit, Graham was allowed to hold a private prayer
session in a large auditorium, though the first official prayer session
was not to be held until July 1991 in the Lenin Stadium in Moscow.
According to the evangelical grapevine, the talk made a great impression on the Soviet leader. A first crack in the Soviet Union's isola-
tionism, the meeting was regarded by many evangelicals as the first
seed of perestroika and as the introduction of a new global order in
a very religious sense of the term.

The story is a typical example of how many strands connect
democratic capitalism and evangelicalism. Major characteristics of
the Protestant work ethic are clearly present in evangelicalism today
and are expressed in causal terms: Faith brings practical, economically productive benefits in its wake. Conversely, productive, democratic capitalistic systems are understood to be the backbone of social
and political support for evangelicalism rather than for modern
secularism.

Even conservative Christianity itself takes on some cultural
attributes of capitalism. Competitiveness, for example, is fundamental to the process. Graham and other evangelicals do not hesitate to

compete for people's spiritual commitment, whether their competitors are liberal agnostics or knee-jerk communists. Two kinds of victories must be won: the winning of people's souls and their conversion to democratic capitalism.

Such themes are regularly reflected among evangelical leadership and in social surveys of evangelicals. The National Prayer Breakfast in Washington, D.C., for example, has as its theme the twofold message that evangelical faith and democratic capitalism are singularly well suited to each other. The political conservatism of evangelicals, which includes a bias toward free-market economics, is also well documented and well represented within Washington circles, especially within the Republican party and in the conservative government of Great Britain.

But what about the role of evangelicalism at the individual level? Do the characteristics of evangelicalism really make any difference in one person's business life? Do evangelical managers think differently about business problems? How do the traditional lifestyle ethics of conservative Protestants—industriousness, thrift, and self-denial—play out among this group? Most important, what does their faith require of them as executives? Are these requirements expressed in concrete deeds, or only in attitudes? Are there any real differences between them and the relativistic and self-indulgent yuppies?

The CEOs who were interviewed for this book indeed have distinctive and discernible approaches to work that can be associated with their evangelicalism. The patterns, however, are often difficult to describe. So we'll begin with the least surprising aspect of the evangelical business philosophy: the so-called Protestant work ethic.

A Brief History of the Protestant Work Ethic

Evangelicals are noted for their emphasis on self-discipline, hard work, thrift, and delayed gratification.[1] It is important to recognize that such behavior reflects a pattern that has influenced the very history of American progress. The conservative Protestant culture of early New England puritanism was embedded in a triple foundation of private faith, economic productivity, and politicalfreedom.

Max Weber's portrait of how conservative Protestantism fueled a capitalistic spirit is the classic explanation of this relationship. Drawing on Benjamin Franklin's persona of a Yankee Puritan, Weber argued that conservative Protestantism supported a way of life that was industrious, frugal, punctual, and equitable in all its dealings. Trifling actions, such as being seen by creditors to be working at five in the morning versus being seen at the billiard table long into the night, were to be regarded as personally and monetarily significant. Good treatment of customers or employees was a must—not just because it made business sense but because anything else was a forgetfulness of duty.[2]

As Weber noted, certain personality traits accompanied this behavior: mental concentration, cool self-control, a certain ascetic tendency to avoid displays of wealth or power, and above all, a systematic and compelling (that is, rational) search for profit.[3]

There are many biblical justifications for the relationship of work to salvation, but the *spirit* in which the methodical, fair, and unwasteful constraints of the Bible were adopted made them more than a utilitarian theology; they were a practical *ethic*.[4] For Calvinists, the disciplines of work were expressions of duty in one's sacred calling—obligations that any devout person must meet in every professional activity.

Weber's early New England Puritans and Benjamin Franklin's fictional Yankee were paragons of personal austerity, self-denial, self-discipline, thrift, and soberness. They shunned anything emotionally, aesthetically, or sexually stimulating. Rigid social prohibitions were the norm: no dancing, no Christmas celebration or decorations, no excessive passion in marital relations, for some of them no sport or theater, and certainly no drunkenness or loose living. As H. L. Mencken put it, Puritanism was the suspicion that somewhere someone was having fun.[5]

This was a paradoxical ethic at heart. The conservative Protestant shunned the pleasures of the world but rejected the kind of monastic retreat from the world that Catholicism embraced. Worldly deeds and mundane details *mattered* in the sense that they were expressions of faith. At the same time, they meant nothing; you could not buy your way into heaven with good deeds. As written in Romans 1:17, "The just shall live by faith." To the conservative Protestant, as exemplified by the Calvinist, faith was a matter of being among the elect, but deeds of worldly self-control and success were important because they were signs of election.

Ultimately, this combination of characteristics produced perhaps one of the Western world's greatest ironies: a social group that completely shunned worldly goods and pleasures but was an economic powerhouse. The orderliness and industriousness of conservative Protestants, along with their severe restrictions on lifestyle that limited the opportunities for spending, led to their substantial accumulations of capital.

As a result, these believers created a methodical approach to organizing the resources needed for economic success. As social historian Simon Schama pointed out in his analysis of sixteenth-century Protestant communities in the Dutch Republic, only the symbols of a well-ordered household (fine architecture and fine furniture) or the symbols of church ritual (the baptismal or the wedding cup) were seen as legitimate channels for private consumption; all other spending was directed by the church toward the good of the community.[6] In Puritan New England, even ornamental objects were regarded with suspicion.

As industrial capitalism became more advanced, it loosened its ties to the Protestant ethic. Protestant asceticism was not incompatible with developed capitalism; it simply was no longer the only way in which capitalism could flourish. Historically, the capitalist work ethic was transformed into a secular version—still emphasizing thrift, industriousness, efficiency, and methodicalism, but no longer dependent on religious justifications or nonconsumptive lifestyles. As sociologist James Hunter noted, by 1900 the theological notion of "calling" in one's vocation had largely lost its appeal.[7]

There have been several notable exceptions, however, to the steady decline in the concept of work being a religious calling. In the 1920s, for example, northern mainline churches were so eager to assimilate with the secular mainstream that they jumped wholeheartedly on the prosperity gospel bandwagon. The poet Edgar A. Guest wrote in *American* magazine that "religion pays." And the best-selling nonfiction book in 1925 was Bruce Barton's *The Man Nobody Knows*, which depicts Jesus as an executive who builds a worldwide organization with his twelve associates.

But with the crash of 1929 such easy fusions of Christ with business ended as suddenly as they appeared (although they had an interesting resurrection among the televangelists immediately before the crash of 1987). Meanwhile, on business and society issues such as organized labor, the church remained largely either silent or supportive of the status quo.[8]

In the second half of the twentieth century, the connection between religion and business grew ever more obscure. American economic activity became increasingly secularized, and religious activity—where it existed—was increasingly compartmentalized into private experience. As sociologist of religion Peter L. Berger put it in the 1970s, "religion has become privately meaningful and publicly irrelevant."[9]

In the twentieth century, at least until recently, the pivotal point for liberal mainline Protestantism was not so much inner spiritual well-being as liberal social activism issues: sexual tolerance or liberation, racial harmony, the peace movement, the environmental movement. Many of these activities were actually antibusiness or proMarxist in focus—for example, the widespread participation of the Protestant and Catholic churches in the boycotts of infant formula and table grapes or their support of various socialist regimes in the Third World. Meanwhile, conservative Protestantism, especially fundamentalist sects, refocused their "this world" attention on private social issues: no drinking, no smoking, no sexual permissiveness.

Given the antibusiness leanings of liberal Protestantism and the concentration on private social issues by conservative Protestants, it has been very difficult to say with any authority what role religious faith plays in the lives of Protestant business executives today or whether the traditional values and habits of the Protestant work ethic carry over into current business activity. The starting point for my research was to shed light on these questions.

How I Conducted This Study

In its first stage, the basic outline of my research was deceptively simple: interview noted CEOs who (1) were evangelical Protestants, (2) were admired for their ethics, and (3) were the heads of successful companies. Preferably I would interview "the best of the best"— those executives who had good reputations for their business acumen and religious integrity.

I chose to look at successful CEOs rather than at a broader sample in order to fulfill two objectives. First of all, evangelicals as a whole have not been especially prosperous in the American business world since World War II. They have been extremely underrepresented among the top leadership of America's large corporations, which mainline Protestantism has dominated. As a group, evangelicals have been among those with the worst economic performance in America. It seemed logical that the successful few who had "made it" would be unusually strong leaders who could provide helpful insights about management and economic cultures.

This suspicion was quickly confirmed as several of my interviewees made the top manager lists of national business journals: Max De Pree of Herman Miller, Kenneth Wessner of ServiceMaster, and Thomas Phillips of Raytheon. It seemed reasonable to expect that interviews with these men would yield some sound management insights. But to the degree that they had not abandoned their faith along the way to success, I expected to find positive information about how the evangelical can keep faith alive at work.

Although the general outline of the research was simple, the actual task was not. I encountered serious obstacles in almost every aspect of the project. First there was the general nature of the subjects under study. Business leaders are, for the most part, doers rather than philosophers. They do not tend to develop full-scale explanations of how their faith motivates or affects their everyday actions. (Does anyone?)

Then there was the time frame. Tracing the behavior and influence of even one evangelical leader throughout one large corporation presented logistical nightmares. At that point I would have a sample of one. It would be necessary to sacrifice "proof" and rely on firsthand interviews with a wider group of subjects.

In making this choice, I was aware that this study would reflect personal rationalizations that were not always consistent with reality. Any mature sociologist, journalist, psychologist, or historian faces the same problems in dealing with reported material. The interviewee's subjective interpretation of events must not be confused with fact. At the same time, the material under discussion was very sensitive. It is difficult to probe for the accuracy of someone's religious claims without appearing to be attacking their beliefs or their ethical character.

In this study, I ran several kinds of unintrusive reality checks on the interviewees' statements in an attempt to compensate for the absence of firsthand observation of their business practices:

- I probed for concrete examples wherever possible.
- I took special note of any contradictions in an interviewee's remarks.
- I checked the general press and public financial statements wherever possible.
- I asked others, when I could, about their opinions of the companies and CEOs represented in the sample.

Given the wide diversity of the interviewees in terms of their denominational affiliations, regional cultures, and types of business, this is not a "pure" statistical sample. A mixture of impressions, opinions, and concrete examples cannot definitively describe the business ethics of a uniform sociological group.

Gaining the consent of the CEOs turned out to be more difficult than I had ever anticipated. I soon discovered that my own background, firmly seated in the alleged secular humanism of Harvard University, was about as suspect as could be and was the worst recommendation I could possibly have for requesting an interview. As a former classicist with a Ph.D. from Harvard, and then a professor at Harvard Business School, and now a working mother with her own consulting firm in business ethics, I stood for everything the evangelical is protesting: relativistic, ungrounded, intellectually arrogant, secular humanism. This stereotype was particularly difficult to swallow, since I had always considered myself to be a devout Christian.

While few actually derided me for working, many mentioned that their own wives had always stayed at home and that this had seemed best for the children. No one let me get more than two minutes into our first phone contact before asking me to explain—in detail—my own religious background and the state of my relationship with God today. One person actually grilled me about my stand on religious issues for two hours before sweetly informing me that he couldn't be of any help.

And then there was my sex. While many evangelicals have women "counselors" and form mixed Bible study groups, they tend to be very cautious about relationships with women outside a lay religious setting. Several turned out to have strict policies about never appearing in public alone with a woman, however close a friend or casual a business acquaintance. One interviewee had to resort to asking his son and daughter-in-law to join us for lunch in order to fulfill this policy, even though we met alone back at his office. Another CEO apologized for not asking me to lunch with him since there were no companions available. (By contrast, others met me for breakfast at nearby hotels—a choice of locale that would have shattered the more socially cautious among the group!)

For three months no one agreed to be interviewed. The Boston evangelical business community, where I started, had recently been scalded by a cover article in a local business journal titled "Christ in the Boardroom." The piece was factually sloppy and was sensationalistically determined to prove that evangelicalism was the greatest threat to basic values and economic opportunity since yellow fever.

Despite the initial cold shoulder, I soon learned how to keep the grillings of my own background to a minimum, and to give out only as much information about myself as I felt comfortable with. Once I completed a few interviews, these same people offered their personal help in locating others and in assuring them that I was not out to do a hatchet job on the business or evangelical community. In several cases interviewees expressed their surprise that they not only had enjoyed the interview but had learned something.

Using this "network" technique for locating participants, I eventually interviewed over sixty-five CEOs in four cities, plus thirty members of the Young Presidents Organization at one of its retreats. A general profile of the sixty-five appears in the tables at the end of this chapter. In constructing this sample, I was able to locate only a few evangelical women executives, and none of them agreed to participate. All of the men interviewed were recommended by other evangelical businesspeople as successful and good representatives of the evangelical community. In several cases the deans or presidents of local evangelical colleges and the pastors of large evangelical churches recommended members of their boards or congregations as potential interviewees. They also provided invaluable help in thinking through the questions on this project. After writing the first draft of the book, I shared my findings with several large groups of evangelical business leaders, including the Dallas Consultation with George Gallup on Leadership in Business and National Life, and many participants in the Laity Lodge Leadership Forum.

What I Found

And so the project began, with a great deal of suspicion on both sides and many inherent obstacles to success. I soon found that there was no one "type" of evangelical business leader that would provide a legitimate basis for even the most relaxed theory of evangelical business values. The group whom I interviewed displayed tremendous variety in terms of denominational affiliation, company size and industry, regional culture, personal lifestyle, and business philosophy.

Nor is there any obvious distinctiveness in their (for lack of a better term) business ethic. It would be naive to try to "prove" here that evangelicals are comparatively more (or less) ethical, honest, and humane than the average enlightened secular humanist in business.

For these reasons, some of the most frequently voiced questions about evangelicals from outsiders are the most difficult to actually investigate and then to try to answer conclusively. Many people, however, *have* voiced these questions in connection with this study. Here are some examples:

- Are evangelicals completely hypocritical?
- Do they really believe all that saccharine piety?
- Isn't their belief system just a repression of normal sexual impulses and a fear of their own fallibility?
- Aren't evangelicals *scary*?
- Don't they act just like anyone else when it gets down to making a buck?
- Aren't they the first to look the other way on basic ethical principles of business?

The evangelicals I interviewed were remarkably weak at defending themselves against such prejudiced charges, even though the charges are frequent. I discovered that these evangelicals were also as unschooled as the general public about what business and evangelicalism have to say to each other. Instead of providing sound theological discussion that is relevant to the complex business problems professional managers face, many evangelical writings offer superficial philosophies of wealth that contradict each other. Some evangelical preachers and theologians emphasize a so-called prosperity gospel not unlike New Age visioning: Just believe, and God will give you material success. Others completely deemphasize or even condemn capitalistic activity; when it comes to wealth, giving money away or engaging in mission work are the only noteworthy acts of faith; wealth *creation* is beside the point. Then there are the quick-fix, cookbook recipes for Christian business practice: ten steps to searching for the *real* excellence! But such advice goes only so far. As longtime Dallas business consultant and counsellor Fred Smith scoffed, "There is no such thing as a Christian business. Christian is better used as a noun than an adjective."

Even in academic circles the evangelical discussions of secular humanism have tended to steer away from the business context. A good example is the excellent book edited by Professor George Marsden, *Evangelicalism and Modern America*.[10] In this volume, thirteen essays by noted theologians and historians address problems in politics, science, the arts, the women's movement, and ecclesiastical organization. The only businesses mentioned are Bible businesses: evangelical broadcasting and publishing. So even though the evangelical is assured that "through Christ's Incarnation God can and has entered real human history and can be known through ordinary human events,"[11] the events of the marketplace seem to be devoid of such messages.

Even business writing by evangelical authors tends to sidestep concrete problems in business such as choosing a product, being effectively shrewd without compromising Christian ideals, dealing with underperforming businesses, and making hard choices about benefits and salaries in the face of performance expectations from shareholders. Robert Greenleaf's admired book *Servant Leadership* is an example of this tendency. Although Greenleaf, an evangelical and a former corporate officer of AT&T, is profoundly eloquent on general principles of leadership, he profiles a college president and a rabbi as his only extended examples of servant leadership![12]

We could interpret the previous lack of concrete attention to sophisticated business problems in many ways. The evangelical business leader who writes about his personal philosophy and sticks only to examples of how he counseled teenagers to get a job or how he proposed to his wife, could be masking the fact that faith really plays no part in his business thinking. He could be unconsciously or hypocritically avoiding a hard confrontation with potential conflicts between the pursuit of economic success and the callings of Christ. He might be confusing conflict with personal religious failure.

No doubt, as the responses of this study will show, these explanations are true for some evangelical businesspeople but certainly not all. For many others, the source of their spiritual dialogue—or the lack of it—is more complex than simple hypocrisy or familiar psychological avoidance mechanisms. Evangelicals, by the very nature of their worldview, have a curious way of crossing categories so that they sometimes appear to be ducking important questions when they think they are answering them. For example, I discovered that when I would ask an evangelical CEO to cite a specific instance of a business situation that put his faith to the test, he was as likely to tell me the story of his personal conversion or to describe a case in which his child misbehaved as to talk about business. Press again, and I might get another story of a personal marital problem, a family estrangement, or a troubled teenager that he had counseled.

While such responses are extremely frustrating to an interviewer, they should not be confused with deliberate obscuring. Such category crossing, which for the evangelical most often moves from the business context to a domestic arena, is a product of holistic thinking and historical trends in evangelical thought. If one's worldview assumes, as does the evangelical's, that every small detail is significant in the larger scheme, then it is not at all preposterous to speak of one's marriage when asked about one's business strategy. The wholeness of his personal psyche, dependent to a significant degree on marital relationships, theoretically has great relevance to the evangelical's decision about whether to embark on a new business venture or not.

The fact that he is unmoved to draw out this connection in a linear, logical way does not mean that no connection is there. Rather, the particular traits of the evangelical that were identified in the previous chapter—*personal, prayerful, relational,* and *intensifying*—tend to direct his discussion away from concrete, single events and toward more emotional, personalized aspects of the decision-making process. This happens in much the same way that a yellow lens would inevitably turn every view of business amber.

Pushing hard enough, I could sometimes get an interviewee to demonstrate how the connections are made, but in most cases, I have had to piece together a more articulated worldview after the fact. In the preceding example about the choice of a new product venture, it may be that the state of this CEO's marriage had a direct influence on how much risk and pressure he was able to take. His prayer life may have actually included this venture even though he failed to mention it at first. He may also have based his decision on whether his potential suppliers or customers were in some way connected to his socioreligious network of believers.

But for the evangelical all of these details will be only secondary in importance compared to the essential state of his faith. And that faith is what will preoccupy his discussion.

Some of the avoidance of concrete business discussion in connection with faith is also a product of history. The evangelical dialogue historically has been anti-intellectual, suspicious of social doctrines, and strongly focused on a personal relationship to God through Jesus. Only the most intimate of human relationships, such as the family or the religious fellowship, provide a topic even remotely competitive with stories of the state of one's faith. Therefore, the evangelical's extreme "domestication" of the business dialogue to include certain private topics is very much in line with mainstream evangelical thought.

We can see the same "domestication" element in evangelical political discussions. These, too, have been firmly biased toward private, individualized contexts: sexual choices, family strength, church attendance, and the state of one's soul.

At the 1990 National Prayer Breakfast in Washington, D.C., Secretary of State James Baker III spoke eloquently of his personal journey of faith. He emphasized the need to forge bonds of friendship through faith throughout the world as a solution to world problems. (Cast in emotionally gripping language, this was a perfect example of applying the evangelical lens piece of the prayerful, the personal, and the relational to a large-scale problem.) Baker made an eloquent argument contrasting the relative weakness and impermanence of political power with the personal strength gained from strong faith. As an example, he quoted the Ninety-first Psalm, which he said was a favorite of his mother's: "A thousand may fall at your side, / And ten thousand at your right hand; / But it shall not come near you" (Ps. 91:7). Commented Baker: "My mother, who taught me so many of the values that give me strength today, drew much comfort from those words, and from hearing her say them, so did I." Baker gave the group two charges: to improve their own responsibility regarding faith and to improve the society that ensures the freedom to practice faith.[13]

It would be wrong to conclude that evangelicals do not care about world affairs. These leaders have, on the whole, voiced a great sense of urgency about what is wrong in this society: It has lost its grounding in religion and has become secularized, crime ridden, sexually promiscuous, morally relativistic, and personally ungrounded in anything besides the self. As an extension of this self-orientation, there is no loyalty to family, and a whole ethic of greed and deceit has grown up in the marketplace.

When evangelical leaders speak publicly on these events, they do not focus directly on business ethics. Instead, they tend to interpret business misbehavior as one more piece of evidence of a general breakdown of traditional values. The examples they most often cite are excessive materialism, divorce, promiscuity, crime, drugs, and abortion. All of these sins are symptomatic of a decay of the spirit (the lens piece again). Charles Colson's book *Against the Night* is a representative sample:

> Material obsession paralyzes the West and political repression grips the East. Scandals and scams are commonplace in our world. Men and women trade character for cash and sacrifice commitment on the altar of selfishness. . . . All around us crime rises, moral values decline, and families fragment. . . . When I became a Christian, I gained a new perspective on the actual influence political structures have over the course of history. I began to see that societies are changed only when people are changed, not the other way around.
>   The crisis is not political; it is moral and spiritual. And so is the solution. That's why Christians are the only ones who can offer viable answers.[14]

Colson and many others, including former British Prime Minister Margaret Thatcher, would focus all issues of group behavior, including business behavior, through the lens of personalized attention to matters of the spirit. Responding to the exaggerated attention to issues and policy that has marked the modern sociopolitical dialogue since at least the New Deal era, they propose that attention be radically realigned to matters of the soul and to traditional private or domestic commitments.

They are very clear on this point: No collective examples of social injustice, criminality or—on the other side—ethical behavior, deserve as much attention as the state of people's souls and their personal freedom. These leaders eloquently urge the churches to more passionately nourish and strengthen an individual's faith rather than attend to social policy. Only when these institutions and matters are revitalized can the rest follow.

Representative of this view among business leaders is a statement by Elmer Johnson, former executive vice president of General Motors:

[This] is a truth I believe to be self-evident: That a society is in a serious state of decadence when its members come to depend primarily on either the market or paternalism or any combination of the two for generating and sustaining an adequate ethic. As one who subscribes to the Judeo-Christian tradition, I believe in the primacy of the life of the spirit, in the incredible power of the God-inspired hero, whether he be the famous prophet or statesman or the little-known teacher or author, to arouse and transform the many from their ignorance and apathy and self-indulgence so that they are enabled to lead lives of freedom and dignity and moral worth. Next to this source of moral power, paternalism and the market are not even poor seconds.[15]

Such a worldview, sharply focused on individual faith and personal responsibility, helps explain both the general political conservatism of evangelicals and the lack of discussion about systemic business problems. As you will see in Chapter 4, free-market economic and social policies are generally supported as the best environment for religious freedom. Several of those I interviewed argued that the democratic free-market system is the logical evangelical choice in that it was historically created by a God-acknowledging public, it celebrates individual liberty and freedom of religion, and it demands self-reliance and hard work to succeed. What evangelicals have been less prepared to discuss, however, was how particular business policies impact the moral health of the capitalist system or the conduct of other employees in their own companies.

These trends in mainstream evangelical thought have introduced a deep-seated irony in the discussion of business among evangelicals: *Although the evangelical business leader has been increasingly evident in mainstream business circles, this has not increased the evangelical community's discussion of his or her main activity, namely business.* While evangelicals are paying great attention to how contemporary issues have struck with full force against the old-time, Norman Rockwell-type domestic culture of America, they leave that most pluralistic and modern institution of all, the large corporation, largely outside the intellectual playing field.

I suggest that the mainstream evangelical dialogue has inadvertently invited a kind of bias against exploring concrete problems in the business and political arena outside family and individual health (spiritual, mental, or physical). As a result, neither evangelicals nor the general public knows very much about the business mind-set of successful evangelical businesspeople. We do not know what business realities they perceive nor what their responses are. There has been very little analysis or understanding of the complex problems that well-minded, faithful evangelical business leaders face in their roles as managers.

This neglect of the economic and managerial life of the evangelical business leader deserves response. I believe that the current emptiness of the business-religion dialogue is a serious lapse, not only from the standpoint of our knowledge of important trends in America but also from an ethical standpoint. The exaggerated focus on personal and domestic relations that is evident both in evangelical thinking and in many of the self-help programs in corporations today has led to a suppressing of discussions of other important factors in the social problems we all face. When noted Mormon writer and psychologist Steven Covey says that one must focus on using a "heal thyself" technique and on influencing a very small circle of relationships, he may inadvertently distract managers from exploring *systemic* factors of business that also undercut personal health. These are factors that individuals have little control over, such as required days on the road away from their families, physical and mental isolation from the poor, mandatory layoffs, or exposure to health-damaging manufacturing or office environments. As responsible business managers, it is also *imperative* to address these kinds of problems.

From a faith that claims to be truly involved in this-world problems, it should be possible to create a more focused discussion of the role of faith in business than one that is restricted to personal wholeness, self-respect, humility, and home life. In the following chapters the familiar domestic themes of evangelicalism are sounded in a variety of ways, but there is also a weaving of these strands with the concrete problems that all businesspeople face. Within this tapestry appear distinctive patterns of thought and behavior among evangelical CEOs that describe, at least in part, the nature of their business lives and their success.

Profile of Evangelical CEOs Interviewed*

- Types of company ownership represented
Publicly owned	21
Privately owned	44
Total interviewed	65

- Religious affiliation
Protestant	62
Roman Catholic evangelical	3
Total interviewed	65

Table 2.1 Type of Businesses Represented

Industry	Small[1]	Medium[2]	Large[3]	Total
Banking, Financial Services	4	3	2	9
Real Estate	3	6	0	9
Manufacturing	7	10	0	17
Service	2	6	3	11
Service & Mfg.	4	1	0	5
Food Service	3	2	0	5
Retail	2	1	2	5
Media/Sports	1	3	0	4

* Note: Sixty-five CEOs were interviewed in the first round of this study. Another twenty were interviewed in groups of five to twelve, but full data on their companies was not provided.

[1] Small = Under $10 mil. in sales, 10-49 employees

[2] Medium = $10-100 mil. in sales, 100+ employees, or significant national recognition of company or brand

[3] Large = $100+ mil. in sales ($500+ mil. for real estate and financial)

Table 2.2 Regional Distribution of Company Headquarters

Northeast	10
Midwest	28
Florida	14
Texas	11
Other	2

Table 2.3 Ages of Interviewees

Age of CEO	Total
Under 35	0
35-42	6
43-50	27
51-60	14
60+	18

Note: In some cases the ages are approximated.

3

Seven Creative Tensions

They do not understand that it is by being at variance with itself that life coheres with itself: a backward-stretching harmony, as of a bow or a lyre.

—Heraclitus[1]

I am traveling on a plane. The person next to me asks me about my work. I tell him I am writing a book on evangelical CEOs. I might as well say I'm working on ancient forms of sexual perversion, to judge from the curious mix of contempt and fascination with which this information is usually greeted.

I have it on good authority after three years of extensive business travel and casual conversations that evangelical businesspeople are assumed by nonevangelicals to fall into one of three categories, depending on the person offering the judgment:

- They are sleazebags who calculatingly use Jesus' name to grease their hypocritical smiles and line their pockets.
- They are rigid, uptight neo-Nazis who exploit friendship to "sell" Jesus and who have no idea of their own destructiveness.
- (This last generalization is usually voiced in a confessional tone of surprise.) They are discovered to be decent, hard-working human beings—in *spite* of their religion.

An example of the last characterization came from a fellow passenger on the Delta shuttle between Boston and New York:

You know, my boss is evangelical. It really surprised me. He's amazing. I really respect him. He always has time for people. He knows the personal life of everyone in the company. Always asking people about their family, their boyfriends. And he's always calm. You know, when everyone else is panicking, he'll just smile and calm us down, and figure out a way to get the business. And he's very straight [that is, conservative]. He works very

hard—no one works harder—but he doesn't seem "owned" by the business.

Evangelicals come in various forms and sizes, and the impressions they make on others vary dramatically. At the risk of general-
izing, we know that everyone has met the snake-oil salesman whose
invocations of Jesus are about as genuine as a tin dime; most people
have been scared off by the rigidity of some evangelicals, whose
uptightness *must* be hiding something that is no good for everyone
else; and some people have met the plausible evangelicals, whose
decency and intellect fall into the "normal" range of human behavior.
Casting such differences into rigid typologies has little point and
would be morally distasteful.

Nevertheless, the fact that there were certain general traits
commonly shared by the CEOs I interviewed suggested that I could
appropriately make some sort of qualified generalization about their
business mind-set. Making such a generalization also seemed to be
a helpful way of moving beyond the knee-jerk reactions that make
up the popular characterization of the evangelical business leader.

To be sure, the group that I interviewed generally emphasized
industriousness and a methodical, rational approach to life and
business. On the whole, though with notable exceptions, these
business leaders were relatively modest in lifestyle. But while they
may have been appalled at a Charles Keating-type three-thousand-
dollar lunch for five at Le Cirque, they were also not John Calvins
in modern dress. They were neither totally unmaterialistic nor
against leisure time. As I noted earlier, some of those I surveyed were
surprisingly modest in their choice of cars or houses, but many others
lived in extremely upscale communities and had large yachts, fancy
cars, and expensive leisure-time lifestyles.

It is not on the issues of materialism, industriousness, or world-
liness that the evangelical CEO can be definitively called distinctive.
On these grounds they exhibit about the same work values as an
ambitious, rational workaholic whom you could find in many secular, not-so-humanistic business circles. The difference showed itself
most obviously in terms of the personal style that interviewees
exhibited *as CEOs*. The "typical" participant was a soft-spoken

person, intimate in manner, more like a minister or old-time professor than a J. R. Ewing. His descriptions about his company tended to favor the small incident rather than the bigger picture—even if his firm was in the Fortune 500 and doing millions or billions of dollars of business a year. His choice of issues in connection with a question about conscience or business ethics was usually about a counseling encounter with a secretary or an hourly employee rather than, say, about environmental policy, product safety, or lobbying for economic policy with other business leaders.[2]

The typical participant carried the personal element identified in the previous chapter to the discussion of business, mentioning his own home life or the sexual habits of employees in what was purportedly a discussion of business philosophy and faith. He took a holistic view of problems, with the result that a discussion about a choice of product was sometimes abruptly punctuated with a story about a family problem. The two topics were reconciled, however, by the belief that it is the spiritual health of the inner, private person that will ultimately determine the moral and practical health of any business problem. There was a fundamental self-confidence to the evangelical that on the surface raised him above being personally agitated by the "little" things of life, however high the financial stakes. He was not your frenetic mover and shaker. He was calm.

This is a portrait of what could be called a domesticated capitalist. He is domesticated not only in the sense that he seeks to tame the more bestial side of modern capitalism (such as Wall Street predators on the hostile takeover scene), but literally domesticated in terms of his household concerns—marriage, child rearing, friendship, and family participation in a religious community—which extends even to the way he understands and arranges his business career. Not one participant failed to mention some important aspect of his home life (satisfactory or otherwise) and of his prayer or other spiritual activities. A good many, however, never got around to describing their product choices, the ethics of the industry in which they operate, or even a specific economic decision.

The personal "style" of the evangelical CEOs who are described in this book may be familiar to the reader, but it does not conform to the general public's expectations about the personal qualities needed for success in business today. A joint study by Korn/Ferry International and Columbia Business School of senior executive views on leadership in the next century revealed that the very characteristics that the participants in my study exhibited were rated *lowest* in terms of potential leadership. (The precise attributes were *"tough, personable, patient, dignified,* and *conservative."*[3]) As that report notes, most of these characteristics are "old-fashioned" values: "They describe the CEO who ushered in the 20th century."[4]

Despite popular opinion to the contrary, the group interviewed for this book represents substantial business success and challenges us to reconsider some of the critical assumptions being made today about the nature of successful business leadership. Whether or not we accept the sincerity or spiritual correctness of these evangelicals, or their general Norman Rockwell style, we *do* need to carefully consider and analyze their effectiveness in the marketplace and the health of their organizations. *The portrait presented in this book is an attempt to test (and hopefully explode) some of the more thoughtless stereotypes held by nonevangelicals and evangelicals alike.*

Briefly, I will show that the successful impact of evangelical faith on business management is best understood as a series of sustained tensions—seven in all—that describe the recurrent issues identified by participants. The running theme throughout this analysis is *contrast.* Evangelicalism, with its focus on the spiritual, the relational, the domestic, and the holistic, poses certain contrasts with the traditional requirements of a large, capitalistic organization. Strong investment ratings do not automatically coincide with people needs inside a company. Competitive pressures do not instantly lend themselves to an attitude of loving one's neighbor. And the pluralistic agnosticism of today's workplace rarely welcomes the mention of Jesus or any other kind of witnessing.

How then does such a faith play a role in this world? Is that role good or bad for business? More to the point, what *kind* of business values are we talking about? What sort of competitive characteristics emerge from participants' visions of good business practices?

As the interviewees probed their own attitudes toward work, career, business success, and spiritual well-being, certain common beliefs about management and Christianity were expressed so often that they suggested a group of core concepts that seem to drive evangelical business thinking. In the pages that follow, I have organized these recurring themes around seven basic tension points:

1. The love for God and the pursuit of profit
2. Love and the competitive drive
3. People needs and profit obligations
4. Humility and the ego of success
5. Family and work
6. Charity and wealth
7. Faithful witness in the secular city

As you can see, the first part of each "tension" describes an important Christian theme, while the second half describes some basic components of business enterprise.

Although all but the seventh tension represent familiar issues of conscience to any enlightened businessperson, these particular seven also betray an evangelical slant that is evident by what is *not* included. Absent here are the larger organizational perspectives— global problems such as overseas bribery, or grand schemes for economic development. Instead, as I have already noted, the interviewees tended to describe their business values in terms of relational or domestic problems—a negotiation with a customer, a small incident with a secretary, a marriage problem triggered by business events, or a situation with an unethical employee—rather than larger-scale political or ethical concerns.[5] In seeking to analyze the role of faith in business, these believers in business, as I came to call them, tended to start with their own behavior rather than with the behavior of others.

What the Seven Tensions Explain

The expression of themes in the form of the seven tensions is somewhat artificial, in that no one specifically identified seven, six, or even one "tension" to represent his business philosophy. And yet the problems these men described, their occasions for prayer, and their understanding of what it takes to be a business success, proved to hinge on these same seven oppositions time and again. Though I did not originally pose these seven as the basis for discussion, they summarize the most frequently mentioned themes in the interviews. They also provide a useful basis for others to explore the role of faith in their own business lives or that of their spouse.

I seized upon the idea of these seven tensions almost by accident. In many cases I found my interviewees making statements that on the surface appeared to be contradictory, and yet I was reluctant, in taking their entire interviews into account, to pass these things off as mere "denial" or hypocrisy.

For example, a CEO might state categorically within five minutes that (1) "Money is nothing—it is God who counts," and (2) "Profit is very important, critical to business." Or a question about business responsibility would often prompt the CEO to offer a series of nonbusiness examples. By giving such examples, he seemed to imply that the economic and practical concerns of business are inconsequential.

The problem was that the participants were men of good standing in both fields. How would I explain that they were regarded as men of faith and that they were demonstrably good businessmen? There were too many participants for me to attribute their business success wholly to chance, and there were too many concretely faith-oriented examples for me to assume that their faith meant nothing in a business context. These men wholly supported a capitalistic system in theory, and at the same time described a set of religious-cultural values that on the surface, at least, were in discord with the basic elements of capitalism.

What was going on here? Was I encountering the world's greatest collection of hypocrites? Or was it something at once more profound and less derogatory?

When the interviewees were confronted with the suggestion that business as they described it posed certain inevitable contradictions of Christian doctrine, many of them sidestepped the issue.

There are two likely but contradictory explanations for this phenomenon. One explanation is that the evangelical CEO has failed to assimilate spiritual concerns into his business activities. Wittingly (in which case it would be hypocrisy) or unwittingly (in which case the source would be some form of intellectual failure or psychological denial), he has not achieved the kind of worldly relevance of faith to which he aspires. The alternative explanation is that an assimilation of faith does indeed occur but is so successful that it is impossible for the CEO to distinguish the pieces anymore.

I, for one, am quite reluctant to pass judgment on people's sincerity. I do not have perfect pitch when confronted with the music of the soul. Nor do many other people I know. Most judgments of religious or ethical hypocrisy rest on serious misperceptions about human fallibility and nonconformity.

Evangelical stereotypes are no exception. It is assumed that every perceived imperfection or ambiguity of character in a self-avowed Christian must be self-serving and therefore unchristian and therefore hypocritical. Short of choosing martyrdom or self-imposed poverty, which are also capable of provoking a cynical interpretation, the Christian business person hasn't got a chance of obtaining spiritual success, according to the public.

By assuming that the fundamentals of economic success are essentially negatives on one's Christian scorecard we fail to address the very affirmative connection that these men see between their careers and their faith. As long as the standing question remains quantitative—that is, How "Christian" is such and such a practice?—resolution is difficult. However, the assumption that there is an automatic complementarity between Christianity and the needs of business flies in the face of the real-world experience of an unforgiving marketplace of shareholders who are in it for the short term.

But if we start with the notion that there are indeed inherent, recurrent tensions between Christianity and business practice in a capitalistic system, we can rephrase the operating question to a qualitative one: How does faith (in this case, evangelical faith) play a role in these contradictory claims on the Christian? This question is the more effective one. First, it faces up to real problems of business behavior among Christians and nonchristians. Second, it admits the concept of the paradox—that is, an apparent contradiction that is nonetheless true.

I concluded that the only way to understand the interviews without shortchanging the real struggles of conscience these men have faced was to recast the remarks of the CEOs in the form of a series of sustained tensions. The ways in which the CEOs responded to specific examples of these tensions varied dramatically, as you will soon see from the character types I have outlined. But the most compelling examples occurred when the participant sustained and transformed the tensions into a *creative paradox,* reflecting the paradoxical nature of Christian spiritual claims and the worldly concerns of profit making.

Three Categories of Responses

Such tensions could be, and frequently are, seen as mutually exclusive by evangelicals and nonevangelicals alike. They can be seen as the ultimate weapon, striking a fatal blow to capitalism from a Christian standpoint, or a fatal blow to Christianity from a business standpoint.

I found a real resistance to the idea of tension itself in many of those I interviewed. Interviewees tended to fall into three basic categories, determined by personality style, intellectual sophistication, theological assumptions, and psychological bias. As I mentioned in the preface, I have named these categories the generalist, the justifier, and the seeker. *The third type—the seeker—is of the greatest interest in this book and, I believe, provides the best example of active faith.* It should be said that a Seeker approach was by far the most frequent among this group of interviewees.

The Generalist and the Justifier

The first type, the *generalist,* never gets down to specific examples from the right-hand, or business, side of the stated tensions. No matter how hard he is pressed, he manages to evade the suggestion that determining the right thing to do from a Christian's standpoint can be difficult or contrary to common practice. A common conviction among the generalists is that there is never a real problem in their own lives between faith and the requirements of the business. Given specific, obvious inconsistencies between an ethic built on honesty and love and, say, an apparently deceptive business practice in his own firm, he might acknowledge the inconsistencies as a problem but would then change the subject back to a reaffirmation of faith rather than discuss the dilemma.

Let's suppose that his company has launched an advertising campaign based on wildly exploitative gender stereotypes. When asked to explain it, the generalist might reply that he "sees no problem with the ad." He has never really had any problems knowing what was right. He will then quickly shift his focus to the general importance of home life and parenting as the real source of values, moving on from there to affirmative examples of times at home that strengthened his own or his children's relationship to Jesus. As one participant commented, "Doing everything according to your faith is not about how it comes out in the wash. As long as your motives are pure, you're okay."

The second type, the *justifier,* is very comfortable with the basic idea that the right-hand sides of the seven tension equations, which typify economic concerns, are supported by the Bible. What he does *not* do is demonstrate how specific biblical injunctions apply to such sticky problems as a hostile takeover or a boss who is unethical or a below-standard wage rate for first-line employees. The justifier tends to see his own economic success as the justification of his faith. For example, if he has preceded his decisions with prayer, asking God to help him "win" a deal, it seems apparent to him that his desire to win is consistent with God's will in that he wins over and over again. Capitalism must be godly. Any suggestion of tension between his desire to win each deal and other requirements of his faith (such as to serve others) is overshadowed by his strong (and often genuine) demonstration of a charitable and sensitive *attitude* in nearly any business decision. Said one CEO, who was unable to specify any of his remarks:

> It's not about what you do; it's about your attitude. Get that right and the rest follows. If you love God, that's all that counts. The most important thing is to make sure your perspective is correct: who you serve.

Another CEO commented:

> I feel a call to do the best I can do with what I can do, with the God-given talents I have. . . . In business I have to worry about a return on every in-

vestment. But I don't see it as a double standard, but rather different degrees of latitude.

So it is not surprising to find that the justifier's choice of examples is either about very obvious cases of law breaking and getting caught or about decisions that were unfailingly admirable: special attention to a secretary, meticulous honesty during a negotiation, charitable deeds in the local community. Most of these examples are supported by an argument of enlightened self-interest. That is, if you do the right thing in business, you will do well economically; if you do the wrong thing, you will be punished by the marketplace. A comment by one businessman from Boston is a good illustration:

> I have a hard time thinking of illustrations simply because business is trying to find people we can help. That requires confidence, and if they thought you were a liar and a cheat, they wouldn't even let you in the door.

When asked how a Christian should handle a situation where his boss is lying and cheating, the same man replied with another justifying scenario: "Those people don't last in business."

More entrenched tensions, such as when it is permissible to "bend" the truth, or how many days should be spent away from the family for the sake of the business, are glossed over much as in the generalist's remarks. Unlike the generalist, the justifier tends to acknowledge that both sides of the tension equation are important to him, but he resists the idea of their being contradictory, recalling only the occasions when business instinct and Christian paradigms seem complementary.

For example, when I asked one particularly self-satisfied businessman if there were any dangers that a young Christian should avoid in the marketplace, he laughingly replied, "You shouldn't run prostitution rings in the city." His implication was that all the issues were already obvious to any good Christian. I tried again. "That's it?" I asked with seeming incredulity. He replied evenly:

> I would say there's very little that's not okay, as long as you keep in mind Christian principles. I mean, you can be a bartender. But you shouldn't be involved in the underworld or do anything illegal.

Essentially, these first two types—the generalist and the justifier—attempt to deal with conflict by denying its existence. They simply cannot imagine, no matter how hard they are pressed, a really problematic test of their faith. The generalist does this by never linking his understanding of Christian ethics (which is dominated by issues of sexuality and one's personal relationship with God) and management in the same set of problems. One wonders at times if there is *any* business decision that would agitate his conscience as much as one hint of illicit flirting. The justifier limits his examples to happy complementarities and ignores the more bothersome aspects of business.

Some of their denial is surely an attempt to put as favorable a light on evangelicalism as possible. They do not want outsiders to get the wrong impression by calling their attention to ethical lapses among the brethren. Others seem to have a theologically naive fear that the very suggestion of conflict between religion and business somehow contradicts a strong personal faith. If the sign of a first-class intelligence is to hold two opposing ideas at once, the justifier and the generalist flunk a basic theological IQ test. To them the admission of a possible dilemma is tantamount to a confession of spiritual doubt. Better to look the other way.

This strong tendency toward denial is a chief reason, in my opinion, why evangelicals are regarded by outsiders with suspicion or misunderstanding. It is very easy to assume that the glossy facade, the unfailing beatific smile all the way to the bank, hides a deep-seated hypocrisy. Evangelicals themselves regard some of their brothers and sisters in this light. As one evangelical CEO told me, "Some of the believers in my workplace are the *last* ones I'd trust."

But while hypocrisy explains some instances of denial, it did not generally seem to characterize the group of CEOs I interviewed. None of them were involved in the kinds of public scandals that would logically result from really venal cynicism—the kind of hypocrisy that was displayed in the savings and loan crisis, for example. Indeed, one CEO was in the personally difficult position of cooperating with the federal government in building a case against his chairman (also an evangelical), who had squandered a local S&L's assets. The CEO's condemnation of such behavior was unequivocal;

but like a true seeker, he also found it very difficult to know how to give Christian love to the boss while essentially contributing to the government's case against the man.

But even if we absolve the generalist and justifier of deliberate concealment or hypocrisy, there is nonetheless a serious problem with their approach in terms of providing models of evangelical leadership from a spiritual and business standpoint.

Both the justifier and the generalizer, even when they are well-intentioned, decent people, fail to articulate any *public* meaning to the Christian's life, including his or her business life. Rather, they exhibit a faith that corresponds to Peter Berger's description of a wholly privatized religion: religious relevance is restricted to one's "inner space," domestic activities, or individual personality traits such as being "nice."[6] This sort of compartmentalization of the sacred and the secular is unsatisfactory to evangelicals because of the holistic orientation of their faith. And so they develop avoidance mechanisms for concealing the privatization of their religion.

And yet the conflicts with faith are there. In most cases, economic success does not come without placing the evangelical worldview and ethic in some jeopardy. Even a simple biblical directive such as not working on the Sabbath is nearly impossible to maintain by an executive in a large firm. In fact, several men said that they drew the line at working on the Sabbath, but when pressed they admitted that they would travel on the Sabbath to get to a Monday morning meeting. There are many such examples of the conflict between faith and the business culture, and between profit obligations and Christian commitments.

These points of conflict are frequently what I call "Siamese twin" problems. Two things are linked together in a way that cannot be maintained. One twin must be sacrificed for the other to live. Such a choice is unthinkable but inescapable. If nothing is done, if you turn your back, both will die.

The evangelical businessperson is constantly confronted with such choices. Should he or she invest in a very good health plan for employees or in product development to ensure jobs down the road? Should the evangelical travel on the Sabbath and get the business or attend the Bible study class on Sunday evening? There is no way to justify "turning one's back" or to expect capitalism to offer an automatic solution that will reward both one's faith and one's business expectations. Nonetheless, a generalist or justifier may not notice that he or she is not facing up to the problem because they have constructed elaborate "blinders" based in part on the strength of their religious belief. What is more, for the most part there is no "ethics doctor" to spell out these choices in inescapable terms. Mature people do this for themselves.

The Seeker

I discovered, however, that many business leaders were, in fact, acutely aware of these dilemmas and prepared to address them. I have called this third type of evangelical business leader the *seeker,* because he is willing to struggle with difficult choices in order to best serve his faith. The seeker, on whom the concept of the seven creative tensions is based, does not try to eliminate a suggestion of conflict between the requirements of the business and what his faith calls him to do or to feel.

Nor does he regard the tensions that most people feel between the promptings of a generous heart and a hardheaded economist as mere trade-offs (the positives and negatives on one's Christian scorecard). As former Eastman Gelatine president Frank Butler remarked:

> Conflict is a part of life. It's naive to expect that your faith will help you find one final solution to problems. But faith tells you the right way to deal with conflicts.

Of the three types of evangelical business leaders, the seeker takes the most dynamic view of the tensions between Christian belief, human failing, and economic practicality. He confronts these tensions, and through prayer and the perspective of faith, seeks out a course of action consistent with Christianity. *Faith itself becomes the mediating factor in these tensions.*

Another reason that I call this type of leader the seeker is that the *process* of his business thinking is as important as the actual deed. He genuinely wrestles with his Christian conscience and business responsibilities in order to seek out as compatible a response as possible, even though he knows that the concept of being a "perfect" Christian doing the perfect Christian deed is beyond any human's comprehension.

In many cases, however, his seeking leads to the creation of third alternatives that are more in line with biblical values and that often are strokes of economic brilliance as well. That is why I refer to the seven tensions as *creative* tensions. To the seeker, business is not simply a temptation that is to be mitigated by making unprofitable economic decisions or that is to be offset by charitable activities. Rather, his business conduct becomes one more *expression* of faith.

Let's look at the example already cited between biblical warnings against a love of money and market demands to focus on making a profit. The generalist would simply duck the problem. Typically, he would respond to this dilemma with assertions about God's love, his joy in Jesus, and how the things of this world don't matter. He would also talk about how proud he is of his work and how close he'd become to his employees. The marital problems of his secretary might follow, or an extended story of his conversion, by which time the original question—about how his efforts to make a profit tie in to obedience to God's authority—would be lost.

The justifier would argue that capitalism is the best mechanism for sustaining a constitution-based society like the U.S., thereby guaranteeing freedom of religion. No problem.

Or the justifier might view a specific conflict selectively, looking only at the seemingly biblical side of the trade-offs—the obligations that are on the left side of the list of seven tensions. So he might spend X amount of effort on wealth creation of an exploitative sort (say, by cheating suppliers out of a fair profit), but it is the Y amount of effort that he spends on giving the proceeds away that captures his attention. As long as the charitable contributions are above the required tithe, his image of his own faithfulness (which is, after all, the real goal) is comfortable. Another frequent response of the justifier is to choose examples in which doing good always pays off in the end, similar to secular arguments about enlightened self-interest. He might, for example, only consider the occasions when he voluntarily disclosed a mistake to a customer and later got twice the business.

The seeker, however, would not duck, gloss over, or compart-mentalize the inherent conflicts posed by modern capitalism's strong emphasis on profit and by the biblical command to submit to God's will above all else. Instead, his faith, already holistic in orientation, mediates the tension in a number of ways. It may help him gain a long-term perspective that allows him to plan and methodically balance his various obligations or help him make short-term sacri-fices for the long-term health of his company, family, or own self. The seeker may draw heavily on the New Testament metaphor of the good steward, or on the Old Testament Creation mandate to increase the land, thereby setting up a quasi-agricultural view of the marketplace that allows cyclical periods of investment, harvest, and fallow seasons. This image builds a certain flexibility into his ap-proach that rises above the make-or-break mentality of short-term survival strategies. He may instinctively or overtly base his own perception of relevant problems on New Testament injunctions to love one another, and therefore strongly favor a business approach based on concrete contributions of value and service in the market-place rather than on something more abstract such as "the efficiencies of the market." Because he is relationally oriented, he will generally steer clear of businesses where the deal is the only product.

In this way, profit is transformed from being an ultimate value to being *a result of ultimate values.* This is not an anticapitalistic or even an economically neutral leadership philosophy. The seeker's overt business actions and values include profit seeking and organized capital investments, but his faith mediates the process to include the "softer," more spiritual aspects of Christianity. So close are these responses to one of "enlightened self-interest" that an outsider usually cannot distinguish the difference that faith makes in the seeker's thinking.

And yet, I will maintain that the seeker's faith does indeed profoundly affect his decision making. By responding creatively, his normal tensions between business and other obligations are trans-formed into expressions of faith. Then a CEO's statement, such as "business is nothing," can coexist unhypocritically with the fact that he spends a major part of his time on business. The evangelical business leader's particular paradox, or series of paradoxes, is a

creative phenomenon in that it leads to productive economic activity
and to productive personal spiritual fulfillment.

In other words, for the seeker the tension between capitalistic
activity and private faith is recognized and sustained instead of denied
or seen as a trade-off to be dealt with in separate allotments of time
and money. The crucial point here is that *the normal conflicts between
the marketplace and Christian ethics are not terminally destructive for either
side of the equation.* In the long run neither economics nor personal
faith suffers from the other's claims, because of the way in which
business is conducted and organized over time. Hence the paradoxical effect.

Where there is an undeniable contradiction between a particular
business opportunity and what the seeker feels to be right in Christian terms, he either has enough slack built into the system to reject
the deal or he finds a way to approach the problem that is more in
line with his conscience. This kind of reframing of business problems is not accidental; it is a product of leadership and prayer.

The suggestion that the evangelical's business experiences as
represented by the seeker are inherently paradoxical should not be
entirely surprising, given the essentially paradoxical nature of Christianity. Many of the fundamental precepts of Christianity are themselves standing paired opposites: in death there is life; humans are
essentially sinful and yet forgiven; heaven cannot be reached as a
result of good deeds, and yet good deeds are evidence of faith. Such
tensions are a fundamental part of the Christian identity. Life is
acknowledged to have definable, inevitable limits, and yet mortality
carries the element of eternal life. The evangelical is human, flawed,
and sinful, and yet has an eternal soul. He or she is humbled by mortal
sin and yet self-confident in being loved by God. By accepting God's
love the evangelical opens the way to becoming a positive part of
God's plan.

In describing the seven creative tensions, I am reminded of an
early Greek pun, attributed to Heraclitus, that asserted that life was
an archer's bow. The pun was based on the verbal joke that the Greek
words for *bow* and *life* were the same—*bios*—only with different
accentuation. The idea behind the pun was profound, because it
described the world as existing in a constant state of balanced oppo-

sites—taut juxtapositions of mortality and immortality, good and evil, light and dark. Such contradictions, far from being mutually negating, were the source of creative power. Another fragment from Heraclitus also expresses this concept of the creative conflict well. He wrote, "War is the father of all things," meaning that creative forces depend on conflict for their procreative power.

For the generalist and the justifier, conflict is almost unchristian. For the seeker, life is indeed a bow, a constant tension between the demands of the world and the promptings of the soul. Faith is the string that holds these opposing forces in balance and that makes the bow work.

The irony is that while evangelicalism can bring about a softening of the more predatory aspects of capitalistic activity and a broadening of personal definitions of success, it also nourishes an extremely powerful, focused economic and managerial expertise such as might be echoed in the most secular of businesspeople. A good example is CEO Max De Pree, noted for his business prowess but quite different in other ways from the average tycoon. He once introduced a cap on the income gap between the highest and lowest at Herman Miller, based on a personally bothersome conversation he had had with an hourly employee. De Pree is an obvious seeker and an outstandingly innovative and successful executive.

What the Seven Creative Tensions Do

The concept of the seven creative tensions provides a springboard for understanding the role of faith in the businessperson's specific worldly pursuits. Given their pervasive nature, these seven tensions outline the major building blocks of the seeker's business and career thinking.

It would be an understatement to say that tracking this process is a very difficult task. It requires identifying qualitative factors and tracing their effects on concrete, materialistic actions. The seekers whose interviews are recorded here did not, for the most part, express their thoughts in neat, paradoxical statements. And yet the *totality* of their statements has suggested just such a pattern.

The following story is an excellent example of the seven creative tensions at work, and of the ways that these reference points of Christian and business obligation can determine a seeker's problem solving. This story was told to me firsthand by Jack Willome, president of Rayco, a homebuilding and neighborhood development company in San Antonio, Texas.

> Several years ago, our company was involved in real, life-threatening consumer litigation. The plaintiff's attorney was very active, and he filed a group action against us. Ultimately, about one thousand families to whom we had sold homes over four or five years were included.
>
> Here's the background. Between 1981 and 1985 we sold about thirteen thousand homes total, and approximately three thousand were sold to a company called Epic. They would hold the homes, renting them temporarily, in anticipation of the high inflation in housing prices which had been occurring in Texas. When oil collapsed, that inflation did not happen. They had made heavy acquisitions throughout the Southwest, and owned about twenty thousand homes altogether. By 1985 they were bankrupt.
>
> Local papers reported that all of Epic's houses would be dumped at the same time, and that values in our neighborhoods would plummet.
>
> So this attorney who advertised on TV, organized through cells with block captains in all our neighborhoods, and filed a group action lawsuit. Initially about a hundred families were involved, and the more publicity it got, the more people jumped on the bandwagon. They were motivated by fear. The truth was, none of these houses was ever dumped. The attorney was on a contingency fee, so he would only be paid on the basis of what he won for them, leaving the homeowners with no financial risk for the lawsuit.
>
> The filing, under an anomaly in the Deceptive Trade Act of Texas, was in October '85, and our sales stayed strong till March '86. So the lawsuit was building to a crescendo just as our business was falling apart. And you have to remember that judges are elected in Texas, and this attorney was very powerful politically, and the judges were looking at two thousand homeowners. . . . So you get all the dynamics.
>
> I wanted to lose as little money as possible for the company. I genuinely felt that the lawsuit was unfair if not downright sleazy. I wanted to be protected. I wanted to win. Those were my kind of gut desires, and that's what I asked for through prayer.
>
> But through dialogue with some good people, I got refocused. We have this conference line, and once a month about ten of us, from all over the country, talk and pray for each other. I told the group about the lawsuit, and asked that they pray for me to win the suit.
>
> And one of them said, "Hey, wait a minute. I can't pray for that. All I can pray for is that you be treated fairly and that the truth come out."
>
> And, of course, he was right. And this really changed the way I looked

at the case. Instead of focusing on how to win, I began to focus on being treated fairly and the truth coming out. So I asked my attorney some questions about the court system and our case. I asked how many of the elected judges (out of approximately eight) would give business a fair trial, and he said maybe two. So right there, it would have taken an act of God to be treated fairly, right? And the second thing he told me was that in the courtroom process attorneys use procedural rules to exclude the truth. So it would take an act of God for us to be treated fairly and for the decision to be based on truth.

And that got down to something I could pray for with integrity and I could ask other people to pray for with integrity.

During a forty-five-day period I sat through the depositions. I wanted to hear firsthand what people were saying they'd gone through and understand what this case was really about. It was very painful for me, but it gave me a perspective that I couldn't have gotten just talking to our attorneys. You know, you just naturally tend to exaggerate your own position.

Ultimately, I came to the conclusion that the more I knew about both sides, the better equipped I was to . . . well, it just hit me that it was foolishness to put the fate of our company in the hands of the jury and a judge in this crazy process. What I needed to do was to inject myself directly into negotiations and apply what I saw of the truth, instead of getting ourselves into this radical position we tend to get into—that I tend to get myself into—of black and white, wrong and right, good and bad. . . . The world just isn't that way.

Ultimately we settled the case. And those prayers were answered over and over again.

That's one of the things I've learned from all this. When I look at things from the standpoint of good and bad, right and wrong, I end up projecting my own garbage on other people. When I look for the guilt in others, I usually see my own guilt. When I look for the innocence, I'll usually find my own innocence. And I believe that where the compassion of Christ comes in is to be able to see the innocence of people who are attacking us.

Jack's account is a moving example of the power of prayer in a CEO's decision making. Moreover, we can see in his story all seven of the tensions that are identified in this book. Let's look at how each of these tensions became a creative force after Jack's views were changed through prayer.

Jack did not ignore the money side of this problem, and yet he created a new solution that he saw as being consistent with and motivated by his faith (*Tension 1—the love for God and the pursuit of profit*). He was acutely aware that the stakes were high and that the company was on the line. At first, he simply wanted to win, in order to prevent the loss of revenue that an adverse judgment would impose. As he revised his view of the problem, however, he began to see the issue as one of both poor stewardship and unchristian self-centeredness in adopting a winner-take-all strategy (*Tension 2—love and the competitive drive*). He did not adopt an *uncompetitive* strategy, because he was always acutely aware that the financial life of the company was at stake. He did, however, radically revise the terms of *winning* and his subsequent negotiating strategy as a result of his changed views.

Note that Jack did not arrive at this strategy through reasoned self-interest (for example, *it simply pays to settle out of court*), but through a sense of love and fairness—a love of God and a love of the people testifying against the firm. As a good steward, as a person striving to serve God, as a Christian commanded to love his neighbor and directed by biblical injunctions not to lie, Jack voluntarily submitted himself to the humbling experience of hearing his company's actions described in the worst, most distorted terms. We can appreciate how difficult it would be for anyone, but especially for the head of a company, to do this face to face. Can you imagine former Ford Motor chairman Lee Iacocca appearing in person at the Ford Pinto depositions?

At the same time, it would be wrong to characterize Jack's actions, though requiring humility, as being passive. Resisting the temptation to win at any cost in order to protect his personal image of "success" required tremendous leadership and self-confidence (*Tension 4—humility and the ego of success*). Negotiating a settlement that would not bankrupt the company demanded strong leadership ability.

Jack's decision to attend the depositions and to seek the truth by listening to people made him sensitive to the double-sided nature of the problem (*Tension 3—people needs and profit obligations*). Whereas earlier he had seen the people in his neighborhoods as being in total and illegitimate opposition to the profit needs of his company, he realized after hearing them that, however unfair the lawsuit, they had a case and a need too.

Later on, Jack's new sensitivity was put to economic advantage. The settlements were never contested. Afterward Jack's organization initiated a new market study of people's expectations in the starter housing market. They discovered a number of surprising preferences in new home owners that led to a very different design and construction strategy. In the late 1980s his firm was able to create a forty-five-thousand-dollar start-up house in southern Texas, and was the first real estate company in his region to experience an upturn in its market, well ahead of other competitors in the area. This combination of charity toward his adversaries and the later creation of a successful new product puts *Tension 6—charity and wealth* into a creative combination rather than into the position of paired opposites concerning the giving and getting of money. What of *Tension 5—family and work?* Jack himself referred to this aspect of his life when he summarized the experience. He reported that his family had been extremely supportive during these events, and that they had given him the strength to endure the stress of the depositions and settlements. He said that they became increasingly close as he went through the trial. This, too, underscored the element of love and truth in the process. As he put it, "The closer I get to them, the more I can tell my family where I *really* am." For Jack—a recovering alcoholic, who had once been isolated and without intimate relationships—this was an extraordinary admission.

Relationships played a significant role also in Jack's attention to his devotional life. Like many evangelicals, he has formed networks of friends (many of them other CEOs) who support each other and pray for each other. As we can see from this incident, these groups are restrictive in a social sense; but they also played a mediating function between the demands of outsiders and the demands of Christian faith (*Tension 7—faithful witness in the secular city*). They helped Jack to *survive* in the real world rather than to withdraw from it.

So it is possible to see how evangelicalism as described earlier (prayerful, personal, relational, and intensifying) became a mediating, transformational factor in each of the tensions inherent in Jack's situation. Jack himself experienced several important inner transformations as a result of his fellowship with the prayer group and their subsequent prayers for him. He went from a win-lose, self-regarding, seemingly hopeless situation to one of truth seeking and, ultimately, accommodation. Also—and this is very much to the point of this study—he developed an economically viable strategy to deal with the crisis.

It's apparent that Jack's faith is what transformed his personal experience of a business crisis into a more humanizing experience, consistent with Christian ethics. His faith was also a catalyst for wealth creation.

Jack's story is a particularly organized display of the seven creative tensions at work. In many other interviews, I had to piece together the creative aspect of the tensions over more than one event to capture the full impact of faith in these leaders' thinking. For this reason, it is important to understand that this study is an analysis of the *process* of evangelical business leadership rather than the *ethics* of individual acts. It is not just an ordering of the facts of a CEO's decision making, but rather an ordering of his construction of reality.

The seven categories, or creative tensions, suggested here give us an organizing framework for understanding how some of the most admired evangelical business leaders in America deal with the profound tensions of modern life and especially of human economic experience. This framework helps us understand also the nature of a certain type of business leadership which addresses key choices that Christians in business face.

Interestingly, when this story and the seven tensions were presented to a group of evangelical CEOs, one of them, who was president of a major fast food chain, found his own thinking changing dramatically about a serious business problem he was facing. He, too, was being sued in a particularly vicious class action case which had been publicized nationwide, accusing him among other things of being ethnically prejudiced. For his part, he felt he was simply carrying out the letter of a contract. After hearing Jack's struggle, this other CEO, call him Tom, changed both the way he himself thought about his legal "enemy" and the way the case was being handled. Against the advice of his lawyers, he met with the man personally and discovered that serious problems of communication had occurred on both sides. They eventually made a settlement. They even became friends.

When Tom's son expressed amazement that his father was

going to meet with the man who had publicly portrayed him in such a negative way, Tom told his son of his own spiritual trials over this case, and his change of thinking. Tom reported that he and his son had never had such a frank talk about religion, and in the end he flew his son to one of the meetings to meet "the enemy."

Stories such as these are not just about the ethics of business or profitable financial outcomes. They show how the evangelical CEO's faith can help him sustain and creatively manage the opposing demands upon him through changing something very deep inside himself, namely his attitudes, his sense of others, his willingness to take risks.

I see the framework offered here as useful even to nonevangelicals who would seek a more domesticated, humanized version of advanced capitalism. Consider the comment of a very successful, extremely driven nonevangelical executive in the financial services world. He was describing the philosophy of his firm and his own managerial style: Motivate people on greed, and as long as you can control the greed to stay within legal bounds, you have an unstoppable economic machine. The only problem, he mused, was that people burned out. The system exploited their strength, then spat them out with nothing left but their bank accounts (if they were lucky). He himself said he felt very fortunate "to have a wife who is willing to spend all her time raising my kids. Because I never see them."

I asked him how long he could keep up the pace. He admitted that, because he was forty-one years old, he had only a few years left. The worry, however, was in deciding what to do next. He couldn't just quit, as a friend of his had done, to farm land in Australia.

> The problem is that I don't want to stop working, and I can't keep up this game forever. But I don't know how to do it any other way. What I need is some sort of mental halfway house.

For the evangelical business leaders of the seeker category—who also are prone to "doing something economic" but are subject to the tensions between hard work, ambition, and the "softer" aspects of existence—Christian faith is that mental halfway house.

4

Tension 1: The Love for God and the Pursuit of Profit

In nothing has the Church so lost her hold on reality as in her failure to understand and respect the secular vocation. She has allowed work and religion to become separate departments, and is astonished to find that, as a result, the secular work of the world is turned to purely selfish and destructive ends, and that the greater part of the world's intelligent workers have become irreligious, or at least, uninterested in religion.
—Dorothy L. Sayers[1]

W hen the great evangelist John Wesley launched his ministry among the coal miners of England in the eighteenth century, he had somewhat mixed success. The converted miners, despairingly poor, abandoned their drinking and carousing in favor of the "spiritual inebriation" of religion, which uplifted their spirits and ultimately their lifestyle. They began to stay home in the evenings, save money, enjoy a new self-respect, and care for their families. But to Wesley's dismay, this new prosperity—a natural result of industriousness and thrift—introduced undesirable tendencies toward indolence and the love of money. Wesley was both heartened by their escape from destitution and fearful that spiritual complacency—or worse—would follow fast on its heels.

The Paradox Defined

Wesley's backsliding coal miners are merely one example of the paradoxical spiritual effects of conservative Protestantism. The very qualities that believers exhibit—hard work, self-discipline, sobriety, and thrift—are the key ingredients to a material success that is the downfall of those not truly committed to God. As the Bible warns, no one can have two masters: "You cannot serve God and mammon" (Matt. 6:24-25).

Is work a curse or a mandate? Are the natural rewards of capitalism—namely, the accumulation of profit—the devil's tool or God's blessing? Commitment to Christ in an evangelical culture invites a way of life that makes obvious good business sense. And yet the demands of business can be a harsh master of a person's time and attention. They can lure that person away from his or her relationship with God.

So while every employed evangelical faces a natural tension between spiritual commitment and responsibility to an earthly job, for the CEO these tensions are particularly keen. The demands of time and energy and the material rewards of successful business conduct are not necessarily evil, but they can sidetrack a Christian from his or her primary responsibility.

The famous warning in Matthew 6 concludes that Christian commitment and an obsession with wealth are mutually exclusive: No one can serve two masters. It's all very fair to argue, as many theologians do, that the passage is not a condemnation of work itself but a warning against *focusing* on work and wealth to the point that it becomes an overriding priority.

But how do you make it in the business world without focusing much time and attention on mundane, profit-oriented decisions? How much is too much? That question leads to at least two others: Can an evangelical legitimately assume leadership of a corporation and still be faithful to his or her primary commitment—the commitment to Christ? Is it unfair to assume top responsibility for a job knowing that you really have a higher set of priorities? And are the successful evangelicals who publicly profess their commitments to Christ really just kidding themselves?

Theologically, the value of poverty versus the value of wealth is a matter of wide debate. Even the value of economic activity is ambiguous. Some Christian ministers suggest or imply that in the hierarchy of "callings," "full-time ministry" comes out at the top, and

business at the bottom. Others deny any hierarchy, suggesting that
each person must work according to his or her gifts.

Many New Testament passages seem to place a special emphasis
on poverty: "Blessed are you poor" (Luke 6:20); "Woe to you who
are rich" (Luke 6:24); and "Do not lay up for yourselves treasures on
earth" (Matt. 6:19). Jesus encouraged his followers to consider the
lilies of the field, which neither toil nor spin but surpass Solomon in
his visible glory. Jesus' statement that it is easier for a camel to pass
through the eye of a needle than for a rich man to enter the kingdom
of heaven is a good indication that, in New Testament terms,
economics and wealth are *potentially* a source of moral degeneration,
an impoverishment of the spirit in the face of material riches. As one
interviewee put it, "I really believe that materialism can separate you
from your God." He cited Luke 12:34 as evidence: "For where your
treasure is, there your heart will be also."

Before concluding that business and Christianity are contradictions in terms, we must recognize that many other passages in both
the New and Old Testaments praise economic self-reliance and the
wise use of resources as being signs of moral health. Despite the New
Testament emphasis on the "blessed" poor and its warnings about
the love of money, other biblical injunctions and parables of Jesus
strongly support resourcefulness and monetary stewardship. In the
parable of the talents, for example, Jesus uses an analogy to describe
the preparation of the spirit for the Lord's coming (Matt. 25:14-30).
Three servants are given a sum of money, each according to his
ability. The first two invest their money and eventually increase it.
They are praised and rewarded even further for doing so. The third,
however, simply buries the money. His master punishes him. The
point of the parable is not actually meant to be a lesson in financial
stewardship; Jesus is encouraging his followers to use their gifts and
abilities fully. But the choice of the good steward as a *positive* example
is nevertheless an indication that absolute condemnation of economic success is not necessarily consistent with Christian teachings.

One thing is clear: The need to work is inevitable. (In 2 Thes-
salonians 3:14, Paul advises Christians to keep away from anyone
living in idleness.) Even in the Garden of Eden, before the Fall, Adam
was put to work tilling the soil. Genesis 3:17, 19 tells us that, after

the Fall, God declared that hereafter humankind must work to win its food: "In toil you shall eat of it [the ground]/ All the days of your life. . . . / In the sweat of your face you shall eat bread/ Till you return to the ground. . . ."

And yet our work is for more than a survival subsistence: Noah plants vineyards (albeit with mixed results), and at various times the children of Israel are rightful masters of enormous dominion. Even Jesus' disciples never stand in bread lines.

The passage in Genesis 3 is sometimes called God's curse. More often it is understood to be a marching order. The element of *curse,* as the *Oxford Annotated Bible* suggests, is that the necessity to work is a sign of humankind's broken relationship with God. Then work itself becomes a spiritual paradox. It represents spiritual incompleteness in one's relationship to God and yet a carrying out of God's willed order. New Testament passages on work and prosperity imply the same paradox: Work is a mandate in God's order, but its meaning is limited from a spiritual standpoint.

So for the evangelical business leader, a career as a captain of industry holds the potential of both weakening the personal relationship with God and fulfilling God's order. What can hold these conflicting aspects of work together is the concept of grace, which moves the evangelical toward the possibility of a sanctified life.[2] By God's grace, humankind has a chance at integrating the sacred and the mundane. The ambiguity and the failure to get it right, however, are very high, and very uncomfortable for many evangelicals.

The Paradox Defied

There are several ways out of such tension. One of them is to separate work from the really significant aspects of one's life. Both the church in some of its preaching and the generalists accomplish this by avoiding any direct discussion of how specific requirements of business (such as gaining financial power) do or do not contribute to a person's spiritual health. In avoiding such issues they inadvertently create a *schism* between grace and mundane economic tasks that is ultimately dissatisfying to the evangelical mind-set, which seeks to link *all* aspects of life to God's grace and authority.

Of course, such an approach fails to provide either the emotional or intellectual support required to integrate faith and work. For the seekers among those I interviewed, any stigma or taboo on the discussion of work was unacceptable. A common complaint from the interviewees was that their clergy never acknowledged or understood the complexity of issues that a business leader faces. As one remarked:

> They [the church] always ask me to head the finance committee, and of course I am able to give a large donation. But that's about all they understand about my role as a businessman: I can do the books. In their eyes, when I'm doing what I do at work, I'm not a real person with a real soul.

Failure to confront the problem of the businessperson as Christian and the Christian as businessperson is damaging to the Christian executive. He or she may view success in business as alien to a Christian worldview, or may feel secretly guilty about work because it is a kind of secondary calling. In either case, the "real me"—the one who prays and communes with God and knows how this-world activities should be conducted—is the one that exists outside working hours. For a business leader, this is a very small part of his or her day.

This kind of schism in one's personal identity can be very threatening. Not surprisingly, the generalists and justifiers have developed a number of coping mechanisms. The most popular is to deny the tensions altogether. As one generalist said to me:

> I do not see any contradiction at all between Christianity and business. I can honestly say that in my thirty years in business I have never felt that I have compromised myself as a Christian. Some of the best Christians I know are businessmen.

The justifiers also expressed a sense of unquestionable moral rectitude about their own choices to be business leaders. Satisfying as this is, it also risks inviting a fatalistic logic between economic success and Christian ethics. This leaves no room for self-examination or any need to question common business practices. The following comments are typical of the way that a justifier understood his choice of a business career:

I don't say all poor people are cursed by God, but I do feel that my success in business, all the blessings that it brings, are a sign of God's favor.

When you look at the success of the American economic system in relation to the poorer countries of the world, you have to believe it's more than good luck. You feel there is some connection with God's will. This country and our way of life were founded in God's name. They reflect the feeling of our forefathers that this was God's will.

The offices of several of the interviewees displayed variations on a picture of an elderly businessman seated behind his desk. Behind this businessman stands Jesus, with his hand on the man's shoulder. Such imagery could merely symbolize the important part that faith plays in the Christian businessperson's decision making. For some of the interviewees, however, it is easy to jump from simply acknowledging God's help to seeing one's business success, like all good things, as one more sign of God's blessing, and thus assuming that God is behind Widget, Inc., all the way to the bank. In fact, for some, any business activity of a believer was beyond question.

A few justifiers in the group expressed belief in what is now called the prosperity gospel. They assume that being a believer gives you special access to God's economic pipeline. One widely read evangelical writer, Myron Rush, believes that the temptations of Christ provide good biblical evidence that Satan wants to take over this world by taking over the marketplace. Among Rush's conclusions are these:

> It follows that Christian businesspeople everywhere must take a strong stand for God in the marketplace. They must be committed to knowing and applying biblical principles of doing business.
>
> As they do, I believe three things will occur: First, they will prosper. Second, the entire business community—and society in general—will be more prosperous. Third, Satan's effort to control the world by controlling the marketplace will be held back.[3]

It is important to note that Rush does not accept an "anything goes" business ethic. He very clearly warns against letting the business be run only by a profit goal:

> The Christian wants to serve, obey, and please God. But he is also some-

times tempted to forget God, roll up his sleeves, and do whatever it takes to compete successfully for business.

The majority of interviewees in my group, however, rejected the prosperity gospel. Elmer Johnson, former executive vice-president of General Motors, made the following comments to a group of evangelical CEOs:

> I am rather repelled, as I am sure you are, by the sight of pious, so-called Christian business leaders who like to crow about the vital connection between their faith or virtue and their business success. I am not so sure that there is much of a connection. If anything, the distribution of sainthood may be inversely related to the distribution of wealth and income. A faith that is viewed as utilitarian is not worth bothering about. Second, I have seen too many effective business leaders who share our human and social values, but who do not share our Christian faith, for me to think that you and I have any monopoly on wisdom just because we are Christians.[4]

Bob Slocum is a Dallas entrepreneur whose book, *Ordinary Christians in a High-Tech World,* was recommended to me by one of my interviewees. Slocum at one time simplistically believed in a prosperity gospel and confused it with the "Puritan work ethic." His reflections on his change of view summarize an opinion echoed by a number of interviewees:

> I began this venture [his own business] with high hopes and enthusiasm grounded in what is commonly called the "Puritan work ethic"—the belief that if you are industrious and work very hard, God will bless you materially. . . .
> Well, the result of the last few years is that I have worked very hard and also avoided sexual sins. And so far the material blessings have not come to pass. Does this mean I am one of God's naughty children? I don't think so. . . .
> It is up to God whether and how I am blessed. I must accept this for my own business venture even though I have high hopes for the future.[5]

When asked about the prosperity gospel, noted Dallas businessman Fred Smith acknowledged that it had been very widespread among believers in Texas in the boom years of the early 1980s. But he said there had been a big drop in its popularity among executives he knew:

> The end of the eighties here in Dallas sure debunked the prosperity gos-

pel. I get former name-it-and-claim-it believers in here for counseling who've lost hundreds of millions of dollars. You're not hearing the same kind of nonsense around here now.

A Seeker's View of the Reasons to Work

When you listen to a seeker's views on work and success, they initially sound like another kind of nonsense. According to the seeker, work is both a necessity and a trifle, a sign of responsibility and personal health, but ultimately a very poor indication of anything. The way in which evangelical CEOs most frequently express this paradox is to say, "My money and career are nothing. My money isn't mine; it's God's. And success is not because of me; it's because of God."

Why, then, do these CEOs work in for-profit enterprises? How do you explain the demonstrable success of people who say their work is "nothing"? (Interestingly, few of those I interviewed had any problem with the idea of being successful businessmen, or any lack of motivation.)

First of all, we must recognize in the seekers' remarks two distinct definitions of success: one earthly and one eternal. Knowing that one's *ultimate* (or eternal) values are placed in God, the accomplishments of this world mean nothing by comparison.

But evangelicals also tend to have a strong sense of confidence and self-respect as a result of having personally accepted God's love. As John 5:24 says, "He who hears My word and believes in Him who sent Me has everlasting life, and shall not come into judgment, but has passed from death into life."

Brian Griffiths, former chief economic adviser to Margaret Thatcher and professor at City University Business School in London, points out the integral connections between evangelicalism, a sense of self-respect, and work in his book *The Creation of Wealth.*[6] Self-respect, argues Griffiths, is a key message in Jesus' famous commandment to love our neighbors as ourselves. Many people's self-respect is tied to their financial independence. The Christian is no exception, and has a particularly strong sense of duty to work and to be successful in that work. As Paul said, "If anyone will not work, neither shall he eat" (2 Thess. 3:10).

John Wesley's conversion of the coal miners, the Salvation Army's campaigns, and Chuck Colson's Prison Fellowship program all carry a similar message: To be a Christian is to know God's love for you. Knowing this love, you can love yourself and have self-respect. To be a Christian is to be *functional*: not alcoholic, criminal, or sexually depraved. To be functional is to be able to support yourself. In other words, to work for material rewards.

Beneath the social usefulness of conservative Protestant attitudes toward work is another layer of interpretation: The seekers seemed to have a *deep personal sense of spiritual meaning about work itself.* Fred Smith had a nice phrase for it: "My work is my worship." His claim is not simply a mechanistic acting out of Christian ethics; it goes much deeper to the creation of an unbroken link between the *process* of working in the world and fulfilling one's personal identity as a Christian.

The effects of such a view are profound. Once work becomes an expression of one's identity as a Christian, it is placed in a larger universe of spiritual obligations that include prayer, sacrifice, and love. This context embraces, rather than denies, the New Testament tension about the meaning of work—that is, trusting God while still taking personal responsibility—and allows the tension to exist in a creative paradox. The anxiety about the possibility of failure is taken away because work and one's own achievements are ultimately "nothing"—and yet one has a sense of fulfillment as a Christian in the task of work. This motivates extraordinary managerial success. And work becomes both productive and fulfilling.

The way in which this fulfillment was expressed by the interviewees was not in some abstract, removed sense, but in seeing God in the concrete, everyday occurrences on the job: the unexpected closure on an important deal, the employee who asks you about your Christian commitments, the lessons of humility learned from one's coworkers. Bob Slocum's initial failures to prosper caused him to seek a deeper meaning of work than simply a source of financial rewards:

> My work is successful as long as Christ becomes real each day in the arena of my daily work.
> I work for and pray toward business success, but, once that I have done

all I can, I am learning to relax in the knowledge that blessings in terms of profit and loss are ultimately in God's hands.[7]

A Case in Point

Chicago senior executive Jack Feldballe's reasons for working are a good example of the seeker's automatic integration of work into a view of himself or herself as a complete Christian. Until recently, Feldballe was president of a very large development firm that built upscale retail-office complexes throughout the United States. He now has his own company that consults with that firm and others on specific projects. Feldballe is in his early fifties.

At the time of our interview, Feldballe, Dennis Sheehan (chairman of AXIA), and I were sitting in the Faculty Club at Wheaton College outside Chicago. We had been talking generally about their business philosophies. I asked Feldballe, "Why do you work?"

Polite up until now, he stared at me as if I were crazy. The next thing I knew, he was quietly crying, and we all fell silent. It turned out that his parents were very poor. "I won't say there weren't people as poor as we, but there weren't any poorer." During the early 1940s there was often no food, and the water was frozen in the faucets. Neighbors helped out as they could with food and coal. "When I think of those good people," says Feldballe, "I can never repay them." I found myself speechless at the profound sensitivity to the plight of the poor that this man expressed after successfully creating some of the most upscale shopping areas in the United States.

As soon as he could, Feldballe was working. First he sold papers. Dropping out of high school at age sixteen to work, he always had a drive to do better. Seventeen years later, working days and going to night school, he completed his MBA at the University of Chicago. Why real estate?

> I don't know. I just always liked to see buildings go up. I worked construction, went to trade school, became a journeyman, and I had a dream to build big buildings. That was my dream, to build the biggest new communities you could build. And I built it. I was lucky to be able to have accomplished what I dreamed of as a young man.

Money, for Jack Feldballe, is not the big motivator: "I don't do it for money." (He drives a Buick, and his philanthropy in the Chicago area is well known.)

Feldballe's description suggests that self-respect and self-reliance are his motivations for work, but in addition he has a basic *creative desire* that his role as a successful businessperson fulfills:

> I don't know why I chose my field. I wouldn't really say it was a "calling" in some Pauline sense. I just loved construction. At eighteen or nineteen I used to stand and watch a new building going up for hours. I was fascinated. I still am.

Now that Feldballe has "retired" from his old business, he is constantly reinventing himself as well as creating something new: he pursued post-graduate work and research in structural design and technology and also cognitive development; started a business on adult learning materials to fight illiteracy, an outplacement and retraining company, and another real estate company. In each case he is not just being economic; he is literally developing a resource—creating, in a very tangible way.

And he still likes construction:

> I'm enthralled watching the Interstate 355 extension. One of these days I'm just going to walk it. You know, you see them excavating down there, the sewers going in and the bridges being built.

Dennis Sheehan nods and says, "There's a high sense of accomplishment when you watch something like that."

Feldballe agrees:

> That's it. A high sense of accomplishment. . . . Not that it matters whether anyone else knows it, but I can still go down to visit buildings I built thirty years ago and point them out to my grandchildren and say, "I built those."

Work and Self-fulfillment

Jack Feldballe's desire to build new communities is the living out of something deeply ingrained in his own identity and personal preference. These personalized values are integrated with his view of himself as a Christian. His work, therefore, becomes a personally fulfilling and religiously meaningful activity.

Jack Feldballe and Dennis Sheehan's strong sense of accomplishment and personal satisfaction in work are typical of the group I interviewed. They loved their work. They were enthusiastic about it. They felt a great sense of self-fulfillment and self-expression in their careers. Their positions as heads of companies only intensified that sense of personal ownership and satisfaction. As Dick Capen, recently retired publisher of *The Miami Herald* and former ambassador to Spain, put it, "I have been blessed with a close, supportive family and with an immensely fulfilling career at Knight-Ridder."

Such views may sound terribly old-fashioned today. The CEOs I interviewed—even those in their forties—seemed to have naturally fused a capacity for entrepreneurism and self-expression, *often in large organizations.* To use an old-fashioned phrase, their hearts are in it. But unlike a workaholic whose sole object for working so hard may be the magnification of his own self-esteem and status, these people work hard without the ego-trip. For them, work has *religious meaning*—religious in the holistic yet personalized, evangelical perspective mentioned earlier. Work is part of God's universal order; it is also a personal opportunity to live like Christ in the service of others. As former Eastman Gelatine CEO Frank Butler said:

> I don't want to become monastic, because the only ethical way is to struggle with the world. . . . I was called to do God's work in working at an Eastman Kodak company.

So, too, Charles Olcott, former president of Burger King who now heads a venture capital firm that invests in environmentally responsible businesses, felt that being in business was not necessarily a "lesser" calling. He remarked:

> I'm not so sure that a ministry in the church is more important than one in the workplace. Your time might be better spent ministering to people in the workplace where your visible witness is very strong.

I found that the enthusiasm and stamina for work that such views generate did not depend on these men's positions in their firms. Their enthusiasm for work, for creating something, has been lifelong and continues in their forties, fifties, sixties, and even seventies, as Fred Smith, who joined Zig Ziglar's board of directors at age seventy-four, will attest. Nor does it depend on the size of a company. Several of these men headed businesses well into the Fortune 500 (ServiceMaster, Raytheon, Pizza Hut, Borg-Warner, Knight-Ridder, Herman Miller, and Chemical Waste Management).

A related motivating sentiment in the group's attitudes toward work is what I would call the attitude of being exemplary. The evangelical, as a witness for Christ, has a special responsibility for the impression that he or she generates. These men took their tasks very seriously. They were earnest about their financial responsibilities and earnest about their responsibility as leaders for employee welfare. To be perceived as anything but hard-working and prudent would not only be disastrous for the business, but more important, it would be a blot on the Christian community's reputation as well.

Part of this earnestness is simply a desire to do the right thing, as Colossians 3:23–24 prescribes: "Whatever you do, do it heartily, as to the Lord and not to men, knowing that from the Lord you will receive the reward of the inheritance. . . ." But, like Paul's concern for the reputation of the early Christian community, there is also an awareness among Christian CEOs that appearances count for a lot. There is a perceived social benefit to being exemplary. Doug Sherman, an author and a spiritual counselor to several of the CEOs I interviewed, writes, "You may embarrass the cause of Christ by living an inconsistent lifestyle at work."[8]

The Valuing and Devaluing of Hard Work

We must distinguish the work ethic exhibited among the evangelical CEOs interviewed in this book from the workaholic ethic of the 1980s careerist. Sociologist and best-selling author Robert Bellah describes this new work ethic in *Habits of the Heart*. He argues that work has become a "segmental, self-interested activity."[9] Many people today express a strong identification with their work, but only in terms of the material goods and sense of winning they achieve. The tasks themselves or the social groups at work provide no source of fulfillment. What counts is a person's position of responsibility and how much money they make. In Bellah's words, work attitudes have become "a utilitarian self-seeking."[10] Many surveys reveal that the actual psychological utility of such an attitude is far from ideal. Since the 1960s, fewer and fewer people past the age of forty are finding that economic and career success provide a satisfactory indication of their "real" identity, however much they originally sought out wealth and power.

Although the people I interviewed worked very hard and had an uncanny sense for making money, they did not seem *driven* by these goals in the overt and helpless ways in which many managers today idealize their career obligations. Rather than simply moderating their impulses for hard work by capping the number of hours spent on business, the evangelical work ethic was itself a paradox. These CEOs simultaneously sustained tremendous personal energy and a sense of accomplishment about business alongside an ultimate sense of insignificance about the whole thing.

A passage from an insightful evangelical volume on work in modern America reveals this attitude:

> On all hands we see people who *need* to be successful in business as a way of reassuring themselves that their lives matter. It is a way of "saving" oneself, peculiarly suited to the modern world. Christians do not need this form of reassurance, having already the deeper reassurance of God's love in Jesus Christ.[11]

True to the creative paradox model, however, this self-confidence and devaluation of work's ultimate meaning does not dictate dropping out:

> We are concerned here not just with high moral standards, but with *personal holiness*. To be a Christian businessperson is to care passionately about doing good. . . . Such a Christian wishes to approach the business world as his or her special calling, recognizing that business life can be a form of ministry.[12]

Jack Feldballe, further, contrasted his career and his faith in paradoxical terms. He felt his work was integrated with, but not identical to, his Christian identity. He acknowledged the tensions that this contrast presents:

> You have religious beliefs deep down inside, that are a part of your very essence. Then you have things you articulate, and then your actions. The deeper those religious beliefs deep down inside, the more tension there may be in the business world.
>
> You now have to reconcile a secular world which is generally at odds with what you believe. For example, in Christianity it's you first, me second. In business, it's more often me first, you second. So we experience two worlds totally in opposition to each other.

Though not all seekers would go so far as to say that they experience two worlds, the ones I interviewed rejected the idea that success or any other aspect of business was automatically a confirmation of Christian goodness. Interestingly, in their devaluations of worldly success, they did not go so far as to disdain material wealth. This is a sharp variation from conservative Protestantism in the past.

The conservative Protestant's classic way of dealing with potential overvaluations of work was to value hard effort and to rigidly scorn material rewards. As Max Weber pointed out, the Calvinist could never allow himself to enjoy the fruits of his own success for fear of losing sight of ultimate rewards. A rigid asceticism of lifestyle resulted. John Wesley advised channeling all of capitalism's material rewards into charity. He exhorted believers to work as hard as they could and save as much as they could, so they could give away as much as possible.

The group that I interviewed did not express strong feelings of guilt about being wealthy. They did not adopt the ascetic life that some fundamentalists seek. They were, however, very vocal in condemning the unquestioned greed and extreme materialism that characterized 1980s yuppiedom and certain televangelists as well.

In not being driven by greed or material wealth and yet not accepting an entirely ascetic lifestyle, the evangelicals in this group represent a modification of the old Protestant work ethic. They work hard and believe in hard work, but they play too. Many had nice or even elegant vacation homes, boats, and fast cars. They were well accustomed to travel.

In creating such a portrait of a modified work ethic among

evangelical CEOs, it is very difficult to trace the source of such values. None of those interviewed expressed revolutionary theological arguments for or against materialism and career success. As good business people, they are sensitive to the trends of the marketplace and instinctively find a way of "fitting in" to the world in which they do business. They wear appropriate clothes; they stay in appropriate hotels. At the same time, they place limits on material concerns. What we can see in their remarks about the value and limits of work, however, is how the evangelical work ethic is consistent with and perhaps stimulated by the evangelical understanding that there is an order to the world, a design in God's plan, that one can either support or fail to support. Humankind's lot in life, as disclosed in the Creation mandate and as supported by Paul's injunctions to the early Christians, is to work. In fact, several interviewees, when asked "Why work?" replied by citing Paul in a passage mentioned earlier: "If anyone will not work, neither shall he eat" (2 Thess. 3:10).

"Hooray for Capitalism!"

The French sociologist Emile Durkheim noted long ago that a capricious economic system could cause profound psychological destruction. Indiscriminate misfortunes such as total market collapses or undeserved good fortune in the form of windfalls were not only disincentives to work; they could even invite a suicidal state of mind.[13] There must be order.

While the interviewees found their choices of work to be ultimately rewarding, they also felt that the nation's economic system of choice should rest on a logical connection between effort and reward. For the most part, the interviewees saw democratic capitalism as the best economic representation of God's order for this world. Said former Epsilon president Tom Jones: "I have an overwhelming sense that an enlightened management, working with people of any and all beliefs, will be most effective in a free-enterprise system. In this environment, the unique gifts of each individual will have the greatest chance of being utilized." They applauded the prosperity of advanced capitalistic economies as an indication of the system's logical soundness, and they were clearly drawn to the individualistic, self-reliant aspects of a free-market economy. Jack Feldballe commented:

> I'm a dyed-in-the-wool capitalist, because the free-market system basically reinforces the nature of man, which is that of me-first—self-centeredness. The system works. We have the highest standard of living and the highest respect for individuals.

The evangelical right is frequently accused of being indifferent to the distributive inequities of capitalism. But among the group that I interviewed, many drew a distinction between their support for a capitalistic system of wealth creation and inherent flaws in the distribution of jobs and opportunities, for which they felt that they and the government had a responsibility. As one CEO said:

> I think capitalism, working within the moral confines of a Judeo-Christian ethic, has clearly been shown to be the most efficient and motivating system of economics ever created. This is not to say, however, that the government should be oblivious to people with needs.

Despite their general support of capitalism and free markets, not all interviewees were politically conservative. There were former Jimmy Carter supporters and a number of critics of Ronald Reagan's economic policies. Many on both sides of the political spectrum decried the national debt as being "uncapitalistic" and life-threatening to the nation's ability to pursue its own interests. None of the CEOs seemed terribly uncomfortable with the idea of making a profit. They saw capitalism's potential for job creation and its subsequent improvement of self-respect as an important part of their own understanding of the meaning of work.

These men regarded their own roles in the wider distribution of capitalism's benefits as dynamic, direct, and almost missionary. Boston's Frank Butler eloquently summed up a feeling expressed by many interviewees:

> I visited with Mother Teresa, and I understood how she was living out Matthew 25 (the commandment to feed those who are hungry and clothe those who are naked). And I felt that God also does these things through good jobs. These things are in sync more than we realize: at least around

here, with a liberal press, *profit* is a dirty word. But it's the greed factor that distorts it and that's why we get under the gun on some of these things.

At the same time, many of those interviewed expressed profound distaste for the state of capitalism in the 1980s. As Butler said:

> I believe in capitalism and free enterprise. But it seems to me that early on it was not so consumer driven. Capitalism was about savings, and community driven. Something's happened so we have a cult or subdivision which is consumer driven. More than the greed of individuals, it's a flawed direction that free enterprise and capitalism have taken.

For many, the problem rested with high leveraging, and the group as a whole was strongly in favor of conservative fiscal policies for the nation and for businesses. As Elmer Johnson remarked in a 1988 interview:

> These people keep borrowing and borrowing, and moving money around. It's the herd instinct . . . I have this awful feeling that we're going to discover that people can't repay this stuff!

Jack Feldballe is one of the few who expressed reservations about the ultimate legitimacy of capitalism itself, which put his business commitment in a larger perspective:

> I've no doubt that a totally Christian world would not be capitalistic. It would share everything. But the world is not Christian. So within the nature of the given world, which is self-centeredness, capitalism works best.

Other interviewees, particularly the justifiers, were much more strongly committed to capitalism as the unquestionably right way. They saw capitalism's theoretical emphasis on self-reliance and individualism as a natural complement to evangelicalism's lay orientation and emphasis on individual responsibility in daily affairs. The rewards of capitalism are a source of self-respect.

If they rationalized their stand at all (many did not), they argued that capitalism supported freedom of religion, hence Christian beliefs.

The Mediating Values in Choosing a Business Career

While the evangelical's sense of personal fulfillment of Christian commitments and identity is one of the most important motivations, faith also imposes certain important conditions on the choice of a business career. Interviewees consistently suggested certain characteristics that their faith placed on their choice of career as captains of industry. For the most part, these were compatible with the rules of capitalistic economy but were not always the norm of American business activity.

If we recall the basis of the first creative tension—the commitment to God versus the commitment to a business career—we can see that for the seekers, at least, several values drawn from biblical sources mediated between these two concerns. Taken together, this interplay of oppositions and mediating values forms a perspective from which these CEOs could determine economic purpose. As these men try to "read God's handwriting," certain touchstone values provide the lenses for determining legitimate business behavior.

The most influential values are *creating* and *serving*. The production and servicing aspects of business were the primary ways in which interviewees resolved the tension between materialistic financial concerns and personal focus on God. For some, the creation mandate in Genesis, where God commands Adam and Eve to till the earth, is a scriptural authorization for this attitude. Jesus' commands to serve others—"Inasmuch as you did it to one of the least of these My brethren, you did it to Me" (Matt. 25:40)—was also a primary motivation for positive, creative economic activity that depended for its success on good treatment of customers and employees. The "good steward" was the most frequently cited metaphor for personal leadership among the group. For these CEOs it implied service, quality, a responsibility to be fiscally productive, and a detachment from self-serving motives.

There were also important guidelines, drawn from New and Old Testament sources, that provided constraints on the more opportunistic or exploitative aspects of capitalistic behavior. Chief among these were the familiar commandments: do not kill, lie, cheat, steal, or covet your neighbor's possessions. According to the interviewees, none of these constraints should be underemphasized or taken for granted in choosing an industry or a business partner.[14] As the evangelical community itself is well aware, there have been many believers who thought their business activity had nothing to do with these injunctions.[15]

These biblical concepts form a framework for the seekers that affects many aspects of their careers. The best way to understand the interplay of tension and resolution between a business focus and Christian commitment is to look at the creative paradox model, which can be summarized as follows:

Tension: Commitment to God and Commitment to a Business Career

- The Mediating Values—Scriptural Authority
- Creation Mandate: Genesis 1 and 3
- Stewardship: Parable of the talents (Matt. 25:14-30)
- Hard work: Pauline exhortations to work heartily, etc.
- Service: End of parable of the talents; serving "the least of these" (Matt. 25:40)
- Constraints: OT commandments and proverbs
- Justification of wealth creation: e.g., Deut. 28:1-4, a godly society that prospers

Economic and Qualitative Outcomes

- Personal fulfillment
- Career choice based on opportunity for service and value
- Long-term time frame
- Financial conservativism
- A focus on quality
- Meticulousness about small details
- Excellent financial performance as an obligation, therefore a focus on efficiency and avoiding waste.

The preceding summary suggests that a number of important outcomes result from the mediated tension between the evangelical's ultimate commitment to God and his or her intense entrepreneurial responsibility to pursue profitable opportunities. While these outcomes were generally not expressed by interviewees as an actual business philosophy, they appeared in the interviewees' discussions of their choices of careers and general approaches to business.

The Choice of a Good Business

If we understand the Christian emphasis on creating, serving, and having a sense of order as a group of informing values, we can draw a tight connection between the evangelical's spiritual outlook and his or her specific choice of careers. The interviewees tended to favor industries that presented opportunities for either creating something or for directly serving people (see Table 2.1). Manufacturing, retail, sports, entertainment, and service businesses were the most favored types of activity.

Like Jack Feldballe's lifelong desire to "build big buildings," these people took pleasure in *creating* something of tangible value or service to others. Few of them saw this as a "calling" in the biblical sense. Rather, they simply had a desire to be constructive.

More abstract contributions to the economy, such as institutional banking, were viewed with suspicion. Many CEOs spoke of current financial institutions with derision. Those who were in banking tended to be in the commercial segment, and those in real estate were very active in local community development efforts.

An emphasis on quality is a logical result. Whereas some company-quality programs seem driven solely by the egotistical desire to win recognition or by a desperate final attempt for improving the bottom line ("we've tried everything else"), the evangelicals I interviewed see quality as an essential factor of good service, as a way of doing the best possible job *for the client.* Equally important is the sense of doing something pleasing in God's sight, which becomes a source of internal pride. In the evangelical worldview, every creation, every action, is spiritually significant, thus the *motivation* to maintain high standards of quality is very strong. Some participants also felt that by building a high-quality company or product they were creating a significant witness for the strengths and social desirability of evangelicalism. As one person said, "Outsiders will know I'm held to a higher standard."

Mark Taylor, president of Tyndale House Publishers (publishers of *The Living Bible*), underscores this emphasis:

> The issue of quality is very important to us. We want superior content, production, and distribution. We help bookstores create one-stop shop-

ping. Our bookshops provide a pleasant atmosphere in which people can find literature to meet almost any spiritual need.

On the surface, Taylor's assertion could be interpreted simply as one more business hype—or, at best, a form of enlightened marketing that exploits other people's desires for quality. But subtle forms of exploitation will not get you to the same place as a Taylor or a Feldballe. Managers have hard choices to make about the quality of their products and their strategies to support those products. Without strong motivation to the contrary, it is easy to rationalize decisions that shortchange quality for the sake of saving money or time for one's company.

It seemed clear that the Christian outlook of many of the interviewees significantly influences their choices in this area. Fred Wacker, CEO of Liquid Controls Corporation, which makes top-of-the-line liquid measurement products, said, "Quality is a Christian concept." Wacker's company mission statement makes two commitments to this effect:

In the design of these products we have a firm commitment to *no planned obsolescence*. All products are designed to provide a needed service and to make a daily profit for our worldwide customers.

Many of the companies represented here—Liquid Controls Corporation, Eastman Gelatine, Raytheon, and Chemical Waste Management among them—produce top-of-the-line quality products.[16] Dennis Sheehan's Jensen Toolkits offered the highest-quality tools in the country. Bill Rentschler, former chairman of The Medart Companies, has been nominated five times for a Pulitzer prize for "distinguished commentary" in the newspaper industry. Talk to any self-respecting garage, and you'll find that Wacker's brake service equipment sets the standard in reliable, long-lasting auto service equipment. Knight-Ridder newspapers win more than the normal share of Pulitzer prizes (their accomplishments include uncovering Jim and Tammy Bakker's business practices), and Herman Miller's Charles Eames chairs are a legend in good design for mass production.

Quality, according to the CEOs of these companies, is not to be confused with upper-niche marketing strategies. Rather, it is based on creation of value for *any* customer. Tyndale House Publishers, for example, has an inexpensive product line for the general marketplace. Jack Feldballe was quick to point out that the eighty-nine-cent tool, priced fairly and available in a mass-merchandising store, may be as effective for certain needs as the upscale thirty-nine-dollar version. Once again we see the Christian ethic at work. Sensitive to the needs of his neighbor, Jack Feldballe understands that not everyone is best served by the Rolls Royce product.

Not surprisingly, the seekers in the group are very opposed to a "something for nothing" ethic, even if the free market allows it. Just as they are turned off by name-it-and-claim-it prosperity gospels, the seekers—whether they were influenced in their earlier years by New Age gurus or by other evangelicals—found no legitimacy in profiteering or other ravenous attacks on the market. They were unanimous in condemning the rape and pillage of assets that was evidenced by the savings and loan crisis. None of them had a kind word for the financial abuses that occurred in the Christian broadcasting industry in the 1980s. One interviewee had actually had a large account with a major televangelist's firm, and withdrew (several years before the scandals broke) when he suspected that things were not being strictly accounted for. Most interviewees expressed outrage over Wall Street dealmakers who sponsored highly leveraged takeovers, which, though legal, were in their eyes simply vehicles for greedy owners to skim off profits by selling the best assets and leaving the rest to wither and die.

For evangelicals who are drawn to the financial services industry, such values prove to be problematic to various degrees, depending on the firm and the person. Many of the bankers I interviewed, for example, were able to point to their own institutions with pride. Their solid balance sheets were the counterexample to the notorious S&Ls. In real estate, people like Jim Seneff saw themselves as markedly "different" from the rest of their crowd. Seneff's firm, CNL, located in Orlando, Florida, has adopted a very conservative investment strategy, with an emphasis on long-term, quality real-estate ventures. Seneff's pride in his company is well-founded; financial columnist and conscience of the industry Dan Dorfmann has praised the company as one of the more solid and better investments in the industry.

Seneff himself is no fast-and-dirty player in the land game. The company's debt strategy is conservative, and its capacity for conducting meticulous, in-depth research is well known in the industry. They strive to acquire a smaller selection of quality properties rather than to amass multiple transactions. For Seneff, this strategy is driven by the stewardship metaphor: "As stewards of investors' money, we put enormous energy into selecting properties with unusual profit potential and then managing them to realize their full value."

Miami-based realtor W. Allen Morris, president and CEO of The Allen Morris Company, is also keenly aware of the speculative reputation of his industry. But he sees the company's purpose differently. Its real-estate investments are not just financial speculation; they are part of the creation of a community. He views the company's downtown Miami projects with pride, and also serves on the Orange Bowl Committee and the board of directors of the Miami Board of Realtors.

At the time of our interviews Morris was very torn about a project that he felt would be a major stimulant to cleaning up a deteriorated downtown neighborhood; unfortunately, the project would go nowhere unless certain restrictions were waived. How hard, wondered Morris, should a company lobby for zoning waivers? Is it right for a person to exploit his own political clout, even when he thinks the project would be ultimately beneficial to the community in terms of jobs and new business creation, and when he knows the opposition is less organized and is divided in its interests? Such questions are hardly driven by the usual profit maximization free-market philosophies.

Morris's conscience over community service was matched in his and his father's definition of the business: The Allen Morris Company is a service business. The company statement of philosophy begins with the client:

> Our clients' interests always come first. It is our responsibility to worry about our clients' needs and problems at least as much as they do. . . . Our

experience shows that if we serve our clients well, our own success will follow.

Gary Ginter, former executive vice president of the Chicago futures trading firm CRT, was in perhaps the most controversial business from an evangelical standpoint. CRT was founded by Joe Ritchie, Ginter's brother-in-law, along with Gary, Joe's brother Mark, and a friend, Ron Bird. CRT was one of the first successful firms to use sophisticated computer models for trading in options contracts. In ten years CRT grew from a $200,000 investment to a $225 million net worth.

CRT's presence was crucial to the establishment of the first modern U.S. options market. In the early days of options trading, CRT was on one side or the other of nearly every trade generated on the Chicago options exchange. Its continued presence was for some analysts a major indicator of the health of these markets. Ginter and others see great value creation in these markets, which have since been copied around the world to generate investment. Some of the trading techniques, hovever, have come under strong criticism. For example, "program trading," in which large amounts of money are to be made out of small, sometimes only minute-long glitches in the options markets, has received a great deal of negative attention. To the detractors, it has symbolized the get-rich-quick schemes of the 1980s—adding no real value to the marketplace, destabilizing stock prices, and reflecting no real evaluation of a company's performance.

Ginter feels otherwise, arguing that the increased volume that has resulted from program-trading ultimately has a value creation in the marketplace. So concerned is he, however, to test that assumption, that he has helped fund research projects by several well-known university economists to track "value creation" in options trading. (The results so far are unclear.)

Ginter is sensitive to charges of greed in his industry. (CRT was actually the victim of an employee insider trading scam.) He himself is the first to acknowledge and condemn basic industry practices, and he sees himself as a reformer. "This is a terrible industry," he says. "We must try to do something to be the salt and light in this business."

Even at first glance it is clear that Ginter and his officers are not your ordinary yuppie dealmakers. Their office is quiet and calm; they share the space with several other traders, and they are not concerned with creating a formal facade of wealth and power. (They still wear corduroys and use tomato juice cans for pencil holders.) A resident of a racially and economically mixed neighborhood in Chicago, the soft-spoken Ginter has poured money into start-up businesses for the so-called underclass. CRT's chairman, Joseph Ritchie, was a philosophy major at Wheaton College and has also stayed close to the evangelical community.

Ginter's view of his choice of businesses is quite similar to that of other evangelicals, despite the industry. It is clear that Ginter and his partners are highly motivated by the idea of creating an outstandingly successful trading program. They get a kick out of making profits for other people—namely, CRT's clients—and they regard that responsibility with the seriousness of a good steward. Ginter does not shirk from hard work, but he also has a larger perspective on his job:

> It takes a special kind of personality to be a successful trader. We tell all our people that they have to learn to be comfortable with failure. An optimum ratio of win-lose is about 5 out of 8. Any more and you're not taking enough risks. Any less and you're probably going for the long shot too often.
>
> But when you have millions of dollars on the line, it's very hard to accept the idea of failure. You cannot have a huge ego. You have to not take it too seriously at some level.

Once again we hear in Ginter's description the seeker's paradoxical balance of an intense work drive and a sense of the ultimate insignificance of economic activity. Ginter's remarks on tolerating failure stand out in sharp contrast to the success-to-excess culture reported at some other investment companies. (Interestingly, the first directive given by Warren Buffet when he became CEO of Salomon Brothers in the reorganization of the company's leadership was that losses would be tolerated, whereas damages to the reputation of the firm would not be.)

Breakdowns in the Paradox

Obviously there are times when even the seekers lose their

sense of balance between their love of God and their commitment to the needs of their businesses. No one among those interviewed claimed a perfect track record or even perfect clarity about what God precisely wanted them to do with their careers. They were always seeking for answers.

In retrospect, their most frequent imbalances could be attributed to either ego or survival. Ego and Christian humility are discussed at length in Chapter 7. The cost in family commitments is obviously another major tension, which is discussed in Chapter 8.

With regard to basic choices in pursuing a business career, several interviewees saw the ego as a real barrier to understanding God's will. Even more distracting were the survival days when they were in start-up businesses or in the early stages of their career. As Jack Feldballe reported:

> I had a full-time job during the day, and was going to school at night. I never stopped working. Was it good or bad? I don't know. But I think I have a better balance now than then.

The passage in Matthew about not serving two masters uses the metaphor of enslavement to express the conflict between faith and earthly commitments. So, too, interviewees discussed the breakdowns of the creative tension in terms of enslavement. They used such phrases as "being too tied to the business" or "being at the mercy of the markets" to describe an unsatisfactory balance.

Debt, whether personal or corporate, was a particularly well-recognized form of enslavement. As CEO Pat Morley said, "If God calls you to a ministry and you are in debt, you cannot go." Several interviewees cited Proverbs 22:7, "The borrower is servant to the lender," as biblical authority for maintaining a conservative debt posture. The CEO whose company has a high debt to finance becomes a slave of the capital markets, which restricts his or her choices about the way to run the business and ultimately restricts the CEO's own sense of Christian values.

Getting Out

It would be inaccurate to expect that these CEOs, however

successful in business, would find vocational fulfillment only in intense entrepreneurism. For the seekers especially, the pull of commitment to Christ is always both a motivator and a deterrent to business. Having a foot in both doors, they sometimes reposition the emphasis of their activities more toward religious or quasi-religious nonprofit organizations.

Such transitions most frequently occurred sometime after a successful business career. Jack Feldballe is funding a number of start-up businesses in minority communities. Dick Capen chose to take early retirement from Knight-Ridder so that he could devote more time to perpetuating ultimate personal values important in life. Soon after his departure from the newspaper business, he was appointed ambassador to Spain by President George Bush.

During his one-year assignment in Spain, Dick and his wife visited more than 65 cities in all 17 autonomous regions of Spain in an effort to share their American values with thousands of Spaniards, many of whom had never met an ambassador. He is writing a book on personal values and has stepped up efforts as a speaker on how to apply values and Christian faith in the world of business and journalism.

Frank Butler, retired from Eastman Gelatine, is giving himself one year's thinking time to decide which charitable institution he can best serve. Patrick Morley entered a full-time ministry that has a vision to help bring about a spiritual awakening in America by organizing city-wide missions and tackling issues like racial reconcilliation. One interviewee, a spiritual counselor to several participants, was formerly in real estate. His friends suggested he put his efforts into Bible groups and counselling, since he had special skills in those areas. He later returned to business.

Bob Buford, chairman and CEO of a cable television service in the Dallas area, passed the leadership of that company over to his managers in order to pursue several heartfelt projects related to the management of large churches. The first of these projects involved videotaping Peter Drucker in a series on managing nonprofit organizations. Buford later began a series of conferences which gather over 500 lay people in high-intensity career situations for several days of education with top quality speakers and idea exchange with their peers. The focus is how to be effective in a life of faith while being successful in the marketplace.

Buford's reasons for getting out of the full-time leadership of Buford Television are complex. The tragic drowning of his only son on a hunting trip prompted Buford to wholeheartedly reexamine not only the future of his business (his son was the obvious successor and had already notched up several entrepreneurial successes), but also Buford's own business activities. A nationally known strategic planning consultant posed the following question to Buford: "You have a commitment to business. And you have a commitment to Christ. What is your primary loyalty?" Buford's choice of the latter dictated making a life of service a parallel career. He could not serve two masters. Effectively, the question posed by the consultant meant that the first creative tension in evangelical business leadership was impossible for Buford to maintain. One loyalty had to be master, the other servant.

Interestingly, however, most of the interviewees who have officially retired from business have not abandoned the creative paradox; their career transitions cannot be regarded as a breakdown of the creative tensions. Despite their shift toward quasi-religious vocations, most of these men have not pulled out of business altogether. Their entrepreneurism still goes strong. Buford is still actively involved in the television company's strategic decisions such as acquisitions. Feldballe still has a real estate company that serves his former firm in a consulting arrangement. Tom Phillips of Raytheon, though assisting a number of evangelical efforts such as Charles Colson's Prison Fellowship program and the Howard Butt Foundation's leadership conferences, is still very active on several large corporate boards. Dick Capen serves as a director of five public corporations.

The Role of Prayer

So far, the discussion of career choice and attitudes toward business has been limited primarily to the indirect sources that influenced the decisions of the interviewees. I have suggested that there is a very strong connection between the evangelical worldview and the Bible's paradoxical statements about the meaning of material success and earthly activity. These statements proved to be influential concepts in the interviewees' own support of and detachment from their business careers.

There were also many sources that directly influenced the commitments of these men to God and to business. One source was the Christian community of businessmen who counseled each other and helped each other find jobs. But the most direct source of influence came through prayer, either alone or with other evangelical businessmen. Many interviewees reported having prayed extensively over their career decisions, and having taken enormous risks as a result. Paul Kuck of Regal Marine left a job in the Midwest and spent his life savings on starting a boat manufacturing business. Allan Emery of Boston folded his family's successful wool business while it was still profitable in the belief that this would best serve the minority stockholders of the company. In so doing, he felt he was applying the Golden Rule.

As Emery, who later served as president for the Billy Graham Evangelistic Association, sought out his next career move, he prayed extensively. In his words, he was seeking to find out "why God had led him into a business with no future." During a trip to Chicago to visit a customer, Emery had dinner with several evangelicals at Wheaton College. Among these were Ken Hansen, who was then president of ServiceMaster. Hansen invited Emery to visit Service-Master's operations in Downers Grove, Illinois. When Hansen, chairman Marion Wade, and then-vice-president Ken Wessner (who is also interviewed in this book) offered Emery a job, he turned them down, thinking that the last thing a wool merchant and commodities expert wanted was a job in hospital cleaning.

Wade was surprised, and suggested that they all pray about it. He led a prayer, and Hansen followed. Emery reports that he suddenly became aware that he was resisting his own promise to go where the Lord led him: "For the first time in my life I saw myself as a stuffed shirt." After Wessner and Emery added their prayers, Emery said he would accept the job. He then wept openly—for the first time in his life.

Emery's story combines the major themes of the evangelical

worldview as described in Chapter 2, and these themes have obviously had a profound impact on his approach to a business career. His choice was based on a context that was prayerful, personal, emotional, and relational. It did not exclude the pursuit of business from the spiritual context, but rather united the two.

Emery's subsequent career was a resounding success, as were ServiceMaster's fortunes. Is there a causal relationship, or could Emery's business acumen be attributed solely to Yankee discipline and a family background in business? Emery himself cites Romans 8:28 to describe his qualitative experience: "And we know that all things work together for good to those who love God, to those who are the called according to His purpose."

Seekers cannot and do not wish to withdraw from the world's work, even as they try to put the insatiable demands of their business obligations into proper perspective. In practicing this double commitment to God's authority and subordinately to the needs of the business, they have found work itself to provide many channels for spiritual expression. As the following chapters will reveal, faith and prayer help open up many surprising avenues for the reintroduction of a religious perspective in the world of business. At times, it also holds that their faith is tested to its limits by the financial and people needs of the organization.

CHAPTER

5

Tension 2: Love and the Competitive Drive

> It is not from the benevolence of the butcher, the brewer, or the baker that we expect our dinner, but from regard to their own self-interest.
> —Adam Smith[1]

I t is a commonly accepted custom that in athletic contests there are winners and losers. Such a fact does not cause general moral concern as long as the rules of the game are deemed fair and feasible, and they are followed. Winning the athletic game is an impersonal act based on objective events: scoring a goal, sinking a basket, hitting a home run. For the occasional hard call, there is a preappointed referee.

Under such conditions, the athletic game remains just that: a game. Even when the game becomes serious play, its competitive struggles are hardly tantamount to a moral strife.

But in business the game is real, and victory often imposes painful moral conditions such as being willing to take the bread off someone else's plate. In many markets, my increase in share is another's loss. My contract or product introduction depends on getting there before the other person, whose own welfare declines as a result. In fact, many managers believe that the only way to motivate business victory is to promote an enemy attitude rather than feelings of benevolence.

These conditions may be within the rules of capitalism, but they are hardly a matter for indifference in the face of Christian obligations to love one's neighbor. For the leader who believes, as did Thomas Jefferson, that "Jesus' system of morality was the most

87

benevolent and sublime probably that has been ever taught,"[2] the competitive ethic of organized capitalism is bound to be uncomfortable. What is more, there is rarely a referee on the spot to tell you when you've gone too far.

One CEO's Story

For the business leaders in this book, the obligation to compete was keenly felt and happily assumed. Some simply wanted to win, and as long as they stayed within the law, felt no urgency to change that ethic. In many cases, however, the modes of competition were profoundly influenced by the apparently contradictory moral precepts of a benevolent Christianity. It is in this latter area that the seekers offered a significantly integrated approach to faith and competitive demands.

A good illustration comes from Jack Feldballe, who was introduced in the previous chapter. Feldballe was describing a business decision that he felt highlighted the tensions he faced as a Christian and as a business person:

> We were in the process of thinking about forming a new consulting firm with an employee of another firm that was in trouble for various financial reasons and was going to close its doors. Were we to create the new firm, it would have to have some clients. There was a client base at the old firm, and the old contracts with these clients had run out.
>
> Using one of the best law firms in town, we determined that there was absolutely no legal obligation not to take on one of the old clients. You couldn't induce anyone to breach their old contract, but you could go after the client for new contracts.
>
> The owners of the old firm didn't see it that way. Perhaps they believed they had rights. Perhaps they were posturing. Anyway, they wanted money. What should we do?
>
> I stepped back and said, "I know what the legal obligation is, but what's the ethical obligation from my set of ethics?" I'm reminded that we're taught very clearly in Scripture that the fulfilling of the law is in part to treat others as you would want to be treated. So that becomes a standard.
>
> So I said to myself, *Wait a minute. If I were sitting on the other side, with great financial problems, I might feel I created and nurtured these clients over a couple of years.*
>
> I thought about this all that weekend, and on Monday morning we made an offer to share the profit with that individual (the former owner) for one year on these clients. She was ecstatic, and not only that, but she

then got on the phone and helped us finalize a contract with that client, which was a large automotive company. And we got a contract out of it.

I don't say it was hard or not hard. Just that I had to make the decision about what my standards were. And just because it was legal did not mean that it was ethical for me.

Feldballe's story describes a situation in which the rules of the game do not require any concessions to the former owner. Furthermore, in the first analysis, any concession would directly and negatively impact Feldballe's bottom line. Ultimately, however, he was moved to find a more just approach to the problem—an approach that involved self-denial, risk to the cash flow of his firm, and respect for another person's point of view, which he did not entirely share. By his own account, the anchor for this approach was his Christian ethics.

A cynic might suggest that Feldballe simply had made a brilliant economic decision that maximized efficiency. Indeed, in hindsight, his decision making was *on the surface* indistinguishable from a rational ethical standard such as enlightened self-interest; it ultimately paid to be generous.

I would reject any such interpretation. Based on Feldballe's own words and on many similar stories, told time and again by interviewees, it seems to me that not only is the evangelical impulse for benevolence real, but it is also based on an understanding of business that is very different from enlightened self-interest.

Feldballe himself reported that his dilemma over whether to accede to the owner's demand was directly influenced by his understanding of Christianity. The weekend consideration of what it looked like from the other person's point of view was not simply a rational calculation of what would make the most money for the firm. Rather, Feldballe rearranged the terms of competition to take into account the interests of the other person, and it is this *unconditional* nature of his thinking that most clearly reflects the element of Christian love. From the standpoint of the lawyers, such a move was gratuitous and even anticompetitive.

It is noteworthy, however, that Feldballe did not tell a story about pure charity in addressing the issue of competitiveness. What is essential for us to understand is that he also was aware that *the decision paid off.* Feldballe seems to have had an instinctively "good business sense" that channeled his moral conclusions into economically productive behavior. It wasn't hard or easy. As he put it, he just did it. Once again we see the evangelical sustaining the tension between fiscal obligation and Christian ethics. And this creative paradox again led to economically creative approaches rather than to a retreat from business or to an acceptance of things as they were.

Whether a person can capture this apparent sixth sense for business in rational terms of management science is a debate to be taken up by others. What I can detail here, however, are the main elements in this kind of thinking—a way that reflects all the hallmarks of evangelical thought as described in the previous chapters.

Jack Feldballe approached his problem with a worldview based on relational thinking rather than on legalistic measures. Instead of relying on the lawyers, whose expertise he nevertheless views with the greatest respect, Feldballe injected himself personally into the problem. He took what social philosopher Amitai Etzioni would call an I&We view of the issue[3]—he was able to project his perspective beyond his own self-interest to include the welfare of other parties in his sense of *what was right for him and his business.* Unlike the generalist, who might never have seen the tension in this problem, Feldballe had a kind of holistic urge to apply Christian teachings to the little details, which initiated his personal weekend deliberations. Without a strong base of faith in "do unto others," he might have simply seized the market opportunity and gone after the client without a twinge of conscience. Doing so would have been unquestionably within the rules of the game. But as interviewee Jim Seneff commented, "We believe God works in a providential manner and is not at a distance. There is a sovereign God, so you have no choice but to be ethical."

We need to consider two other points in assessing the charge that Feldballe might be simply thinking of his own interests. First, *either course of action would have made him money.* Refusing the owner's demand would have saved him much-needed cash in the short run.

Second, when this incident occurred, the business was in the start-up stage. The resources of a company are usually quite constrained at this point, and Feldballe's company was no exception. It

**Mediation of Faith:
"Do Unto Others" as
Scriptural Authority**

4. CEO reflects on other side's point
of view even though he felt originally that it was not legitimate.
5. CEO adopts a relational solution:
calls person directly, does not admit
wrongdoing, but offers compensation beyond law.

Competitive Problem

1. Outsider objects to company's
competitive behavior and demands costly concession.
2. CEO addresses claim: asks self
and others, Are we doing something wrong?
3. CEO runs a legal test: Do we
meet legal guidelines and fall
within common business practice? Answer: yes.

Outcome

6. CEO gains cooperation
of "enemy."
7. CEO gets new business.

Figure 5.1
The Steps in Jack Feldballe's Decision-Making Process

is particularly difficult to think in the long term and err on the side
of generosity under such circumstances. Adopting a "survival scenario" mentality, a businessperson is more likely to cite the old saw
"We can't afford ethics at this point." In fact, many CEOs would have
categorically refused to take on the problem once the threat of legally
imposed penalties had been removed.

Feldballe's case is an outstanding example of the love-and-compe-
tition paradox, and is similar in many ways to Jack Willome's response
to the group action suit against his firm, described in Chapter 3. The
steps in Feldballe's thinking are illustrated in Figure 5.1.

The steps on the left side of the figure represent common
business practice. While a manager with no scruples and an overac-
tive aggressiveness might never even get to the second step ("So let

them sue!"), most conscientious managers would respond precisely as did Feldballe through step 3. At that point, the dilemma would appear to be resolved: Going after the former owner's clients is legal and well within the gray standard that we call the rules of the business game.

It is at this critical point that Feldballe's faith kicks in and causes him to continue to explore the problem. It is a critical juncture, a watershed, because it is the socially and legally acceptable point at which to stop. Going further, changing course, requires new momentum and personal intervention. Scriptural authority and the evangelical bias toward personal, relational thinking—the very things that motivate Feldballe's hesitation about rejecting the claim—then suggest a very different course of action. Feldballe makes a personal call, expresses his empathy as well as his concerns for the business, and suggests a tangible, serviceable response. As a result, the former owner cooperates, and even goes an extra mile by helping the company to get the new contract. Christian love, it appears, is contagious—at least in this case!

The Sense of Detachment from Business

It is striking to note Feldballe's own sense of detachment from the situation even as he works through the problem. Because his heart is clearly not focused entirely on the business, he is capable of responding empathetically to someone who directly threatens his company. And yet he also doesn't fail to exercise sound financial stewardship.

Feldballe expressed this same paradoxical approach in his statements about the real estate business. He carefully distinguished that approach from an enlightened self-interest philosophy:

> I don't sit there thinking every day about how do we behave, but the attorneys are always commenting on us. They're astounded at how we'll work with the other side. It's good business. But I don't do it because it's good business.

His final sentence is crucial. Feldballe and other seekers are not like the businesspeople who calculate economic purpose based purely on personal gain, even though they may look the same on the surface in any one decision. For Feldballe and many of the other CEOs I interviewed, the attitude of service and love is so deeply embedded in their business thinking that it can be described only as gut impulse. It is a values-driven response rather than a rationalistic consideration of risk and consequences alone.

At the same time, these CEOs are not claiming that the interests of the firm are nothing. In the preceding quote, Feldballe unabashedly admits that his actions are "good business."

Former ServiceMaster chairman Ken Wessner, who died in 1994, vividly explained the difference between the worldview described here and that of enlightened self-interest. He held up two fingers and said this:

> Here are two realities. One finger is the secular, rationalistic approach to the world. The other is Christian. One is oriented on self-interested motives. The other is oriented on love and service to God. You're either here or there. You can't be in both places. And depending on where you are, you approach things differently.

The "difference" that Wessner described is represented by the central category in Figure 5.1, illustrating the dynamic role that faith and Christian ethics played in Jack Feldballe's problem solving.

To those two elements we should add other hallmarks of the evangelistic worldview: personal involvement, relational thinking, and emotional intensity. There is a strong element of "personality" in the evangelical's business approach to problems such as Feldballe's. To call it charisma would be to overstate it, but injecting the personal element clearly contributes to the way the evangelical first perceives the problem and then its solution. Personality is a profound way for the evangelical to assimilate Christian precepts concerning love.

The Importance of Detachment

Once again the potentially profitable capacities of Christian commitment are also moderated by the same virtues: The evangelical's heart is committed to God, and that commitment ultimately imposes an iron detachment on an evangelical's dealings with the marketplace. As Feldballe's story illustrates, you don't give up "loving your neighbor" just because it might cost you something.

This detachment from the bottom line, however, has a paradoxical effect in that the intervention of faith reaps its own economic reward; by not getting too emotionally involved in "winning," the evangelical is capable of taking great risks with the business and keeping cool under extremely hot negotiating situations. As one CEO put it, attributing the idea to Peter Drucker, "You lose the anxiety of ownership and take on the responsibility of stewardship."

One person I interviewed had a $100 million deal at risk at the time of our session, and his cash flow was deteriorating fast. A key player called him during our interview to tell him that the deal was not yet close to being worked out—that several new problems had arisen. The CEO took the call with extraordinary calm, asking several perceptive questions about the details, all of them based on a "What do *you* need?" approach. At no point did he whine or storm about the pain that the delay was causing him. Either he was the biggest bluffer I've ever met (which is always a possibility), or the detachment that he himself had described elsewhere was clearly helping him to maintain a service attitude that was more likely to move the negotiations along. As retired Miami builder-developer Charles Babcock told me, "If we think that profit is the only success, we'll probably make mistakes with the customer or people we're dealing with, and that will eventually hurt the bottom line. So if you focus on *your* profit first, you'll probably make bad decisions."

Ironically, the detachment from ego that frees the evangelical to consider the customer's interests also imposes a strict discipline on the evangelical's relational impulses. Friendships, for example, should not be allowed to interfere with the fundamental rules of legitimate competitive activity. Several interviewees objected to the behavior of some believers who tolerate unethical behavior toward nonbelievers in the marketplace. The fact that in some cases the wrongdoers were friends made it all the more important to draw the line on such activities. Similarly, if a friend is a competitor, none of the rules of business should be suspended. Said Gary Ginter:

It's like playing against a friend on a football field. We're in the game and we enjoy it. With capitalism, there are more bumps and grinds, but in the end we're all better off for keeping the game going. If a friend goes bankrupt because he wasn't disciplined about the business, then maybe the system is better off without that business.

A Covenantal Approach to Competition

In a previous book I have suggested that two very distinct approaches to the moral problems of business must not be confused with each other: the "enlightened self-interest" approach and the "covenantal ethic" (see Table 5.1).[4] Briefly, market approaches that emphasize self-interest—from Adam Smith to Milton Friedman to Peter Drucker—share a basic set of problem-solving assumptions. The enlightened self-interest approach defines a corporation as a legal entity engaged in financial transactions for the benefit of its owners. It thereby places a high value on efficiency and return as the purpose of business.

The management assumptions behind the enlightened self-interest philosophy can be boiled down to these four:

1. The basis for decision making is one's own return (self-interest).
2. There is an agreement to obey the laws and customs of the land.
3. If everyone follows assumptions 1 and 2 in the marketplace, the economic return to the common good will be the greatest.
4. The primary focus of decision making is efficiency.

In other words, a company's own competitive success is the first criterion in deciding the purpose and priorities of business. But by playing so strongly to self-interested motivations, *such a system fails to stimulate a felt concern for other people such as customers or even employees.* So a manager motivated by this mind-set is likely to be unresponsive to customer needs that don't automatically enhance his or her own balance sheet. The manager sees a customer complaint, for example, as a cost in time or a pain in the neck rather than as a source of information about how to better serve the marketplace.

Similarly, the "right thing to do" is based on a calculation of consequences to the bottom line and on narrowly defined legal constraints. A decision on a potentially injurious product would be given two tests: (1) Is it legal? and (2) Will doing nothing cost us much in lost sales? In other words, in this very I-oriented system of so-called enlightened self-interest, the welfare of the other side is a secondary concern unless *outside* constraints such as the law or another competitor's superior product force the business person to think of the "other guy."

Such an approach is almost bound to be counterproductive in the marketplace, because capitalism depends so heavily upon voluntary exchange and social trust. A transaction requires the cooperation of two parties with separate interests, and that cooperation is best met when there are benefits on both sides. But in a self-oriented approach, it is very easy to forget about the other party, even if that party is the potential customer. Sensitivity to outsiders is low.

Detroit's spectacularly poor market sensitivity during the first wave of Japanese imports is a case in point. When the only spoken goals are growth and efficiency, product quality and honest design go out the window. Furthermore, the system invites wasteful lawsuits; if consideration of responsibility to people other than the shareholder is regulated only by the law or by a calculation of how far it will advance the bottom line, these same people will demand costly replacements for trust, such as high litigation, unwieldy contracts, and regulation. In business as in marriage, if someone is considering your welfare only insofar as it helps him or her, it's best to call in the lawyers!

Not only is the self-interested approach self-defeating from a market standpoint; it is also morally very weak. The fear of getting caught and suffering a penalty replaces internalized concerns about fairness or customer welfare. Such fears are easily silenced or overridden in the large organization, isolated from the immediate consequences of its actions. For example, when the laws or regulatory agencies are not perfectly geared up to prohibiting certain types of injury—say, to the environment or to personal health—what motivation is there to stop the questionable practice? And what prevents the exploiting of employees during a recessionary period?

In contrast, a covenantal ethic begins with an I-We orientation and bases problem solving on a very different set of assumptions:

1. The primary goal of business is the creation of value for others.

2. There is an agreement that the system will ensure that such behavior receives an economic reward.
3. Service to others will achieve these mutually satisfying economic
   ends.
4. The primary focus of decision making is the creation of mutually enabling relationships.

This covenantal ethic approaches the marketplace through relationships and a concern for the mutual welfare of the parties
involved. It assumes that a capitalist economy rests on a bargain
between the various parties in our society—a bargain that demands
mutual obligations and a concern for the general welfare. These
elements of the bargain extend well beyond legal constraints and
beyond what a person can get away with in a pluralistic and at times
discordant social environment.

I have chosen the term *covenantal ethic* because of the covenants
of the early New England Puritan communities, which bound
neighbors together in a search for the common good and bound
everyone to God. In a covenantal ethic, the first question asked is
not, How much money did we make? but How is the customer
faring? Maintaining a specific product is not a sacred duty; maintaining a beneficial relationship is.

Theoretically, both the self-interest and the covenantal approaches are compatible with capitalism, but the covenantal business
ethic is qualitatively different and morally more compelling.

It can also be effective in the marketplace. Some noteworthy,
highly respected, and economically successful companies operate
according to a covenantal ethic.

Johnson & Johnson is one example. Its well-known Credo is
constructed around four relationships that the management must
maintain and service: (1) customers and other business relations, (2)
employees, (3) the community, and (4) shareholders. Profit, as the
last line of the Credo states, should be a natural result of successfully
fulfilling the other obligations. The Tylenol incidents are just one
illustration of many such decisions at that company: the welfare of
the public, of past and future customers, was an overriding and
immediate priority despite the risks to the bottom line. The mainte-

nance of trust (of customers, regulatory agencies, and employees) was a beacon for action.

At the same time, these relationships needed to be mutually beneficial: Tylenol was reintroduced, and the campaign became a marketing classic.

Covenantal Ethics among the Evangelicals

Many of the executives interviewed for this book expressed their understanding of business purpose and competitive ground rules as described by the covenantal ethic. Overall, they described business purpose in value creation terms, defined problems very much in relational terms, and saw a service mentality as the key to business success.

The element of Christian love is an obvious complement to this approach. The covenantal ethic makes a number of assumptions that allow the businessperson to incorporate love and benevolence into decision making without giving up the profit motives.

Many interviewees had created documents or statements of business philosophy that reflect this ethic. Max De Pree, already mentioned in previous chapters, used the term "covenantal thinking" in his excellent book *Leadership Is an Art.* According to De Pree, a true leader needs to engage in covenantal thinking in order to meet business obligations:

> Corporations, like the people who compose them, are always in a state of becoming. Covenants bind people together and enable them to meet their corporate needs by meeting the needs of one another.[5]

De Pree's covenantal approach requires that the business leader first develop an understanding of business purpose that goes well beyond economic return to include "a concept of persons."[6] It is this relational aspect of evangelical business philosophy that most distinguishes its approach and allows evangelicals to include values such as love in the business context.

But how do the basics of competition fit into this approach? First of all, De Pree prioritizes goals over financial rewards, and outlines a series of corporate goals that emphasize accomplishment and the development of people. Innovation, excellence, and the fulfillment of individual goals are the guiding values behind the organization of resources and the development of products. De Pree's understanding of the "concept of persons" is essentially a thoughtful philosophy of human interaction—the *relational* element of the corporation.

For example, it includes "the recognition and celebration of diversity," which prevents a CEO from being entirely self-reliant and keeps him aware of the human potential of the firm. At the same time, a leader is expected to "provide meaning, fulfillment, and purpose" to others in the organization. Leaders not only owe the owners a solid asset base that outlasts their tenure; they owe them "relationships and a reputation that enable the continuity of that financial health."[7]

Most strongly, De Pree has a keen sense of responsibility to enable others to develop, make a contribution, and have a sense of fulfillment about their work. His use of the term *covenant* is well chosen. He describes in his own philosophy a series of relationships that go deeper and further than the law, including a respect for other people's welfare.

All of these concepts are expressed in the Herman Miller mission statement, which converts the concept of persons into a statement of competitive purpose. The Herman Miller slogan is "Innovation and excellence through participative ownership." The first covenant expressed in the mission statement is the creation of innovative designs and solutions *for* customers and to "meet our business challenges." A direct result was the massively innovative decision during the Depression years to bring to market the open office plan system designed by Robert Propst. Distinctive, people-oriented design has continued to be a backbone of the company's success.

The final value in the mission statement concerns leadership: "We can lead best by enabling others and by being dedicated to achieving our corporate vision." Interestingly, this value echoes the primary decision-making focus of the covenantal ethic—that is, the creation of mutually enabling relationships.

Many other CEOs expressed a similar perspective on the marketplace. *Enabling relationships* was not always the term they used, but the idea was nonetheless present. Former Knight-Ridder chairman Alvah Chapman, a man with a joking style that sometimes belies his very serious sense of purpose about Christian attitudes in the marketplace, summarized his emphasis on mutual welfare by quipping, "You can't sell peanuts at a funeral!"

Chapman's unconditional concern for community welfare was well illustrated by his support of an anti-casino lobby in Florida. Though as a newspaper publisher he was well aware that such a political stand would be controversial, he nonetheless proceeded, feeling that any increase in gambling activity would not only result in direct rip-off of the poorest in the greater Miami area, but that it would also be bad for healthy business development. Legitimate businesses might be scared away. When a group of reporters and editors from Knight-Ridder's *Miami Herald* approached Chapman with the objection that the corporation's contribution to the lobby might compromise its professional abilities, Chapman replied:

> My job is to do what I think is right for this company and this community. Yours is to report the truth, including the truth about what we do.

Although there was a firm policy at Knight-Ridder not to interfere with reportorial independence, Chapman wanted to make sure that the reporters did not misunderstand his position. In this case, as in all others, he expected them to apply their own high reportorial standards to their coverage of the story.

Current Knight-Ridder chairman James Batten, a practicing Protestant, echoes the same covenantal perspective on people and relationships in his descriptions of the business:

> As we work to solidify newspapers' niches in people's lives in the late 1990s, I think we need to work not only for respect but for affection as well. Those bonds of friendship between newspapers and readers can help keep us healthy and vibrant in the years ahead. Carefully nurturing those bonds in ways big and small, day in and day out, is one of our most important jobs.

Batten is a bear on customer orientation in an industry that has not always been successful at a market orientation. Batten asks:

Are we fanatically determined to please our customers with an engaging, lively, entertaining, well-printed paper, delivered when they want it delivered—and where they want it delivered? Or are we subtly dominated by other, more inward-looking priorities?

The latter, he asserts, is a risk that every business runs to its own disadvantage: defining excellence or quality in its own terms rather than in terms of the delivered value to another.

Translated into action, the Knight-Ridder papers are not only a service to the Miami community; they are a celebration of that community. Two of interviewee Dick Capen's most memorable accomplishments as publisher of *The Miami Herald* were his weekly column celebrating the local heroism and dilemmas of people in the community, and the creation of one of the largest daily Spanish-language papers in the United States, which continues under the leadership of current publisher David Lawrence and Roberto Soarez.

This kind of coupling of community service with the main activities of the business can be seen in many of the firms represented in this book. Herman Miller, for example, has extended its commitment to excellent design to the provision of world-class monuments and architecture in the small town of Zeeland, Michigan. The late Jim Beré, who was chairman of Borg-Warner when I interviewed him, said that when he was being considered as president of that corporation, he was asked if he was willing to commit himself to the communities in which Borg-Warner operated. His own perspective was a natural fit.

Beré felt that it was necessary to put such principles into a written statement of corporate beliefs. As head of a large and diversified public corporation, he did not attach his personal religious commitments, which are evangelical, directly to the company's mission statement. Nonetheless, he initiated a company-wide process of reexamining the company's purpose and standards, despite initial resistance from his managers to do so.

The values that Beré himself brought to the discussion and to his own management philosophy are yet another reflection of the evangelical's sustained tension between people-oriented values and business efficiency. Beré listed the values as follows:

A sense of belonging	Citizenship
The work ethic	Shared power
Competitive zeal	Gratitude
Company loyalty	Belief in the economic system
Rational decision making	Risk taking
Employee ideas	Diversity
A self-identity as an agent of change	

Value provision, creativity, and people are also prominent elements in the mission statement of Chicago-based ServiceMaster, which is perhaps one of the best-known evangelical companies in the United States. The late Ken Wessner, formerly ServiceMaster's chairman, was eloquent about the expanded sense of mission that directs the company, whose name is a shortened form of its first purpose—"Service of the Master."

At ServiceMaster the concept of stewardship as the driving force of business is particularly evident. Ranked as the most profitable management service company in 1985 by *Forbes* magazine, Service-Master manages support services for hospitals, schools, food services, and other industrial companies. It also has franchises in heavy cleaning and lawn care.

ServiceMaster's basic strategy rests on people. Harvard Business School professor James Heskett has described ServiceMaster's approach as a "quality wheel," in which employee development and satisfaction lead to high motivation, which leads to a high level of service quality, which leads to great customer satisfaction, which leads to increased volume and increased rewards, which further fuel employee satisfaction and an ability to develop new people.[8] Employee development comes first. In the words of the president, Bill Pollard, "Before asking someone to do something, you have to help them be something." This kind of development includes whatever is needed to do the job—everything from sophisticated literacy programs to counseling from a hygienist on personal cleanliness (a must in food and hospital services).

ServiceMaster's statement of business philosophy is, not surprisingly, strong on the basics. It is definitely *not* a stakeholder statement of responsibility of the enlightened self-interest type. Rather, it reads:

> To honor God in all we do.
> To help people develop.
> To pursue excellence.
> To grow profitably.

And what is the connection between the top and bottom of the list? Says Wessner:

> We believe that God has created all things and that we honor him when we honor his creation. We do that when we create an environment in our business dealings that will help people—whether our own employees or the people we serve—to become all that God has intended them to be. . . . It is a spiritual motivation.

And how does Wessner understand the meaning of profit?

> It is not an end in itself. It is a means to accomplishing our other objectives.

Pat Morley, founder of Morley Properties, Inc. in Orlando, Florida, and author of several books on the personal struggles of the evangelical layperson, also feels that his business mission goes beyond profit. He bases that understanding on traditional evangelical concepts: family, service, relationships, and love. Morley describes his business as

> . . . more than a company; it's a family. It has a heart and a soul.

His company mission statement cites as one of its guiding principles "an all-pervasive attitude of caring, . . . a spirit of helpfulness, . . . a genuine desire on each associate's part to perform in a more excellent way."

All this may sound like a sequel to *In Search of Excellence,* but the underlying structure is clearly reinforced by more than a performance objective. In Morley's mind, the corporate mission is supported by specific biblical injunctions. Chief among these is Jesus' command to go the second mile. Under Roman law a centurion on an official mission was allowed to force a Jew to carry his armor and supplies for one mile. Jesus said that when someone forces you to carry his burden a mile, carry it two miles (Matt. 5:41). Morley argues that the marketplace automatically forces you to go a mile, but that the extra service rests on the "undaunted" spirit that Jesus prescribed.

Is this all hype, or is there an element of truth here? When a Morley or a Wessner pulls out his mission statement in which God and the company's product are associated, is this leader just manipulating his own public relations? When a Jim Beré devises a corporate statement of beliefs that make good business sense, is there anything more there than a humanistic refinement of ordinary business practices?

The answer can be partly constructed from their own remarks. The values that these men emphasize have an internal consistency that shows how strongly they rely on Christian ethics in devising business strategies. How explicitly each person or business attributes this philosophy to God or to Jesus was a matter of great debate, as we saw in the mission statements mentioned earlier and as we'll see in the discussion of the seventh tension in Chapter 10 of this book.

What we can conclude here, however, is that evangelical faith affects and transforms the activity of profit making for the interviewees in several important ways. Its strong emphasis on service and people stimulate product innovation and top quality. Values about hard work, cleanliness, orderliness, and aesthetic appeal prohibit a sleazy, half-hearted effort. The evangelical CEO sees work and financial self-sufficiency as a healthy sign of self-respect. Because he has faith in God's love for him, he feels little angst about the idea of making a profit or being in business. Consequently, he has a great deal of entrepreneurial energy.

At the same time, his commitment to God first, and therefore his detachment from his own success (a typical phrase was, "It's not my money—it's God's"), not only affect the level of significance that he attaches to profit making, but they allow him to take unusual risks with his products and his career.

Most important, the Christian concept of love plays a strong role in a variety of things from customer sensitivity to the personnel commitments of the firm. (For a discussion of the latter, see the next chapter.) The source of this process is also varied: specific biblical passages play a part, as in Morley's mission, but just as influential is the overall evangelical worldview.

This kind of worldview can be a messy but exciting conception of what business is about. As Elmer Johnson, a senior partner of Kirkland & Ellis and former executive vice president of General Motors, said:

> Our firm's ultimate purpose is not to maximize profits for the partners; it is not to be one of the top firms in average number of hours per lawyer per year and thereby ensure that we all become the dullest of bores. . . .
> On the contrary, because our goals stress quality of service and difficulty of challenge, the character of our firm could perhaps better be described as one of constructive turbulence.

Such corporate strategies do not forget about efficiency but simply consider the role of efficiency as *one* aspect of service among many others. Providing value and a good price to customers or providing a good return on investment to shareholders depends in part on efficiency, and the evangelical CEO is aware of that connection.

Efficiency itself was rarely cited as a driving virtue by the interviewees. Nevertheless, their typical Protestant thrift and their sense of order found real joy in the efficient use of resources. Raytheon's uncharacteristic lack of wastefulness is well known in the defense industry, and it is a source of pride to its directors. Max De Pree takes special joy in the three ponds that grace the Zeeland, Michigan, site. Not only are they pleasing to the eye, but they play an integral part in the water conservation program of the company: they collect the runoff from the buildings on the site, acting as a flood control device, and they furnish a ready supply of water in case of fire. De Pree himself describes the role of these ponds in holistic terms: they are a justifiable expense because they serve useful functions, but just as importantly, they symbolize the company's attitudes toward people and the work environment—attitudes that are ultimately played out in the award-winning office product designs at Herman Miller.

Tyndale House Publishers also prizes efficiency because it is a sign of not wasting resources as seen in this excerpt from their mission statement:

> Each of us can use our time wisely, or waste time. We can work together, or we can slow each other down. We can use supplies wisely, or we can be wasteful. We can treat equipment carefully, or we can misuse it.
>
> As we operate profitably, we can continue the ministry God has given us. But if we operate at a loss, the ministry will eventually cease.

Indirect Signs of the Evangelical Approach

While there were very clear signs of the relationship between Christian love and the evangelical's approach to competition, I would not suggest that the evangelical CEOs chant "Love your neighbor" or "Do unto others" fifty times a day between each phone call. Rather, they have developed a competitive worldview out of their faith that is relational and covenantal.

The values or actions that are influenced by faith are not usually subjected to a deliberate statement of faith. CEOs are doers, not philosophers. Therefore, the outsider who wants to see the relevance of faith in the business context must look to external, behavioral, or organizational signs that are consistent with both the marketplace and the evangelical worldview. We can find several such signs in the competitive approach of the CEOs interviewed, and they are described in this section.

Promoting Orderly Growth

Behind the evangelical CEOs' corporate mission statements are an ordering of meaning and a sense of individual worth that have had very healthy business consequences for their companies. First among these is the ability to impose a sense of order and direction on corporate objectives, in contrast to the frenetic diversification in which companies were engaged in the 1970s and 1980s.

For example, when ServiceMaster faced the need to identify new areas of profitable growth, the questions that Ken Wessner put to himself were limited and orderly. He laid out four readily understandable choices in a matrix. The two axes were expertise (current and new), and markets (also current and new). And so the choices for the company ranged from completely diversifying in a new area (with new expertise and a new market) to staying the same and trying harder (with the current expertise and the current market). Bucking the diversification trends of the mid-1980s, Wessner decided that the idea of unlimited choice (unintegrated diversification into completely new businesses) was unwise.

Though it sorely needed growth to fuel its quality circle of employee development, ServiceMaster would seek to adapt its own expertise to new markets rather than try something entirely new. It soon identified a thriving business opportunity in the facilities maintenance of educational institutions. Several large contracts, including one with Duke University, followed, and the company then added the acquisition of a home-cleaning management service. In both new business areas there was a deliberate choice to pursue growth, but not at the expense of the company's past establishment of a business order.

In talking to Wessner, it was clear to me that he felt a strong sense of possibility in his own people but also a strong sense of limits about what the company could do. Call it perspective or just plain common sense, it also is consistent with the evangelical emphasis on fiscal conservatism and the tangible creation of value.

A Long-Term Vision

Another significant business outcome of the evangelical worldview is an increased capacity to commit to the long haul rather than the tendency to provide the quick fix. No interviewee exhibited a capacity for orderly, patient growth more dramatically than Tom Phillips, the retired chairman of Raytheon. A quiet man, Phillips has nonetheless been an outstanding supporter of evangelical business leadership and a tireless deviser of programs, such as the First Tuesday breakfast group, to help Christian CEOs keep a Christian perspective on their activities.

As we now know, Raytheon, under Phillips's direction, continued to slog out research and development on the Patriot missile system throughout the 1980s, despite being outside the better funded and politically favored Strategic Defense Initiative program, otherwise known as Star Wars. From 1983 on, with army support, Raytheon worked on expanding the Patriot's capability from hitting enemy aircraft to targeting short-range missiles as well. Their progress was slow and steady and, in advanced weapons circles, decidedly pedestrian. Meanwhile, Star Wars was, in the *New York Times*'s own words, "a zig-zag effort," "a frantic search," in which candidates came and went. As one former White House official reported, "There was a lack of internal and external coherence in what we were trying to do."[9] In the U.S.-Iraq conflict of 1991, the success of the Patriot was celebrated. It was the world's only working antimissile system.

Long before the Persian Gulf crisis, I asked Tom Phillips how as a Christian he viewed his leadership of a defense company. He didn't duck the question but acknowledged the difficulty of his position. At the same time, he said, most of Raytheon's products were in radar systems of some sort. They were on the defensive versus offensive side of the equation. Furthermore, Phillips felt a very strong sense of protectiveness toward the United States and the democratic system. Like many other evangelicals, he understands American democracy to be the form of government that is most likely to protect religious freedom and allow for self-expression. Keeping up a strong military was the best defense possible, and in his view the most likely deterrent of even worse violence.

What Phillips did not defend, however, were some of the more notorious contracting practices within his industry. He felt that the responsibility to keep up high standards was a double one between industry and the U.S. government. (Raytheon has been remarkably free of scandal in this area relative to other firms. According to *Business Week,* "In the often wasteful and sometimes fraudulent defense business, the company gets high marks for performance and ethics. 'Raytheon is absolutely the best prime contractor,' according to Thomas S. Amile, a civilian technical systems expert working for the Air Force."[10]

Phillips cited two hallmarks of his own sense of business mission: providing something of value, and having relationships mean something in the company. Therefore, it's not surprising that Raytheon's policies typically include the guarantee that if a long-term employee is about to be laid off, the company must place that employee elsewhere.

Shortly after the close of the Gulf conflict, I saw Phillips again. I reminded him of our conversation about the need for a strong defensive system, and complimented him on his Patriot missiles. He grinned wryly and said:

> It's just like an insurance policy. No one wants to pay for it, no one likes you when you come to the door to sell it, but after disaster strikes, people are glad you're there!

It would be impossible to relate all the examples of a long-term business vision as reported during the interviews. But a comment by one participant demonstrates the discipline, patience, and felt need to do what is right that undergirds the evangelical CEOs' ability to do business for the long term:

> If you're focused right in the beginning, you can tell what is necessary for the business and your values. For example, we've had to go before a certain zoning board to get permission to do business. It's well known that of the nine people on the board, three will take money, and two are often the swing vote.
>
> If your policy beforehand is to do the right thing in the context of your faith, you have to go into that situation recognizing you might lose. Interestingly, I've lost two or three times on very big business projects, and had to go back to court to get the zoning. In one case that took three years.
>
> Well, it turned out I was in a lot better shape financially three years later when I finally got the zoning. It worked out better because of the inflationary spiral. So it worked out to our benefit, even though that was not our intention in refusing to try to influence the board with payments.
>
> It's amusing to think of how we could try to account for this in our annual plan. So many of us look for a short-term fix, and so we do things we should not. Then we suffer long-term.
>
> You also get to be known for your business standards. It would be very unusual for a county commissioner to ask us for a bribe now. They know it won't work.

Emphasizing the Details

The evangelical emphasis on compassion and service expresses itself competitively in many ways besides strategic focus. For evangelicals, who see significance in everyday events, the small details count, and that includes the small details of business performance. Believing that the supernatural is not closed off to human history but rather very much alive,[11] evangelicals tend to get excited about the little event, occurrence, or verbal exchange. Although they can attribute supernatural influence to everyday events ("Praise God! You called at just the right moment!"), such a view did not appear to stimulate a *passive* belief that God would solve every problem. Instead, it motivated among the group interviewed here a passionate and active perfectionism. When Ken Wessner showed me around ServiceMaster's headquarters, for example, he stopped to point out a window between the cafeteria and the kitchen. It gave him obvious pleasure:

> We put that in because we think it's a good idea in food service. A window helps remind everyone about the importance of cleanliness to customers.

Even the pictures on the office wall demand attention. An oil portrait of the three successive chairmen of the firm at the headquarters building includes their spouses—a decision made with great deliberation, according to Wessner.

I went to Dallas to visit the Mavericks' general manager Norm Sonju at his place of work. There had been a freak snowstorm, and I couldn't get a cab in town. Fred Smith, another participant in our interviews, personally drove me to the arena at great inconvenience and danger to himself and then politely left.

I followed Sonju around before that night's game against the New Jersey Nets. Sonju provided a simple meal at the stadium for all the press people who had to come early. Consisting of soup and cold cuts, it was not an ostentatious free ride, nor was it cheap. He simply met the practical needs of the people working in the building and got some good will for the effort. After he'd seen them all off, given his pregame radio interview, and checked a few other details, we continued the interview in his office. He took his time to consider my questions carefully, and we didn't even enter the arena area till after halftime.

There we joined his wife, who was a terrific fan. She and I talked for a moment, and then I turned to Sonju. To my surprise, he wasn't watching the players. He was looking up at the ceiling. Then he turned to me, half-embarrassed, to explain:

> I notice there are several light bulbs missing from the scoreboard. That shouldn't happen. The fans come to get a show, and having all the bulbs on is part of it.

I later mentioned the conversation to Sonju's assistant, who nodded and laughed: "And don't think we won't all hear about those bulbs tomorrow!" Sonju's concern for detail is palpable. He really *cares* to get it right.

Though I'm no psychiatrist, such emphasis on detail, recommended by every management guru from Tom Peters to W. Edwards Deming, does not seem to be just some kind of obsessiveness. First of all, as in Sonju's case with the light bulbs, it's motivated by a concern for the needs of others, not out of some personal tendency to hold back. Obviously, this combination of values—service and detail—have a tremendously positive impact on the business. But to understand their nature, it is important to see that they are the product of a gut tension in the ordering of the world between the mundane and the supernatural. To the evangelical, who sees God's order in all things, the state of the light bulbs can be just one more indication of an ordered, godly attitude—or the absence of one.

The evangelical's emphasis on getting the details right appeared to be motivated also by the relational, service aspect of evangelicalism and of Christianity in general. For example, there was the time that the Dallas Mavericks were planning to honor Kareem Abdul Jabar. Sonju, who greatly admires Kareem's piety and his athletic prowess, had personally picked out a sculpture from Africa to present to the superstar. He also had a special table built for the event, which still stands in a corner of his office. (Sonju can't bear to throw out anything that might be useful, and he sometimes uses the Mavericks logo on the table as a backdrop during a TV interview). It looked like any presentation table, but it was about eighteen inches higher than most. Explained Sonju, "You don't honor a man and then make him have to stoop to receive your gift."

It sounds reasonable, but the execution is not all that common. I am reminded by contrast of a conference of business ethicists that I once attended. At the end of the event, the organizers were presenting a large bouquet of flowers to the secretary, who had taken care of operating details. Although she had a serious knee problem, she was forced in accepting the offering to descend an entire flight of auditorium stairs and then approach the stage by climbing the stage stairs, which had no railing. I saw her wince as she completed the task. Both of the people who were responsible for the flowers knew of the knee problem but just hadn't thought of it till it was too late.

Sonju's attention to detail, coupled with an extraordinary ability to empathize with another person's needs, expresses itself in the small details such as a presentation table, but also in the overall picture as well. Sonju has been very active in urging the sports industry to adopt policies prohibiting the use of injured players. Drawing on the agricultural analogy mentioned in an earlier chapter, the good steward does not try to overwork the land, or harvest too early to the destruction of the crop.

The same philosophy applies just as much to a takeover situation as it does to an athletic team. Many of those interviewed were profoundly disturbed by the sleaze-and-squeeze strategies that often have followed takeovers. Skimming off the prime assets and leaving the rest of the company to die a slow death is not in their vocabulary of responsible profit-making.

Cleanliness counts too. Many of the businesses described in this book appeared to be a reaction to disorder and dirt. ServiceMaster, for example, is not only in the cleaning business; it teaches its employees cleanliness. Chemical Waste Management, with a strong market presence in hazardous waste disposal, is a mega-cleanup company. Herman Miller's cleanness of design is another variation on the theme, while many of the people interviewed specifically mentioned the importance of having a clean and safe workplace as one of their chief responsibilities.

Promoting Quality

Given the biblical command to work heartily as if for God, the emphasis on detail, and a sense of the business belonging to God that many interviewees (though not all) expressed, it is not surprising that quality itself has become a competitive framework for their businesses. Quality, the job well done at a good price, is not only a service; it can even produce something pleasing in God's sight, which becomes a source of internal pride. So the other-orientation of quality becomes paradoxically a self-enhancing one as well.

Competing for a Personal Position

Author Charles Kelly, in his book *Destructive Achiever,* suggests that within most corporations there are all too many executives who assume and behave as if success must be achieved at the expense of their colleagues. In the quest for a leadership position, competition becomes synonymous with the destruction of the other person. Many organizations even reward such behavior.

How do evangelical CEOs, admonished to love their neighbors and to turn the other cheek, deal with the bloodthirsty ambition that often stands between them and the top? Many asserted that if that is what it takes to compete, they'd rather fail. Several were cited for their notable *lack* of sharklike qualities. Allan Emery, for example, described Raytheon's Tom Phillips as follows:

> He's not a self-promoter. And there's not many of those around. He's remarkable. He's a modest, humble, competent man. He's gotten where he has through performance rather than through politics.

One participant, who for obvious reasons must remain anonymous, got very specific about the tension he felt in this regard. A true seeker, his search for an answer to the problem took seven years. We'll call him Andy.

When Andy was promoted to vice president of a major division of a large manufacturing corporation, he became one of three top managers at his company who were in line for the top position. Meanwhile, a new boss came in, and in Andy's eyes he was the classic destructive achiever: he claimed credit for other people's ideas and was extremely unpleasant about foisting off his own mistakes on someone lower in the organization. He covered up poor quality, and he abused employees. And yet he got ahead. A Harvard and MIT graduate, he was part of an old-boy network to which Andy was a stranger.

Andy could hardly stand it. As he put it, "I finally allowed myself to hate him." Andy was preoccupied by the injustices he was witnessing, and angered that such behavior was producing bad results for the business. He was very troubled by these thoughts:

> Here I was, a Christian. I knew the Bible says very clearly that if anyone loves God, whom he hasn't seen, and hates his brother, who he has seen, there's no light in him.

And yet the hatred went on. Andy would sit in church and feel very guilty. He assumed that everyone else around him, "with their nice smiles on," couldn't possibly harbor the kind of thoughts he harbored. And he felt he couldn't talk to his minister about it, because such thoughts were so unacceptable.

Some people would have felt no hesitation at trying to discredit the hated colleague, especially if there were plenty of evidence to that effect. Andy did not go so far as to actively discredit his competitor, but he continued to hate him and to feel guilty.

A Bible-study class with a lay ministry group became the vehicle for bringing his faith to the problem. Andy confided his problems with his boss to a minister who worked with the group, and at one session the minister challenged Andy to share his problem with forty men whom he did not know. The group's reaction was mixed. Some were shocked at the admission of hatred. But before the day's session was out, most of them came up to him and admitted having similar conflicts at work. That experience led Andy to realize that he had a calling as a lay minister, and it also led him to believe that the hope of solving such problems once and for all was a misguided one. He saw that the problem of hatred is always present and that the struggle will come up again and again.

Andy came to the conclusion that Christian love meant that he should try praying for the hated boss. That realization was transforming. As he put it, it is very hard to hate someone when you are praying for his good and not his bad.

The event effected a powerful change in his attitude toward the boss. Andy still disagreed with many of his decisions, but he no longer was preoccupied with proving him wrong. Nor was he as subject to the factionalism that was occurring in the plant. He found that he had the patience to say, "The fate of my career and this man's are in God's hands, not mine." Quite suddenly one day, Andy was promoted over the other man, who was allowed to "retire."

As he analyzed the event, Andy felt that the crucial qualitative change in his personal competitiveness from hatred to love rested on the admission of a darker side to his own personality. The Bible-study group and Martin Israel's book *Smoldering Fire* were powerful factors in this process. Ultimately, his self-sickening preoccupation with his boss's blocking of Andy's own progress was subordinated by the Christian experience of God's forgiveness. Andy was able to pray for the fellow's welfare. As Andy remarked:

> We all have a darker side, which we must face up to. Too many evangelicals are afraid of ever admitting doubt or conflict. But instead of denying our dark side, we must affirm it passionately. Only then can it be brought before God and healed.

Constraints on Profit Opportunities

The positive strategic investments in people and value creation that have been described in this chapter, and the personal transformation of competitive hatred to compassionate love, are, in their conceiver's eyes, more than a matter of simple financial sense or careerist maneuvering. They are expressions of Christian duty and order, resulting from a sense of the supernatural in everyday life. And yet they make good business sense, as the returns in these companies indicate.

To the degree that profit and Christian values go together, we might question whether there is really any tension at all for the Christian in pursuit of business. I have tried to show how the seekers' struggle to follow Christian teachings permeates their basic approach to business and career, and usually sustains a creative paradox in the marketplace.

But not every contradiction has a happy, creative resolution. What about situations in which Christian values clearly run counter to profit opportunities, however attractive from an investment point of view? What about the occasions when common industry practice or financial constraints are so strongly oriented toward the unethical course that the choice is to either go along or go out of business?

Even though the decision to terminate a business opportunity may look easy to the general public or to theologians with anticapitalistic biases, it is not a matter-of-course decision for the seeker. It is an ongoing personal struggle to know how far or how self-denying the Christian concern for others should go in terms of risking the financial returns of the business. Those CEOs who really took their corporate responsibilities and Christian responsibilities seriously could not be complacent about these ethical quandaries.

The seeker's first strategy when faced with a survival trade-off is not to accept such a trade-off as inevitable. He or she builds slack into the firm's business mix and debt profile so that doing the right thing will less likely put the firm out of business. The seeker searches for a new statement of the problem that may lead to the development of a different product. Or, like Jack in Chapter 3, who was caught in a life-threatening lawsuit, he or she follows a compassionate course of action as far as possible and makes a financial comeback the next time.

None of these responses is "shalt not" obedience to a few rules. Those rules, as Jack Feldballe noted, are relatively easy to determine: no law-breaking, no lying, no bribery, no killing. He also likes to quote Micah 6:8; "And what does the LORD require of you / But to do justly, / To love mercy, / And to walk humbly with your God?"

The positive covenants that threaten the bottom line are the ones that are more difficult to deal with. A good example is the welfare of the less fortunate. As Feldballe said, it is not in the charter of corporations in our society to satisfy the needs of the poor. Though Feldballe himself is personally very sensitive to his Christian obligation to feed the hungry and clothe the naked, he is much less sure where corporate responsibility lies in that area. He also noted that it was a remarkable irony that other institutions such as hospitals, universities, and the government have charters much closer to this goal but rail against the corporation for not taking more of the responsibility off their shoulders. His approach to this problem—it could hardly be called a solution—is typically directed toward the internal workings of the firm:

> Provide where you have some ability. Create and maintain a safe, nondiscriminatory workplace; create jobs; provide a material benefit to society.
> But it's a delicate tension to satisfy other demands: the capital needs you have to stay in business, the different desires of stockholders. I'd just as soon they increased our tax for the benefit of those in need, and allowed the free market to handle the provision of services required.

How far did the interviewees go with their willingness to sacrifice profit for the sake of serving God's will? No one spoke of deliberately putting his company out of business for reasons of conscience, but there were many recollections of turning down contracts or products. George Gallup, who was not interviewed personally for this book, has told evangelical groups that his company, which begins each meeting with a prayer, turns down "several" client proposals for surveys each week for ethical reasons. Another former CEO, whose company had recently gone bankrupt, recalled with dismay how close friends, including evangelicals, had urged him to fudge on his financial representations in order to save some money out of the business for his family. After all, if ever there was a survival scenario, this was it. But he refused. "I owed these people money," he said, "and it is my obligation to carry this out as accurately as possible, whatever the cost." His wife told me that she fully supported his position—a far cry from the six million dollars in personal bonuses declared for Drexel Burnham's managers only days before it declared bankruptcy!

Ken Wessner, chairman of ServiceMaster, also recalled an important business opportunity that fundamentally opposed his sense of Christian values. SeviceMaster had taken over a substantial hospital cleaning contract in the Northeast. The hospital's chief administrator turned out to be a very abusive person. He had a drinking problem and a bad temper, and he used language that in Wessner's terms was simply unacceptable. This man especially abused his own staff. One day he even threw a wet tray at one of the ServiceMaster cleaners (trays were supposed to be dry). The ServiceMaster manager in charge went to Wessner and expressed his concern for their staff.

Wessner agreed that it was unfair to ask their people to work under such a personally abusive situation. Wessner withdrew from the contract.

It would be wrong to see Wessner's decision as a simple act of charity to his employees without a concern for profit. ServiceMaster is a business, and though it is explicitly dedicated to "Serving the Master," no one in top management has suspended the ordinary benchmarks of good business judgment and financial stewardship. The decision to withdraw, however, was based on the *long-term success* of the company, *not the short-term threat to profit*. Continuous sound business judgment, a good plan for the future, a very consistent philosophy of employee development, and the fact that there were many contracts in place, all built a financial slack into the system that allowed Wessner to cut bait without forcing the company into a survival scenario. Having that slack did not make his decision any less ethical, for the slack itself was a product of the same set of values that had caused him to withdraw on that particular contract.

Jack Eckerd is perhaps the most well-known evangelical leader who turned down business for the sake of Christian values. Though I was not able to interview him personally, he has written extensively about his business philosophy in his autobiography. Many other evangelical CEOs cited Eckerd as their number-one example of an admired Christian leader in business. Starting with a single drug-store, Eckerd eventually headed a billion-dollar chain.

In looking back on his career, Eckerd himself is not entirely comfortable with the competitiveness and drive that he exhibited as he built up the company. But there is one decision that he is certain he was right about, and that was the decision not to carry *Playboy* and *Penthouse* in his stores. Eckerd made this decision only a few days after his religious conversion. As he tells it, he suddenly saw the magazines in a different light, and found them completely incompatible with a "family" store such as his. "The Lord would not let me off the hook,"[12] he said. Though the direct cost in lost sales was several million dollars a year, the magazines were taken off the racks.

Eckerd then began a campaign, writing to other drugstores about his decision. Eventually an organized consumer coalition, the National Coalition Against Pornography, joined in with him, and several major chains dropped the magazines. Others modified their packaging and display locations to enforce an adult-only rule.

Dennis Sheehan recalled how a former employer had been about to withdraw from producing a tracking part for armor that was being used in Vietnam. The device triggered a radio signal that would attract a certain kind of mortar. Placed in weaponry, it would be activated after a weapon was stolen and supposedly taken to a guerilla enclave. It was learned, however, that the arms were also being stolen by children and taken back to villages, blowing up innocent civilians when the charge was activated.

Just when the company was debating its involvement, the army decided to discontinue using the device. They had discovered that the Vietcong were throwing the weapons over U.S. compound walls late at night, and when the mortars were set off, they'd come straight back down into the company's midst. Sheehan called the incident "a self-correcting situation," and with characteristic modesty claimed no great morality in being willing to wrestle with the dilemma.

But the fact that seekers can even recall such incidents indicates how seriously they confront conflicting impulses in Christian ethics and business. The generalizers and justifiers had a much harder time identifying any such problems.

For all three groups, the easiest acknowledgments of the irreconcilable tension between profit and Christianity were, not surprisingly, instances of sex and blasphemy. Several interviewees condemned advertisements that use sexy models to sell a product. One retailer, who was dangerously close to being a generalist, reported that he'd never had any trouble reconciling business practice and his faith. But was there nothing in normal business practice that he wouldn't do? After a long pause, he confessed that he wouldn't sell racy underwear in the lingerie section. When asked about some of the less savory practices of retailing, such as putting extremely disabling pricing conditions on small suppliers, not paying bills on time, or returning unsold merchandise with false damage claims, he simply said his company never did such things.

Fred Smith of Dallas recalled asking a group of evangelical CEOs the question, If you weren't going to be a Christian tomorrow, what would you do differently in your business? There was great silence, an indication to Fred and to the group of just how compatible good Judeo-Christian ethics are with a well-run business. Finally, one fellow replied, "Well, I'd occasionally cuss."

The generalists were the most resistant to acknowledging personal responsibility as Christians for even overtly unethical practices. Their denial of involvement in "un-Christian" business activities can be attributed in part to the evangelical worldview, which tends to look at signs of faith through the person rather than through the institution. The personal bias has a great upside in terms of the evangelical executive's interactions with employees, or of his service attitude to the customer.

But this same perspective carries the danger of creating blinders about the ethics of institutional decisions. The generalist, for example, is a master at creating cognitive smoke screens to protect himself or herself from accepting responsibility for obviously profitable but ethically questionable business practices. Like magic, these potentially disturbing conflicts are buried in a rhetoric about personal faith.

A good example came from a New York executive, a very honest man, who was demoted in a takeover scheme. Now he has less say in the business, and the new owners have few moral scruples. They continually go back on their word with clients, renege on deals, and stretch the financial facts. When asked how he could stand working for them, he replied, "I don't work for them. I work for God."

It's hard to believe it's that simple. Surely there are times when this man is directly involved in some of the activities of his partners or is indirectly responsible for bringing unsuspecting clients into their clutches.

Another example of the generalist's inability to confront conflicts between standard business practice and Christian values was evidenced by one interviewee's reaction to his own advertising literature. We'll call him Ted. Ted was a highly respected senior statesman for evangelicalism and business growth in his region. During our interviews he displayed an uncommon capacity for listening and caring about others. His interactions with his employees were respectful, and it was clear that they cared about him too. A folksy sort of person, he displayed in his office a prayer that one of his neighbors had embroidered for him. His workplace was safe and immaculately clean.

Ted reported that he was terribly angered by the growth of pornography in his region, and had joined a Christian coalition of businesspeople to enact stricter laws about videos. He also served on an anti-abortion council. His family feelings were strong, and at least two of his children worked for him.

Ted's business, which I have disguised here, was in the manufacture of a leisure-time product. A quick glance at his advertising literature gave me a start. The copy pitched the product as "good family fun." The photos showed scantily clad women and men (no children) draped around the product in a typical singles-set scenario. Ted was selling sex appeal, and none of the models looked like good, clean family fun. In fact, the women looked like they'd be customers at the abortion clinic in a month or so. I asked Ted gently what he thought the message of the ads was. He replied, "Good, clean family fun." He then went on to talk about the breakdown of the family and his own work on anti-abortion laws.

I don't think Ted was a hypocrite in the normal sense of the word. He seemed genuinely unaware of the contradiction between his values and the message he was pushing and profiting from in the marketplace. What made this blindness possible was his absolute restriction of his worldview to *personal* expressions of faith. For Ted, and for most generalists, faith is a personal motivator of attitude, but is not necessarily linked with external actions. It masks the problematic conflicts between Christian values and *institutional* norms on profit making. Like the New Yorker who worked for God and was therefore not responsible for the ethics of his bosses, Ted was so secure in his personal abhorrence of sexual promiscuity that he failed to see its presence in his own advertisements. These ads were well within acceptable standards from an industry standpoint.

By contrast, the seekers have deliberately developed a viewpoint of personal responsibility that includes their companies. Their most obvious expressions were in the creation of corporate credos or mission statements that outline the fundamental values of their firms in ways that are consistent with their own individual ethics. But as recounted here, they were also able to identify and act on specific instances in which institutional activities defied those values.

Returning to the worst-case scenario, in which a CEO is faced with the choice of going out of business or going along with un-Christian practices, I found an interesting insight into the dynamics of faith from Jack Feldballe. Feldballe acknowledged the necessity of facing up to such issues and also the need for spiritual guidance. Reflecting once again his strong relational approach to problems, he did not think that business leaders should have to shoulder such responsibilities alone, or that they had all the answers. He confessed that he had no special formula for deciding such things, but he was adamant about the need for his religious leaders to acknowledge conflict as much as the businessperson does, and to help put it in a spiritual perspective. In this he found the religious leaders wanting:

> Now, you do get situations where either you accept a business as it is [i.e., against your own sense of what is right, based on a scriptural orientation] or you shut down. And I have no grand insights into what is the best thing to do, but *that's* where the clergy don't understand. They'll just say, Don't do it, don't shut the plant down. No sense of dilemma. And they can't give you any help. See, ideally, when I face these problems, I should be able to take them to my clergyperson and talk things out so as to give me some insights. And my personal experience is that very few can do that.

Feldballe's point is crucial to understanding the moral and practical concerns of the evangelical business leader. Certain trade-offs and tensions will constantly recur, and human frailty almost guarantees that the answers will never be perfect.

But in the experience of those interviewed, it seems there is much more that representatives of the faith can do to help bring Christian perspective to these problems. If the two ends of the bow—Christian commitment and competitive success—are to be transformed by faith into a dynamic tension, it seems appropriate for the clergy to be much more active in helping to drive the arrows.

Table 5.1
Comparison of Two Business Ethics[13]

SELF-INTEREST ETHIC

- Purpose of Business: Increase own interest (profit)
- Social Contract: Obey laws and customs of the land
- Primary Assumption: System brings greatest good to greatest number
- Problem-Solving Focus: Efficiency

COVENANTAL ETHIC

- Purpose of Business: Creation of delivered value
- Social Contract: Receipt of an economic return
- Primary Assumption: Business is a service
- Problem-Solving Focus: Enabling relationships

6
Tension 3:
People Needs
and Profit
Obligations

Assembly workers are
the lowest on the totem
pole when it comes to
job fulfillment. They
don't think they have
any skill. Some corpo-
rate guy said, "A mon-
key could do the job."
—President,
Lordstown Local,
United Auto Workers[1]

W hen I asked the evangelical CEOs if they were religious at work, the most frequent reply was something like, "Well, I like to think so. I mean, I have a good relationship with my employees." Many also said that the strongest linkages between their faith and their work were in the area of manager-employee relationships. Employee relations were just about *the* distinctive area of spiritual relevance for the CEOs—second only to their personal psychological state resulting from a personal relationship with the living God. They drew consistently from employee relations to give their most concrete examples of faith influencing work.

So "how you treat your employees" became both the representation and concrete test of faith at work. Take, for example, a letter I received from John Snyder, Chairman of Snyder Oil Corporation in Fort Worth, Texas. Snyder had participated in a group interview at a Young Presidents' Organization fellowship retreat, and was voluntarily following up with a copy of his corporate philosophy. That document defines a series of relational commitments to a variety of stakeholders. Several values, including "achieving long-term growth," appear ahead of employees.

But as Snyder's comments revealed, in thinking about the *meaning* of that document in his organization, his first concerns are more specifically focused. He had underlined certain precepts and commented on them in the margins in order to clarify for me his perceived areas of success or still-to-be-worked-on goals. *All of his personal notes had to do with the treatment of employees.* The content of his letter literally constituted an employee relations scorecard as the sign of his religious belief. And he was very rigorous with himself about his track record.

Or take the comment of Fred Roach, former president of Centennial Homes in Dallas. Roach is a modest fellow about how well he lives out his faith at work. Here's his self-evaluation:

> I usually have to hook what I do onto a Bible verse, though I try not to proof-text. I like Romans 6:13, "Give yourself completely to God, every part of you."
>
> If you approach it that way, that simply, that brings order to the rest of these things [the seven tensions described here] and a comfort level. I believe that a businessperson who doesn't get to that point is not as effective. There is tension because there is disharmony.
>
> But if I can get to that point, and I mentally say that to myself, then the adrenaline is flowing, your mind's sharper, you stand taller, you breathe better, *and you're much more effective in dealing with your people. You're a better motivator.* [my emphasis]

Roach's train of thought was typical. In analyzing the role of faith at work, most of the participants tended to discuss their relationship with God first, and with other people at work second. This latter relationship is a test not only of Christian values but of managerial success. The CEOs saw little incongruence between the two—at least in theory.

Even the most resistant generalists exhibited some self-reflection and concreteness in this area. There was one man, for example, who was particularly prone to sweeping generalizations and made endless, preachy personal testimonies about the love of Christ. In his interview, which lasted over an hour, I pressed him again and again for a concrete case of faith working or failing on the job. He cited only one specific example of a work situation: he had flared up at a secretary's incompetence and had felt that this had not been the way a Christian should act. But, he pointed out, though he was still impatient, faith had indeed made a difference:

> Twenty years ago I wouldn't have thought about this. Now, at least I think about it, and it bothers me.

Though the evangelical business philosophy is usually expressed in personalized rather than systemic responses, many of the "people values" that CEOs hold important have been formally incorporated into their mission statements. ServiceMaster's four-part corporate objective puts honoring God first, and "to help people develop" second (excellence and profitable growth follow). Morley Properties' corporate mission statement expresses the priorities in a different order ("Create a customer by solving client problems" and "Earn a profit" are the first two), but the third and equally important commitment is "to provide people—our associates—with an opportunity to fully express their potential." Herman Miller, Inc., outlines a commitment to, among other things, "quality relationships based on mutual trust and integrity."

Jerry Dempsey, former chairman of Chemical Waste Management, brought such concepts to life with a very personal response during our interview. He said, "I am blessed with fine people. This business is intense and growing fast. We need extraordinary people. Our people are very qualified. They know what the business is about."

Conceptions of Work and "People Values"

These expressions of "people values" seem a lot less remarkable in the 1990s than they would have twenty-five years ago. As organizational theorist Fritz Rothlisberger pointed out in 1968, most managerial theories offer a correlation between employee satisfaction and employee productivity, but managers adopt radically different approaches to employee relations depending on their various concepts of work.[2] For some people, especially those with past attitudes toward "labor," work is an unpleasant task, an effort, something "taken out" of a worker. Proper motivation then rests on overcoming a natural distaste for the task and on providing compensation for the effort expended. In this view employees are like little productivity chips in an organizational computer: valued solely in impersonal, instrumental terms, they are best managed, organized, and rewarded when their natural feelings have been divorced from the job at hand.

For others, work is something that satisfies certain basic needs beyond the securing of a livelihood. With this frame of reference, the employee becomes a *person,* a complex social creature rather than a mere physical embodiment of a production operation. In this view, employee policies are motivated not just by a desire to obtain effort, but by a desire to obtain personal commitment as well. Quite different from a steam engine, the worker must be managed, organized, and motivated with a regard for a complex set of *human*—emotional, physical, and intellectual—needs.

This latter conception of work, stated here in secular terms, closely represents the evangelical's view as described in earlier chapters. Work is a theological certainty of the human condition. Commitment to hard work is an expression of obedience to God's order and an imitation of Christ. As I have already noted, the interviewees tended to internalize this idea to the point that work well done is a self-actualizing expression of Christian—and therefore personal—identity.

By extension, the interviewees draw on the same assumptions and values to motivate other employees. These assumptions and values, of course, include meaningful work.

The Provision of Meaningful Work

William Rentschler, former chairman of The Medart Companies, and now a consultant/business broker to private firms, is an eloquent spokesperson and living example of the CEO's responsibility to provide meaningful work. In the early 1980s, Rentschler put together a small group of investors to buy up struggling low-tech manufacturing companies and make them profitable again. His motive was partly patriotic and partly humanistic: he has an unswerv-

ing conviction that American strength is rooted in its industrial
underpinnings and that there is nothing more personally rewarding
than to give "more good people the chance to do 'work worth doing'"
(he consciously uses Teddy Roosevelt's phrase).

As Rentschler watched thousands of small to mid-size companies flounder and fail in the wake of the high-leverage megamerger
mania, his conviction reached urgent proportions. In 1981 he decided to start a search-and-rescue operation in America's sinking
industrial heartland. Medart, Inc., a homely little Mississippi manufacturing firm employing 151 people and in Chapter XI, was the first
purchase. With lots of "hard-nosed management fundamentals and
entrepreneurism," Rentschler and his team got Medart back on its
feet, and began the same process with other small companies. The
best sign of success? In Rentschler's terms, it was job creation; at its
fifth anniversary, the Medart group of companies was employing six
times as many people as they did when they started in 1981.

Since then Medart has continued to buy small, low-tech companies that are, in Rentschler's words, "the prototype of the sort
written off and consigned to the industrial graveyard by the heavy
thinkers." Medart currently makes lockers, range hoods, bifold
doors, hand trucks, and basketball equipment. When Michael Jordan
scored his record-setting sixty-three points at the Boston Garden, it
was on a Medart backstop made in Greenwood, Mississippi.

Rentschler's focus on job provision is almost a fixation. Quoting
Teddy Roosevelt's Labor Day declaration at the turn of the century,
Rentschler once stated in a public address:

> Far and away the best privilege that life offers is the chance to work hard
> at work worth doing.

Rentschler continued:

> Deprived of that "prize," a human being is a mere shell of what he or
> she is, was, or might be. . . . To be deprived of "work worth doing" is the
> ultimate putdown, castration, embarrassment, the final defeat which strips
> that person of all human dignity.
> It is also the failure of an affluent society, a condition we cannot con-
> tinue to tolerate.[3]

Unlike many of the interviewees who tended to avoid talking about national economic policy in favor of personal or company-based solutions, Rentschler sees the need to put the private and public sctors in tandem as the only real solution to the job problem today. His agenda, which he has shared with his friend, U.S. Senator Paul Simon (D-Ill.), rests on the same two elements of his personal view: a *changed attitude* and a *changed set of actions* concerning job provision. He has long advocated a mandatory universal service requirement for all youths, recently adopted in the Clinton Administration, that would offer a variety of options, from military service to public works endeavors. The goal would be to cultivate higher motives through work: "To inspire among our youth a certain sense of idealism, selflessness, and giving in a materialistic age."

Rentschler also advocates a broad-based national public works program based on local public-private partnerships to strengthen the decaying infrastructure. While such recommendations for job provision and a revitalizing of American manufacturing productivity were being suggested by both the left- and right-wing politicians in the early 1990s, Rentschler was advocating and living out that agenda throughout the 1980s.

In assessing the attitude and actions of Medart's former chief officer, we must recognize that Rentschler is constantly maintaining a tight tension between people needs and profit (that is, efficiency and cash flow) requirements. It would be a mistake to overemphasize either side of the equation. According to Rentschler, Medart's corporate philosophy is to do whatever it must do to stay profitable in order to stay in business so that it can both preserve and increase jobs. Although his choice of new companies was indeed often based on saving jobs in a commonly abandoned industrial sector, he is not economically irrational: he carefully chose markets based on competitive conditions and on perceived opportunities to provide distinctive value. He freely acknowledged his decisions in this regard ranged "from brilliant to dismal."

Medart is also prepared to make certain trade-offs to invest in whatever it takes to meet the hard-nosed realities of profit making. This includes purchasing bar steel from Brazil and England despite a preference to "buy American." It also means investment in high-tech equipment, but not to the point of becoming robotic. In a replay of Wal-Mart's implausible combination of high-tech communications strategy and people-oriented retailing, Medart installed high-tech transceivers and computer-aided punch presses, but only in order to facilitate communications between plants and entry into new fields. Robotics was rejected as an option because it is seen as a threat to jobs for some categories of employees.

Once again the question is raised, Is all this simply enlightened self-interest? Does Rentschler simply have a good nose for hunting out underutilized employees? Certainly he recognizes and fully acknowledges that there is a big payoff in a rescue-and-repair operation:

> Our employees generally trusted us. Many have been through hard times. When we take over a company, we tell them our aim is to preserve and expand jobs by making a profit and growing. We have kept the faith. Within reason, I think most of our people would walk over hot coals to give us a good day's work, to help in a crunch, to give a little extra when called for.

The *words* Rentschler uses to describe his motivations are only partially about enlightened self-interest. They are biased toward people solutions versus the manipulation of debt or extreme technological efficiencies. In this bias they also reflect Rentschler's deep, unconditional commitment to the welfare of others, and his intrinsic respect for individuals:

> The good people are out there in abundance, eager to take the reins, but most need a little help, which we must provide. . . .
> When I die, I hope whoever delivers the eulogy will remember me as one who sought always to provide steady, decent, challenging jobs, which allowed good people to support their families, build and retain their self-esteem, and "work hard at work worth doing."
> I would consider that among the contributions that make a life worthwhile.

The type of employee philosophy described by Rentschler should not be underestimated as being "obvious." The mere recognition of a profit opportunity does not automatically invite the kind of people stewardship that he advocates, which can be risky in the extreme. Rentschler notes that his kind of entrepreneurism stands in sharp contrast to the spirit of the 1980s, which he termed "the unjustified sacrifice of working people for short-term gain and the ethical delinquency of unbridled greed."

Dignification

According to the interviewees, business should be organized and employees treated in such a way that work provides an opportunity for emotional fulfillment and social acceptance. The best single summary of the evangelical's translation of this approach is the word *dignification*. In attitude and actions, a common goal and baseline is the promotion of people's dignity. To refer back to the covenantal ethic, this is another "enabling relationship" for which the evangelical CEO has responsibility.

The concept of dignification, which takes many visible forms, most certainly has at its base the New Testament emphasis on the universality of God's love and the Christian's obligation to "love your neighbor."

The nurturing of human potential at every level was a repeated theme and was translated into two basic responsibilities for the evangelical CEO: to personally treat employees as human beings rather than as cogs in a money machine (the attitude), and to dignify employees by providing them opportunities to develop skills to accomplish meaningful jobs (the actions).

The metaphors that the interviewees used most commonly to describe their roles in this process were those of nurturer, friend, or servant leader. All of these terms have somewhat familial or even paternal connotations. A CEO, like a good parent, is responsible for the development and growth of his or her children; their success gives the CEO great personal joy as opposed to a sense of having been "taken," as it often is in the more combative assumptions of most formal labor situations. Elmer Johnson vividly exemplified the nurturer approach when he used parental language to describe his personal satisfaction in developing his employees:

> When I got to be about forty years old, I was no longer focused primarily
> on seeing how good a lawyer I could be. That was no longer enough to

satisfy me. My new source of satisfaction was thinking about the new generation, including training and delegating.

Tom Jones, former CEO of Epsilon in Boston, similarly speaks of the CEO's "responsibility of empowerment." Pat Morley calls his employee relations philosophy "the opportunity to express potential." In the interviewees' comments about employees, the centrality of such notions as empowerment, dignity, and the actualization of human potential suggests that these CEOs are extending their application of the parable of the good steward in the Gospel of Luke from the *stewardship of things* to the *stewardship of lives.*

In extending the stewardship concept to employees, however, these men are *not* devaluing people as "productive human capital" in a dehumanizing, mechanistic sense of stewardship. Rather, they are *combining* their relational Christian attitudes toward people in general with their values about financial productivity and work. Thus humanistic values such as universal respect, personal kindness, and individual productively are as central to their approach to employee issues as the notion of making a person's economic potential happen. And the concept of potential itself has many carryovers from the protestant ethic. As Ed Yates, owner of Highland Park Cafeterias, commented:

> You have to be careful how you talk about this, because it sounds self-serving.
>
> We have a concept: every individual who comes to work for this company has to be improved by being here.
>
> That's not just the disadvantaged. It can be your white college grad. I find they have to be taught character mostly, how to be a good citizen. We just feel that that's just a part of it. We talk about a philosophy. We try to persuade people to adopt a philosophical belief that they will not steal. You don't have to worry then about all the proceedings. Same about keeping clean—that's very big in our business. You have to keep on watch for dirt.
>
> We like to teach this as a philosophy. You'd be surprised how an educated person responds to this.

Yates's comments and others like it represent a qualitative refinement of the human capital concept of employee relations touted today. As De Pree writes, "Words such as love, warmth, personal chemistry are certainly pertinent."[4]

On the surface, this approach bears many resemblances to so-called New Age theories of worker motivation, which also rest on the concept of treating workers as people and giving them autonomy, training, and responsibility in such a way as to make work "self-actualizing"—that is, fulfilling in terms of individual needs and goals.

The evangelicals would hardly disagree with New Age organizational behavior concepts such as "empowerment" or "enabling activities" to describe their view of employee development. But the evangelical approach departs from New Age theories both in the range of activities entertained (fire walking, meditation, and other "pagan" exercises are definitely under suspicion) and in ultimate goals. The individualistic motivations of New Age thought are anathema to the evangelicals.

Instead, they are suggesting an approach that channels the needs of the individual worker into a productive harmony with the needs of the group *to the fulfillment of the organization's purpose.* They "align"[5] organizational purpose with the purposes of God's order—which brings them back full circle to relationships between people. On the one hand individual dignification is essential; on the other hand, the *relational* aspect of employee policies, the welfare of the *team,* is equally crucial. The business leader seeks not just to dignify individuals but to provide a social culture in which everyone respects each other, and business purpose is outwardly directed to serve the customer.

The tensions in carrying out a philosophy of employee empowerment are clear: Christianity requires unconditional and redemptive love. Fiduciary obligations and the needs of the corporation's internal society require a disciplined view to the bottom line as well.

Once again, it is the paradoxical nature of Christian thought itself that intervenes and helps the seeker walk a tight course between serving employees and being subservient to financial necessities. In Christian evangelical thought, each person is unique and important, and potentially capable of God's personal redemption. And yet everyone on earth is comparatively "nothing" in the larger scheme of things. To a Christian, self-respect, humility, and self-sacrifice are complementary notions. So the evangelical tends to have little crisis of conscience in putting the needs of the business above any one individual, and yet he or she succeeds in maintaining an extremely strong commitment to the individual dignification of all employees—a commitment that requires investment and the sharing of the company's good fortunes.

Is this a hat trick? On the contrary, like many of the other creative tensions, the evangelical sustains his or her attention to conflicting responsibilities through an intellectual double focus, which is creatively managed so that it produces a partial reconciliation of competing interests. The two chief means of reconciliation—or call it creative management—are to seek a commonality between the goals of the organization and those of individuals, and to channel the dignification effort into the shaping of employee character traits that are "good for capitalism."

An example of the first means of reconciliation is the development of a universal employee stock-ownership plan, like the one instituted at Herman Miller, Inc. An example of the second means is a training program that develops people's skills while educating them on their responsibilities to be disciplined, hard workers. This kind of employee development can be reinforced with greater decision-making power, as in self-management through teams, but also with greater accountability for results. None of these latter qualities are inconsistent with the evangelical's self-concept as a good person.

Service to outsiders is the third essential condition of the evangelical's successful discipline of employee development and organizational fiduciary needs. Steve Reinemund, president of Frito-Lay and an extremely thoughtful advocate of the "people values" in his firm, nonetheless has developed the "Rose Bowl Test" to make sure of this outward direction. Says Reinemund:

> It's easy to get insulated. You develop your own jargon, your own perspective. You like your people, you respect their opinion. But you can get too closed. So we apply the Rose Bowl Test: how would this strategy look outside the comfort of our organization? What if we put it on the 50-yard line of the Rose Bowl before 100,000 people?

Thinking in Terms of Relationships

Generally, the effective Christian business leader has an obligation to invest heavily and often in the dignification of each employee, but also to ensure that the welfare of the whole enterprise is maintained. This is not accomplished so much through some new kind of systems analysis, but rather through the cultivation of "old-fashioned" values like hard work and an extremely strong emphasis on the relationships themselves.

F.J. Rothlisberger's theories about the effective motivation of workers, dated to the late 1950s and the 1960s, are particularly relevant to the evangelical CEO's philosophy of employee relations today. Rothlisberger suggested that human needs were best satisfied for workers "through their relationships with other individuals and groups of individuals at work." His observation corresponds very closely to the relational orientation of the evangelical worldview. Like Rothlisberger, the interviewees tended to assess their employee policies in relational terms—both their personal relations with others, and the formal relationships that are established by compensation, communication, and benefits policies.

Relationships and the Holistic Tendency

Max De Pree, Herman Miller's retired CEO and a pioneer in innovative employee relations, describes his framework as the building of "covenantal relationships." By this he means a concern for mutual welfare that goes far beyond contractual relationships that depend only on "cash bonds" (sociologist Elton Mayo's apt description of the state of personal relations in modern business). For De Pree, the covenantal approach reflects "the sacred nature of relationships" and includes such values as freedom, shared commitment, and unity. Though he celebrates the individual, this is a harmonizing concept of employee-manager relationships rather than a fragmenting one. It rejects the motivate-on-personal-self-interest approach that has been the keystone of many employee policies.

Several structural or cultural themes follow with great regularity. Foremost is the tendency to shun impersonal, rigidly hierarchical, status-oriented organizational systems. In a mind-set where riches and authority are less susceptible to overemphasis ("the first shall be last," and so on), and where poverty, humility, and devotion sometimes raise the lowest above the highest, love and humaneness between people become *the* harmonizing elements (Matt. 25:40, "Inasmuch as you [fed and clothed] one of the least of these My brethren, you did it to Me").

Therefore, most of the interviewees strongly favored relatively egalitarian approaches to their own corporate societies and participative, open communication systems. Such measures, though currently favored by many management experts, may or may not make the best financial sense, but they fall well within the generally accepted notions of good employee relations. The interesting thing here is not so much whether these policies are revolutionary, but rather that the interviewees saw them as being consistent with Christian commitments.

Furthermore, we can find subtle, qualitative differences in the rationale that underlies employee development practices. Certain practices help the evangelical businessperson to both invest in and place some constraints on the use of company resources to meet human needs.

For example, many interviewees conceived of employee growth in holistic, character-forming terms that reach well beyond job skill. Jack Turpin, then-chairman of Hall-Mark Electronics, professed a strong feeling of responsibility in this area, and related it to his own religious faith:

> I'm a good believer in one day at a time. I love every day, not that it's all a bed of roses. But that foundation [that is, one's faith] gives every person an approach to every single day, which can bring them the ability to grow. That is vital.
>
> We have a responsibility as heads of companies to make sure people grow. I hope not just in their career, but in their relationship with God, hopefully in their relationship with Christ, and in their career and their family.

John Snyder, of Snyder Oil Corporation, also stressed his obligation to respect the "whole person." To that effect, his corporate code makes a commitment to paying competitive wages, maintaining reasonable working conditions and hours, and recognizing personal and family needs.

Tom Jones, who used the word "empowerment" to describe his attitude toward employees, also sounded the holistic theme. He saw development in terms of job skills but also in terms of personal conscience and autonomy:

> It's important to be concerned about your people, their welfare. It's important to empower them to do what they think is right and to participate in the process of innovation and change.

Ken Wessner of ServiceMaster, commented:

> Training, indeed any management directive, is not so much about what we want people to do, but rather what we want people to be.

At ServiceMaster personal dignification through training comes in many forms. As mentioned in Chapter 5, the company offers counseling on hygiene and extensive teaching in reading and language skills (there is even a training program in Polish). In addition, the training program for the managers requires them to participate in first-line jobs such as cleaning floors.

The floor-cleaning requirement is a good example of how the Christian emphasis on equality and humility also encourages financial productivity. Why have the *managers* clean floors? Wessner said that a manager who hasn't personally experienced what it's like to wear a green uniform and be treated like a nonperson can never fully understand the importance of his or her responsibility to see that all employees are treated with dignity and to make sure that the job itself is dignifying.

Such firsthand knowledge frequently has its own economic fallout, however. After personally experiencing how backbreaking and inefficient the traditional floor-cleaning equipment was, ServiceMaster managers hired engineers to develop a patented machine that cleans much more efficiently, thereby saving on costs and increasing the quality of service—as well as making the cleaner's job physically less wearing.

The Long-term View

Some other elements of the evangelical worldview reinforce the attitude of holistic "people" stewardship and help managers make hard decisions about employee welfare when the bottom line is in jeopardy. One obvious factor is the evangelical emphasis of the long-term view. None of the training programs or stewardship attitudes mentioned here are financially justifiable unless they are based on a long-term calculation. One striking example of this sort came from Norm Sonju, general manager of the Dallas Mavericks. At a critical point in the season, Sonju discovered that one of his players had a substance abuse problem. Sonju could have delayed instituting treatment in order to squeeze out a few more games. Instead, he chose not to exploit the athlete, and immediately withdrew him from play to begin a rehabilitation program. Sonju's action was clearly consistent with Christian ethics about "love your neighbor," but he had also reasoned that it was better for the long-term health of the player, and better for that player's ability to later contribute to the team.

Is this action just a rational, enlightened calculation of the company's self-interest? Some managers would like to restrict the explanation of such decisions to completely morally neutral factors. They would argue that Sonju was simply "making long-term financial sense." But in listening to Sonju himself, you hear not only the logic of his decision but also a basic attitude of love and respect for the individual employee as a person created in the image of God.

Despite its long-term logic, Sonju's decision flew in the face of the view of many other sports managers—a view that has produced economic rewards for those owners. Their view is that professional athletes are expendable. Sonju rages at this norm, and has pushed hard for an industrywide effort to provide athletes with opportunities for skills development in areas other than sports:

> The fact is, if all your self-respect is wrapped up in the sport, then there will be nothing when you retire or get injured. We have a responsibility to develop the athlete as a person.

The Wrong Approach

We can appreciate just how hard it is to achieve what a Bill Rentschler or a Ken Wessner has done simply by comparing the employee policies record of a major American corporation like General Motors. In his 1983 epilogue to the fourth edition of *Concept of the Corporation,* Peter Drucker criticized General Motors for having fallen behind in its employee relations approach.[6] The old-style formula that had worked so well in the past for Alfred Sloan and that sounded like Max Weber's social economy—"Money plus discipline equals productivity"—had created a nightmare at the Lordstown plant in the mid-1960s. The workforce was rebellious and demanding, and its productivity was steadily dropping while its wage demands climbed. Discipline was gone, and no amount of money was able to buy it back: by the 1970s, GM's labor costs were nearly 50 percent higher than the average American manufacturing industry, and its defect rates were still rising.

Drucker felt that GM's own convictions blinded the top management to the fact that productivity and labor costs were related. The top managers thought of themselves as the "experts," while workers were a group to be disciplined or bribed into obeying orders, not into thinking. Attitude, a strong evangelical theme, was clearly a contributing factor here. By many accounts, GM's top managers were arrogantly secure in their belief that laborers were "inferior"— devoid of any ability to perceive and solve problems on their own or to engage in self-governing activities. Charles Wilson, former CEO of GM and right-hand person of the legendary Alfred Sloan, tried to change the top-down arrogance of GM's management and union leaders. He failed.

In the 1980s, Elmer Johnson, an evangelical who is frequently mentioned in this book, joined GM as executive vice president after serving as one of its main outside legal counselors. Johnson also sought a change in the GM culture, and especially in the top managers' attitudes toward hourly employees. Like other evangelicals in this book, he emphasized an attitude of respect, along with an insistence on the values of the protestant work ethic: hard effort, self-discipline, and accountability. Johnson recommended a number of sweeping changes in GM's employee relations policies to realign responsibility between management, owners, and union workers. Chief among his recommendations were less bureaucracy; more participative, team-oriented decision making; employee stock ownership; and retraining.

Johnson also failed. As he put it, "The golf course way of doing business is not easily changed."

The Debunking of Hierarchy

Johnson's highly publicized departure from GM sharply exposes the differences between a philosophy of employee collaboration and a philosophy of control. Johnson's comments and his failure at GM to sell these ideas underscores how the interviewees' approaches to employee relations, though based on "old-fashioned values," are really quite innovative, especially in a manufacturing context.

In the old-style, hierarchical organization, control from the top was quite rigid. Differences between levels were emphasized and reinforced by many structural elements, from the ways that information was restricted to the creation of elaborate and extreme status systems. So authority was assigned to an elite group, whose education seemed to merit the responsibility. Management expert Rosabeth Moss Kanter describes this approach as "segmentalist," and argues that it tends to not respond to innovation and entrepreneurship precisely because it sets up so many barriers to the flow of information.[7]

To the evangelical, not only does the segmentalist approach make bad business sense, but it goes against the relational and holistic values that are an essential part of his or her Christian worldview. In the newer participative approach (Kanter uses the term *integrationist*), managers deliberately attempt to break down the barriers between levels in order to make better collaborative use of the skills of all the people within the organization. Knowledge and relationships are the chief levelers: teams and communication are important, and the line worker is recognized as having a formidable capacity for knowledge.

This capacity is further developed through training and through increased access to production, inventory, or pricing information.

The late 1980s marked a dramatic swing toward participative management structures. Many outstanding companies are making all-out efforts to transform their cultures into this responsive ideal. But as many companies have discovered, producing such change is difficult. Authority and accountability must still be managed in deliberate ways so that employee skills are neither stifled by too many restrictions nor overestimated so that employees are left with too little direction and guidance. Likewise, effective communication between management levels is an extremely tricky process.

Although my strategy in writing this book did not include observing and reporting the details of these companies' training, communication, and decision-making structures, the comments of the interviewees revealed one very important aspect of managing participative, responsive organizations: *such changes in organizational behavior are unlikely to occur unless a complex set of relational conditions are in place.* Simply opening your door does not automatically create a participative culture; someone still has to want to walk through it.

Many of the companies represented in this book were on the cutting edge of participative, open-communication management styles long before the concept had widespread interest. Borg-Warner's Jim Beré, for example, launched an attack on the company's autocratic decision-making structure as early as the 1960s, when he as a new group vice president went around the division heads and met directly with customers to better understand their needs. At that time this was considered to be a wanton, ungamesmanlike invasion of turf. But it was just the first of many disruptive steps that Beré took to break down the closed communication and self-protective hierarchy in the firm. By the mid-1970s, the company's manufacturing units were working jointly with the research center to develop new products—a product-development strategy still considered revolutionary today.

Changes in Attitude

Outsider accounts of Borg-Warner called the new culture more open and constructive. Beré himself attributed the changes, which led also to a positive turnaround in the company's balance sheet, to an *attitudinal shift* among the top managers toward wanting to satisfy the needs of all the people in the organization:

> I wanted everyone who is part of Borg-Warner to understand that providing for the employees' well-being is a Borg-Warner objective—for good business reasons.

So, too, Ed Yates's approach to extensive employee training, clearly emphasizing empowerment, rests on a profound attitudinal joy in other people's development. To repeat a phrase used earlier, it is the Christian's welcome "stewardship of lives." As Yates said:

> I like the restaurant business because it is an entry-level place to work. It's interesting to see someone come out of the back woods of east Texas and find for themselves that they've got good sense and intellect and abilities that can be developed. That makes it worthwhile. I like individuals as individuals. Many of my best people are the ones who come from that circumstance. That's very fulfilling.

Nowhere has the need for deliberate attention to the attitudinal, relational factors of participative management goals been underscored more dramatically than in the events at General Electric, where chairman Jack Welch devoted his 1991 annual letter to shareholders to the topic of participative leadership. In a widely publicized letter early in 1992, Welch decreed that the company needs "every good idea from every man and woman in the organization," and therefore "we cannot afford management styles that suppress and intimidate." These words make sense, but they represent goals that require fundamental personal changes in managerial thinking. As one longtime observer noted with amusement about Welch himself, who was known for his authoritarianism, "He would need a therapist—not a consultant—to change his management style."[8]

The evangelical CEOs interviewed for this book offer many highly relevant contributions to the attitudinal learning that must occur if participative management is to be achieved in the large organization. Assuming an egalitarian nature of human relations, the interviewees favored not only status-minimizing cultures and infor-

mal, unrigid authority structures, but also personal relational abilities: politeness, the personal touch, respect, and a willingness to
listen. Respect, they said, includes a deep commitment to fight
"isms": racism, sexism, or classism. As Elmer Johnson said:

> I have this spiritual demon in me. I can't stand it when people are not civil
> to others.

Johnson has even been known to conduct a civility audit peri-
odically in his law firm, asking the most experienced secretaries to
comment on how they are being treated. Anyone who fails to pass
the civility test is quietly called in, told of his or her reputation for
being a so-and-so with the secretaries, and reminded that this is not
the way to advance in the firm.

Many other interviewees told stories about a personal friendship with someone from a so-called lower position in the firm. Again
the relational element was high. Ken Wessner felt that it was one sign
of his success as a leader if the people on the shop floor stopped him
as he walked through their area, and shared their stories of private
victories or sorrows. Paul Kuck, chairman and CEO of Regal Marine
in Orlando, had pictures in his office that were given to him by
employees, and as I walked with him around the building, it was very
clear that he personally knew everyone there.

Some firms even institutionalize the setting for the personal
touch. When Max De Pree was CEO of Herman Miller, all the
senior vice presidents were required to meet once a month with
fifteen to twenty employees over a brown-bag lunch.

Management consultant Michael Maccoby points out that
heavily bureaucratized workplaces contribute to the devaluation of
workers by emphasizing hierarchical differences. Many of the CEOs
I interviewed were vehement about breaking down the traditional
symbols of hierarchy as a conscious part of the dignification effort.
Tom Jones talked of dismantling the "we-they thing." One of the
actions he took was the removal of segregated parking spaces at
Epsilon. At the time of our interview, Jones was reviewing plans to
have his office redesigned as a general meeting room for other

managers to use when he was away. (He also converted the "executive" area of the headquarters into a training center.)

Jones's rationale for these actions was partly philosophical and
partly practical in a typically conservative, frugal way: he is mostly on
the road or walking the halls, so the space is wasted if it belongs only
to him. Besides, from a psychological standpoint, he says, he doesn't
feel the need to isolate himself behind a plush desk within an office.

Jack Turpin's egalitarian viewpoint is revealed in the great stress
he places on individual potential. His own background—a star athlete in high school who rejected the trappings of the athletic hero in
college—can be heard in these comments:

> I have a strong emphasis on excellence. I define that as being the best that
> God enables you to be or do. *It is not about being better than anyone else or win-
> ning, but being the best God enables us to be.* I personally strive for it and I
> hope everyone else does.
>
> We've had many cases of young men in the warehouse, just handling
> the product, shipping it out, who we would hope would choose to go to
> night school and expand their abilities. And we'll fund that, all of it, if
> they'll do it. So that's enabling them to grow. [my emphasis]

The Fight Against Degradation

Of course, these egalitarian tendencies and respect for human
dignity also surface on racial, ethnic, and gender issues. Many interviewees expressed concern about racism and have worked to overcome it in their workplaces and communities. At Wyndam Hotels,
president and CEO Jim Carreker takes care to train Caribbean
employees in the difference between service and servitude. "One is
good business," he said. "The other is demeaning and has no place
in our company." When Dick Capen became publisher of *The Miami
Herald,* he insisted that he learn Spanish, and did so, as a sign of
respect as well as for practical reasons. Many other interviewees
stressed their determination to hire regardless of race. (A few mentioned gender.)

While it is admittedly easier for a CEO than for a line manager
to be consistent with his personal Christian values in fighting occurrences of employee degradation, some interviewees had to buck
long-standing corporate cultures for the sake of these values. Elmer

Johnson tried, but found the prevailing corporate culture too strong at that time. Another striking example is Charles Olcott, former president of Burger King. Upon becoming president, he immediately addressed the problem of abusive language and behavior in the headquarters building. He took the unusual stand—from the culture's point of view—of making it well known that he would not tolerate such language or demeaning behavior from anyone, including senior officers. Olcott is no sissy. But in his view the supposedly macho saltiness of the prevailing speech patterns were degrading to clerical workers and invited an attitude of sexual and racial abuse. After a few confrontations on this topic, the top managers began to suppress their habitual crudeness.

Olcott was also willing to make a personal sacrifice for the sake of these values. His abrupt departure from Burger King was precipitated when the senior management asked him to endorse a financial projection that he felt was unrealistic. When the choice was to either vote unanimously or leave, he left. Olcott is far from down and out, however. After a year and a half of searching, he committed resources to a start-up firm that has a new technology for processing—you guessed it—no-fat beef. His next and current venture is a trout farm that produces fish in totally unpolluted water.

Max De Pree told the following story (slightly disguised here) as an example of the unconditional attitude of respect for human dignity that is insisted on at Herman Miller. It is a good illustration of how the personal touch, egalitarianism, and openness of the leader work together on an issue like racism in the workplace.

> People deserve to know what you believe before they accept you as their leader. And you have to let them know how you feel, and say it. One woman who works with us, who is black, is a good friend. We talk from time to time. One night she called me at home, and said, "Max, we've got to get together." So we did at the start of her shift the next day.
>
> She told me we had a bigger racial problem than I'd realized—that there was a supervisor, white, from a small town nearby. In her words, "He thinks because he watches TV he understands my people. And he's too superficial to do the job well."

De Pree asked more questions and then invited her advice. She recommended that he personally stand up at the next monthly meeting with work-team leaders and "tell everybody what you believe about diversity." De Pree did, and later received from the woman a handwritten note saying he'd made a difference.

I asked De Pree where his faith came in. He replied that his faith was what had started the whole process; it was why he believed in diversity and was so against racism. He reported that he had openly shared these thoughts in his meeting with the group in question:

> I put it in the context of my faith, that we were talking about God's mix. They know where I stand. The Bible tells us that we're all made in the image of God. We know we're all different, and we have to keep in mind that we're different for reasons we don't understand but God does. God makes the universe, not we.
>
> And the federal government also has a stand on this. It knows you and I are fragile in this area, more than we realize sometimes. And we have to make sure we comply with the law.
>
> Now someone who is less secure in their faith or in their job might choose different words. But if people want to be Christian and faithful, they have to define where their faith is in these issues.

De Pree's strong belief in the *ultimate* ethical authority of this view motivates him to take personal action on racism when someone with a very relativistic viewpoint might approve of waffling despite a lot of talk about disapproving of racism.

Hard Work, Good Pay

While the evangelicals' general attitude toward employee relations is one of respect and stewardship, none of those I interviewed implied that they are giving up their conservative protestant emphasis on hard work in seeking to nurture the dignity and growth of their employees. Far from it. Work itself, in the evangelical framework, is a self-respecting activity, as John Wesley used to argue to the Scottish coal miners and as Chuck Colson's Prison Fellowship program argues today. In the mid-1980s, Elmer Johnson had suggested to GM that it needed *tighter* rewards and punishments in regard to productivity and attendance.

Many of the interviewees insisted on hard work from their employees, but they also said that the leader should provide good financial compensation in return. We can compare this contractual emphasis on mutual benefits to ancient Hebrew traditions about labor relations. Rabbinic law emphasized a kind of covenant between employer and worker that is similar to something that was suggested earlier in this book: that employees owe the company a contribution of value and that they should be guaranteed a return for doing so.[9] The laborer must, according to Jacob, work with all his strength, but also should reap great reward. He should not, for example, jeopardize his energies by excessive moonlighting. The employer has an obligation to provide a fair return for such commitment: wages paid on time (so as not to endanger the very life of a worker), severance pay, and so on. A lax attitude toward safety would not be tolerated under Jewish law.[10]

Hebrew tradition, which was highly contractual in nature, generally established an exact set of guidelines on the contributions and rewards that each side made—when to pay for what, when to ask for greater effort from an employee, and under what time frame these obligations were to be carried out. The employment contract of the interviewees (as opposed to the relational aspects of the employee covenant) do not radically differ from Hebrew assumptions: Hard work and fair pay are ethical obligations. Safety and clean workplaces are highly valued.

These expressed goals of mutual accountability seem unremarkable on the surface, but in a large organization the mechanisms of accountability are often the management issue that is most subject to arcane and seemingly irrational practices. Borg-Warner's Jim Beré became a legend when, as a group vice president, he actually announced the operational and financial record of each division at a meeting of division presidents. This had never been done before, and it provoked widespread discussion within the company as well as a verbal reprimand from then-president Lester Porter. But Beré persisted in his push for more open and accurate accountability between divisions—a move that led eventually to the strategic decision to withdraw from some of the less profitable businesses whose performances had not been completely understood until that time.

What is so interesting about the Borg-Warner experience is that these tighter controls on accounting for financial performance were introduced alongside a "softening" of the company's formerly hardline autocracy over employees. Said Beré:

All of this depends on your view of man's potential. If you believe in that,
as Christian belief says you should, then you can build an organization
that trusts its people and develops their talents without giving up any of
the sound business practices such as good financial controls.

Tom Gerendas, CEO of Temptronic, a liquid-controls manufacturing firm in Newton, Massachusetts, is an extremely egalitarian
manager who keeps an extremely egalitarian, open environment in
his office building. (There are no doors on any manager's workspace,
and beautiful grounds are a must in considering any new plant site.)
But no one would accuse Gerendas of being "soft" on hard work. It
was only half jokingly that after stopping to introduce me to some
of his employees, he sternly suggested that it was time for everyone
to return to work.

Many CEOs emphasized that they expect employee discipline
and contribution, which can be summed up in a covenantal statement that employee contribution of value requires the guarantee of
adequate compensation—and vice versa. The CEOs often used this
"formula" as a springboard for other values. For example, one CEO's
Christian aversion to racism was communicated to employees
through economic and performance arguments, once again demon-
strating the evangelical's ability to reconcile values of faith with
values of business. As John Snyder wrote:

> Employees should be judged and acknowledged on the basis of their per-
> formance, and not on race, color, creed, age, or sex. Therefore, we must
> ask ourselves, What have they done and what contribution have they
> made?[11]

Related Conflicts

Despite the logical economic relationship between the concern
for employees and the concern for the bottom line, the interviewees
commonly cited several areas of conflict in which doing the right
thing has presented difficult challenges. The conflicts mentioned the
most frequently were in wages, growth (especially with technological
changes), labor negotiations, and the underperforming employee.
Each of these conflicts tests the Christian commitments of the

evangelical CEO against the hard realities of the bottom line and traditional corporate practices. Some of the solutions, innovative at the time they were instituted, conform to what would be regarded today as top management practices. Other solutions are a creative step ahead of even current practices.

Determining Wages

Compensation is a stickler for several reasons. The idea of a system based on achievement is viewed, on the whole, as the best way of encouraging individual autonomy and responsibility. It is also consistent with Old Testament principles that connect contribution and reward. But the extreme differences in income in America—the so-called wage gap—have been very problematic to some of those interviewed.

Max De Pree is perhaps the most famous revolutionary in this area. Long before Bush went to Japan and the CEO compensation question was generally recognized as an ethical one, De Pree recommended to his board that it institute a limit on the cash compensation of the CEO directly related to the average wage in the company. Specifically, the CEO could earn no more than twenty times the average wage, no matter what the bonus plan was. This was a sharp deviation from the American norm: most surveys put the average CEO compensation gap (including stock options) for the top five hundred companies at about eighty-five times that of the average factory worker. Furthermore, performance is a crucial ingredient at Herman Miller. Whereas many multimillion-dollar CEO compensation plans, like those at Chrysler and at GM, have been criticized for bearing little relation to the company's performance, the senior executives at Herman Miller receive 60 percent of their compensation based on performance incentives.

Today it is no longer outlandish to suggest that executive compensation is an ethical issue or that some top salaries are a national outrage. By 1992 even the Securities and Exchange Commission was proposing fuller disclosure on executive compensation in order to facilitate shareholder questioning. But when De Pree first instituted Herman Miller's decreased wage gap in 1985, the proposition was revolutionary. A few members of the board of directors had a slight problem with it at first but finally agreed after he insisted.

The Herman Miller situation is a good example of how the relational, egalitarian attitude of the evangelical business leader changes the prevailing custom, not by withdrawing from competition or performance, but by creatively rearranging the stakes. This situation also illustrates just how dependent on relationships and universal respect the evangelical response can be. De Pree reports that he initially addressed the compensation question after a janitor had casually asked him what another officer was making.

Discussion of the new policy, which seems to be a very positive factor in employee relations, has also been unabashedly frank. De Pree had instituted a common custom in all Herman Miller departments that anyone who wanted to talk with an executive could do so. The employee could simply call the executive's secretary and request a time slot for lunch or coffee.

One day the pattern shop called and said they wanted Max to come meet with them. (Characteristically, De Pree calls this group of tool-and-dye makers "the cream of the crop of factory work.") De Pree tells the story as follows:

> We got into the coffee and rolls, and they were a little nervous. They said they wanted to talk about Mr. X's salary, who was a senior vice president. They'd seen a newspaper clipping about him selling stock. They are all stockholders, and wanted to know what was going on.
> So I explained he was selling stock to raise capital to exercise stock options. They understood. Then I said, "I admire your good manners in saying you want to talk about X's compensation. You really want to talk about mine."
> So we got into the multiples policy, and we talked about the book of Amos—how God says he expects leaders to take care of the bottom rung first. When we got all done, one worker said, "That makes real sense. It's so great to have you come out and explain it to us. And I'd like you to know that I really like it that I'm in my job and you're in your job."
> That's pretty great. So that's one of the ways in which we need to express a Christian standard in a secular world.

Other executives, while not instituting wage caps, have managed to resolve their egalitarian concerns for employees and stockholder demands by instituting employee ownership programs.

Herman Miller and ServiceMaster were among the companies reporting significant employee stock plans. Jim Beré, when he was
chairman of Borg-Warner, reinforced his introduction of a new
corporate values statement with an issue of stock to every employee
in the company. Elmer Johnson is reported to have advocated the
same policies at GM.

Such a stand may have a rational explanation: employees who
share in the results care about the results. This is a controversial
theory, however, that has gained only partial legitimacy in American
business. Professors Joseph Blasi and Douglas Cruse point out that
whereas the general index of 205 companies reporting employee
ownership does indeed, on the average, outperform the Standard &
Poor's 500, the record varies by industry, with financial and industrial
industries doing the best and employee-owned consumer noncycli-
cals doing the worst.[12]

Herman Miller's economic record was phenomenal until the
real-estate recession with its subsequent slowdown in office
equipment purchasing in the early 1990s. But De Pree, like
Johnson and Wessner, does not rely on a justifier's argument for
his stand. Rather, he is very frank about the Christian source of
his ethic, and sees it as being somewhat independent of economic
rationales even when it makes economic sense:

> This is a chief difference in being a Christian—that you accept the idea of
> moving capitalism in the direction of making it possible for everybody to
> be a participant, to be an insider. Many companies don't allow people to
> get genuinely involved in equitable—not equal—distribution of results.
> Thousands of people get to be millionaires, but millions stay close to the
> poverty level.[13]
>
> If top management takes care of itself first, that's wrong. You are sup-
> posed to take care of the bottom of the ladder.

But was De Pree sacrificing or even abandoning economic
motivations in suggesting his famous wage policy? He said no, and
offered this explanation:

> As long as you are willing to be very open about the nonmaterialist side of
> life, it's not difficult [to motivate people and to attract good managers].

We have a guy who's a top officer. In his annual review, I said, "Do you want to talk about compensation?"

He said, "No, that's your responsibility. I really don't want to talk about it."

I said, "That's fair, but what relates to that in your mind that you would talk about?"

He said, "I want a chance to be involved with a company that could be great. I want to be great. That's more important than the money."

Determining Growth

Growth was also a problematic concern for the interviewees. Although growth is a primary measurement of corporate success in the minds of most managers, expectations of growth also pose trade-offs between Christian and financial duties in the eyes of some interviewees. As one interviewee said:

> I'm not so sure that growth is consistent with the Christian context for so-cial order. I mean, it might be better to embrace the idea of staying the same and living in harmony. To grow you have to innovate, and that means pain to someone. Is Christianity about pain?

Technological change was one of the most frequently cited problem areas of growth, because it often makes employees' skills obsolete and results in job loss rather than job creation. Few evangelicals in the interviewed group were comfortable with the idea of committing to employees only as long as the company can get something out of them. The interviewees expressed a sense of personal responsibility for the blood that has been shed when new market conditions have demanded technological changes.

Their most common resolution of the resulting disruption of employees is, not surprisingly, procreative: to nurture new job op-portunities inside or outside the company. Training is an obvious course of action. So are sophisticated job placement mechanisms.

Tom Jones, for example, had instituted an automated voice-re-sponse system that was projected to replace the jobs of a large portion of the clerical staff (250 people) in his Boston company. He justified the move in terms of both the bottom line and client service: it was five or six times more profitable, and it met client needs with more predictable accuracy. Jones felt a good deal of loyalty to the staff, even though the company had no relevant jobs to offer. He resolved the problem by setting up extremely generous severance policies, giving affected employees three months notice (again the openness value), and he brought in a firm to do outplacement and to hold job fairs. He reported that they placed the vast majority of the employees.

What if the same problem had been in Dallas rather than Boston? Jones says he still would have automated, but "the number-one thing is to be honest and open to everyone." He then cited a business colleague, who used to say that "everything has its natural flow." Apparently the evangelical belief that bad times as well as good are part of God's order helped the CEOs accept downside conse-quences even though it did not ease the immediate pain of such situations. In fact, no one claimed that being a Christian guaranteed an individual or his company freedom from pain, including the pain of layoffs. At the same time, the CEOs' equanimity over fluctuations in performance also helped them to prepare for the long haul and to keep people on longer than average in anticipation of a renewed turn upward. "To everything there is a season."

Negotiating with Workers

Other areas of tension between Christian ethical commitments and business necessity have been both posed and resolved by similar appeals to biblical principles. Fred Smith of Dallas, for example, cited the traditional ethic of enmity that accompanies labor negotiations as a real challenge to his Christian values. Smith was management negotiator with the United Steel Workers for many years. At one particularly acrimonious point in the negotiating process, he was prepared to sue the district director because of slander, and according to Smith, the judge indicated he had a case. Like the proverbial act of hitting a donkey on the head to get its attention before speaking kindly to it, Smith filed the suit. However, he then backed off from the enmity of the law courts. Instead he went to visit the man personally in his office. Explained Smith:

> At that point I felt it was my Christian responsibility to go to his office
> and say, "The employees are going to suffer. You and I will not. Can't we
> become respectful to each other?"

Smith claims that from that time on they developed a tremendous friendship that worked in everyone's favor. He cites as illustration the fact that they went through two national steel strikes without losing a day.

Where did his faith come in? In taking the risks in the first place:

> I could have been badly humiliated. If I hadn't been a Christian, I would not have gone into that office. But I did it on faith.

Smith's words ring true. The significance of a management negotiator entering the office of an extremely hostile labor leader who has been engaging in personal slander should not be underestimated. That personal touch has been notoriously absent from the labor relations of many companies and unions. Several interviewees expressed their resistance to organized labor in their companies on this rationale: that organized labor demands an unchristian distancing hostility between workers and managers in order to facilitate "fair" negotiations.

Other interviewees saw organized labor as a fact of life and have worked to reform the relationship. I recall a story that Philip Caldwell, retired chairman of Ford, once told me. Caldwell is not strictly evangelical but is a devout protestant who has professional connections with several CEOs interviewed for this book. Shortly after Caldwell became chairman of Ford, he invited the union leader at Ford's River Rouge factory to visit him in his office. The man arrived and after a few moments wandered over to the window. He fell silent, obviously overcome by some great emotion. Finally he turned to Caldwell and said:

> In thirty years of representing the workers, I was never invited to this office before. I didn't realize you could see "The Rouge" from your window. . . . I think we're going to be OK.

Now, Caldwell obviously had an economic rationale for inviting the man to his office. He wanted to establish a more compatible relationship between labor and management in order to get the job done better. This was particularly crucial at that time because Ford was developing many new changes in production methods for the Taurus design and for the "Quality is Job 1" campaign. It needed the Rouge's cooperation in making these changes.

But just as obviously, Caldwell's approach to labor relations, based on personal relationship and respect rather than on debasement of the enemy, is not something that is produced automatically by rational self-interest alone. It is produced, as Caldwell himself said, "from a whole way of thinking."

Dealing with the Underperforming Employee

Of all the situations that have severely tested the interviewees' sense of what is right according to their faith, the underperforming employee has been the hardest one. As already mentioned, covenantal expectations of contribution from employees are strong for the evangelical. As John Snyder put it, "Management must be proficient in building an atmosphere where each employee understands, shares, personally cares for, and seeks ways to contribute to the company's purpose and objectives."

Tom Jones, of Boston's Epsilon Corporation, also supported the idea of a covenantal relationship between employee and employer, with mutual contribution and support being the key factors. He described this relationship as an intrinsic value rather than strictly functional responsibility, but acknowledged its contractual nature:

> In some ways I do view employee relations as a quid pro quo. I treat ten-year employees differently from new hires. Loyalty is important, and we try to return it.

Jones is uneasy, however, about the conditionality of such a covenant, and sees it as necessary for capitalism but posing a tension with Christian values.

For the justifiers, if there is a breakdown in the employee-employer covenant, there is no problem: The nonperformer should be fired. But for the seekers, such as Jones and others, the tension is more acute. In such situations their belief in a business covenant bumps hard against other Christian values of love, compassion, and forgiveness. Responses range all over the map, and many interviewees confessed that they were not sure they'd gotten the balance of commitments right in their decisions.

Fred Smith, for example, kicked himself for having been too lenient at times, as had his friend Zig Ziglar, whose own motivational work is particularly strong on reinforcing and encouraging the positive sides of people. When Smith joined Ziglar's board, he insisted on a hard review of management contributions, to the point that some people were asked to leave. Ziglar later confessed that he could not have made the decision without Smith's support. Said Smith:

> Sometimes I think we Christians forget our real duty. We don't like to think of ourselves as being mean or hard. People can take advantage of that.

Fred Roach told the following story:

> I had an employee who was stealing from the company. It happened once, twice. Each time I'd talk to him. He'd go right out and do it again. The third time I fired him. He came to me and said, "You're not being a good Christian. You're supposed to forgive seventy times seven, as Jesus said, and you've only forgiven me twice!"

When the group being interviewed heard Roach's story, the general feeling was at first very hard-nosed. Several CEOs said they would have fired the employee the first time. As one CEO said:

> People assume Christians don't confront. We should confront everything God confronts, with the same assurance. Anything he says is wrong, we can say is wrong. If someone steals, you have the responsibility to confront that.

As they talked, however, there was growing unease, not about being hard-nosed and confronting wrongdoing, but about firing people. Fred Roach, CEO of Centennial Homes, then offered an alternative—one that I feel is a good example of the creative paradox. It also appealed to everyone in the group: Why not a sabbatical? Roach recounted the time that he had a cheating employee who was claiming sales he had not made. There was no doubt that the man had lied about his performance and had accepted commissions he hadn't earned. After speaking with the man, Roach offered him a choice between being fired or paying the money back and taking a three-month sabbatical without pay. If he would take the time "to get his life together," Roach promised to take him back. The employee went to counseling, took a rest, and came back as the top performer at the company, a record he still held three years later. Roach mused:

> Maybe I'm too easy, but I thought he deserved a second chance. Work was part of his problem, so I forced him to stop working for a while. After all, I had once benefited from his overworking; I was partly responsible.

On hearing this, Fred Smith replied thoughtfully:

> I used to joke that I hire workaholics to make them happy. But then one of my alcoholic employees went to a clinic, and afterwards he told me that his workaholism was a part of his overall sickness. I never made that joke again.

Jack Feldballe, of Chicago, also raised the issue of the second chance, and felt that it was an important Christian duty. His interview group then mentioned several examples of successful second chances. Dennis Sheehan told of an employee who was arrested for selling drugs on the company loading dock. Sheehan's first instinct was to fire him on the assumption that he would just repeat this behavior, but after a talk with the man's general manager, who recommended keeping him (it was his first offense), Sheehan relented. He admits that it taught the employee a lesson. Having lost his driver's license, the man had to walk three miles to work every day until he found a closer place to live; he stayed off drugs, and was participating in the company's tuition reimbursement program in order to further his education.

Sheehan told the story with characteristic modesty and compassion, but like the other stories, it has the parable quality of evangelical testimony. Not ready to accept the idea that forgiveness always turns out well for the bottom line, I asked him what accounted for the success of this event. He replied:

> I'm inclined to believe there is some formal Christian support there, because he's done so much. I'd like to believe there is.

So, too, another Chicago CEO recounted his crisis of conscience over an underperforming employee, and again Christian compassion paid off:

We had a woman who was not getting the job done. I told her to take time off, and her parents had told her the same thing.

It turned out she had cancer, and it wiped us all out. We really would have liked to let her go. We couldn't afford her nonperformance, and we felt she needed full rest. But as a Christian in business, I just could not do this. It had to be an act of faith to keep her on. So we just carried on; she worked three days a week, so we didn't give her full compensation. Now she's in full remission. It wasn't a disaster. That often happens. You think things mean disaster, but then you just get it behind you and it's all right.

An Assessment

The tendency of the interviewees to emphasize the happy ending and the economic payoff of their Christian beliefs was particularly strong in their discussions of employees. Though bordering on justifier-type narrative, this tendency may be attributed to several other things.

First, it is the nature of employee relations policies to be less subject to hard economic assessment than are other aspects of management. Claims of effectiveness are hard to dispute, and are, therefore, more easily made.

Second, the "people" aspect of employee policies is so obviously relevant to Christian ethics, and so consistent with the evangelical emphasis on relationships, that it is a natural area of concern and management expertise for the evangelical CEOs. Whereas Hebraic tradition is filled with specific advice about contractual obligations concerning work conditions and pay, the New Testament emphasis is on obedience and kindness. Paul's letter to the Ephesians is a good illustration:

> Bondservants, be obedient to those who are your masters according the flesh, with fear and trembling, in sincerity of heart, as to Christ; . . . as bondservants of Christ, doing the will of God from the heart, with good will doing service, as to the Lord, and not to men. . . . And you, masters, do the same things to them, giving up threatening, knowing that your own Master also is in heaven, and there is no partiality with Him. (Eph. 6:5-7, 9)

So in this chapter the idea of tension is somewhat less insistent than it is in some other chapters, and yet we have seen that there are many choices and struggles that the seekers encounter in trying to adopt a Christian approach to their own workforce relations. For the generalists, an attitude of love is considered as a sufficient expression of faith. As one generalist put it:

> It's not so much what you say or do with employees; it's your attitude that counts. If you have the right attitude, then the rest will follow.

What was "the right attitude"?

> That you are saved.

For the seekers, attitude is important but not enough. They struggle with many of the internal *activities* of the corporate society, and in several instances have devised procedures that clearly buck the prevailing trends in big business. While no one disclaimed his right and responsibility to be the ultimate decision maker of the company, a strong egalitarian attitude promotes both the openness of their communications and, in several instances, the structure of compensation and work autonomy. Almost all of these CEOs favored participative, team-oriented decision structures. The common dignity of all God's people invites dignifying efforts within the corporation, especially in the area of training. And, as always, there is great significance to the small detail; the personal friendship, and even the little event or conversation with an employee, occupies their attention as much as the corporate incentives, structures, and rewards.

If there was any blind spot in the otherwise strong tendency toward participation and egalitarianism among the interviewees, it was—not surprisingly—regarding the subject of women. As you will see in Chapter 8, many of the interviewees have a so-called biblical view of gender relationships that assumes that women should take a subordinate position of authority in their marriages. Some interviewees clearly felt the same about women employees.

These attitudes were not often overtly expressed with regard to female employees, but there were clearly some unconscious stereotypes about the relative differences in power between men and women in some of the examples that the interviewees gave. Such differences are also a reflection of reality: for the most part, women are *not* in positions of comparable power and top authority in business. Among the wide evangelical network that I tapped for these interviews, I was able to locate only one woman evangelical CEO, and she was unwilling to talk to me. Many managers had no senior officers who were women—a choice that they said was not deliberate—but they maintained strong personal friendships with female secretaries and junior executives.

The interviewees' descriptions of employee relationships with women were regularly dominated by the language of kindly paternalism. Some typical comments were those of manager X, who cited arrogance toward secretaries as a prime example of the uncaring, unchristian executive. As X put it:

> I love the secretaries. I really care about the little people.

Similar stereotypes of exaggerated weakness can be heard in this description of how a Christian at work should or should not disguise the role of faith and prayer in the office place:

> Say you have a secretary who is a believer. And her boss asks her to type up a letter which she knows contains information which is deceptive and which will harm the receiver. She thinks about it, and worries about it, and prays about it, because for years she has held a little prayer time during her lunch hour.
>
> And finally she goes in to her boss, trembling, scared, shaking in her boots. She's never spoken up to him before, and you know, her voice is halting. And she says, "Sir, I want you to know that for years I've had my own private prayer session, and I've never told you about it. And now I've been praying about this letter, and I think it's wrong." Well, I've got to believe that that boss would respect her and that God would somehow make her words persuasive to him.

What particularly strikes me about this story is that it was the *only* concrete example that this person could offer about the role of his faith in a business context, despite being pressed several times to give examples. The only real detail is about the secretary's weakness, and the moral is that God gives her the words and the CEO becomes kind. (Presumably she herself is constitutionally incapable of formulating a persuasive argument to her boss.)

Such comments beg for further analysis and personal questioning. Disabling or condescending paternalism rests on the perception of a relative inequality of ability that again, does *not* characterize the majority of the interviewees' attitudes toward employees. Given the interviewees' frequent bias toward paternalism in its most nurturing, constructive sense, how are they able to avoid the pitfalls of this stance? For most of them, the key controlling factor is *ego*—or the lack of it—and it turned out that our interviewees had much to say on this topic as they contemplated the characteristics of Christian leadership in the corporate world (see the following chapter).

Summary

The covenantal principle of mutual contribution between employee and employer places certain development responsibilities and certain hard constraints on employee relations. These constraints put employee policies in tension, if not in contradiction, with the unconditional love of Christianity. In fact, I found that many of the executives interviewed for this book were somewhat reluctant to acknowledge the legitimate existence of limits on their concern for others, no doubt in response to the psychological tension that such a statement would impose.

Nevertheless, the evangelical approach to employee relations should not necessarily be in constant tension with profit concerns. Their approach makes good business sense, given a marketplace that increasingly dependent on flexibility and people.

As with many other examples in this book, the evangelical's worldview toward employees has practical and profitable paybacks. Dignity, for example, has been cited by employee relations expert Michael Maccoby as the key ingredient in the future success of adaptive businesses.

Many of the interviewees understand that their attitudes invite a good payback in terms of performance and loyalty. As John Snyder said:

> To be successful, a business must be made up of people who build and create. Therefore, the company must develop and maintain an environment that will reward the innovative individual.

So we might expect to have heard many justifier arguments in the discussion of employee relations. Surprisingly, that was not the case. Though many interviewees believed that their attitudes and actions toward employees were the key to their business success, they rarely expressed this in terms of a payoff. Perhaps they instinctively shied away from viewing people simply as a means rather than as an end in themselves. Elmer Johnson attributed his long-standing advocacy of "people values" to something beyond self-enlightenment, even though he has been an eloquent advocate of the financial rationale for more egalitarian, participative organizations:

> It's the religious or moral drive that makes the difference in how much you stand up for employees. It's not enlightened self-interest. Besides giving you courage, this religious thing causes you to think of others. That's what makes you a reformist.

As Dallas executives Vester Hughes and Fred Smith both argued, if you hang your treatment of employees entirely on the idea that you have to be good to employees merely for business reasons, then you risk losing the power of your belief when you're not getting a payoff. Commented Smith with his characteristic wryness:

> It's always easier to be good when there's a labor shortage. But that's not the basis of a Christian attitude.

Christian love. Enabling employee relations. Business profit. No seeker would suggest that finding a balance between these three will be easy. Nonetheless, in searching for the right solutions, the participants often create policies well ahead of common business practice. Policies that—as with Max De Pree's compensation policy—later become widely regarded as the latest advance in good business practice.

7

Tension 4: Humility and the Ego of Success

The executive vice president for marketing at the Cadillac Division of General Motors is on the phone. . . . Cadillac, it turns out, is interested in cooperating in the production of a new superstretch limousine that would be named the Trump Golden Series. I like the idea.
—Donald Trump[1]

T he general characteristics of the seekers' employee relations practices, described in the previous chapter, are very similar to current prescriptions for the management style of the future. From General Electric's Jack Welch to Peter Drucker, there is a widespread call for empowerment and an end to treating employees as baboons.

This new approach redefines the employee as a thinking human being who is capable of making personal contributions. It also redefines the relationship between top managers and others. If open warfare and mutual disrespect are out, then so is the courtly position of CEO as king of the castle. Fiat and fear are being replaced by freedom and friendship.

Such changes demand a different style of CEO. The days of the glamorous autocrat have passed. Down-to-earth democrats are leaving their limos and rolling up their sleeves. In the 1980s it was the Robert Campeaus and the Ross Johnsons who set the tone. The business press was constantly celebrating executives who had made it to the top through self-promotion and a self-gratifying ethos that might best be described as "greed to succeed." In the 1990s the new role models are the late Sam Walton or Home Depot's Bernard Marcus—the down-home, unpretentious sorts who don't act as if they are superior to everyone else.

This new style of leadership, descending quickly on the heels of the insider-trading convictions and the sudden downturns in financial performance throughout the *Fortune* 500 elite, requires dramatic changes in many CEOs' habitual assumptions and activities. CEOs who were once seen by shareholders, customers, and employees only on video or as they stepped out of the executive lunchroom, are rushing to acquire more personal skills. They receive coaching on how to be more folksy. They privately rehearse entering an employee's office and saying, "Great job. I'm really impressed."

Many of the CEOs interviewed for this book have been practicing down-home, folksy, personalized management for a long time, and they do it well. Even some of the seemingly austere CEOs I interviewed are known for their personal touch, for their caring attitude. This folksiness goes beyond the superficial question of style or interpersonal technique. It is a function of a finely balanced sense of ego that rests on two paradoxes: (1) a strong competitive spirit but an accommodating, egalitarian view of human relations; and (2) a value on achievement, including the achievement of economic success, along with the belief that such accomplishments are relatively unimportant in God's larger order.

We might say that such juxtapositions are simply unbelievable. How can a person who is so good at "winning" not see himself as superior to others? Isn't it hypocritical for a man who makes over a million dollars a year, spending the vast majority of his time on business matters that affect hundreds of thousands of lives, to claim that all of what he does is "nothing"?

Unbelievable as such differences between attitude and action may appear on the surface, they describe quite well the ways that seekers personally integrate biblical authority and individual drive. The seekers' sense of ego is essentially a paradoxical view of personal accomplishment and leadership: The man of Christ has tremendous energy and capability, but ultimately all such worldly achievement is insignificant.

Two statements about success illustrate how these men consciously reject the stereotypical grandiose models of business achievement. Jack Willome, who had to restructure his business when the real estate market went bust in San Antonio, said:

A lot of life is about turning loose. To be able to dream is to turn loose of old dreams. I used to think it was very important to build two thousand or more homes a year. That was something that was really important, being the dominant builder in our area. But to survive, we had to turn loose that stuff, see ourselves differently.

Jim Carreker spoke of the self-confidence he had as a Christian, and felt it definitely colored his priorities about growth and ego. This change also had real economic fallout in his opinion:

Once I became a Christian, there was this whole pressure release. It's the acceptance of the gift, and that takes a lot of pressure off of being success- ful in business tomorrow, and having to win every single point of every single issue. It gave me peace, confidence, a resource, an outlook, a per- spective, a calmness, in the turbulent world of retailing.

Once people see that you are not totally out for yourself, that you're out for the betterment of people you work with and their lives—an unsel- fishness—then you don't have to fight to lead; people just follow. Once superiors see someone following somebody, they will promote that per- son. I don't think unselfishness, a servant's heart, is a human trait.

This psychological coupling of self-confidence and humility reflects a fundamental ordering of values and priorities around the inherent paradoxes of the human condition as described in both the Old and New Testaments: Humankind is inherently flawed, fallen since Adam and Eve, and yet unequivocally forgiven and loved by God. We are made in the image of God, but we are not to confuse ourselves with God. Christianity further dismisses worldly distinc- tions between people by having made its community open to all kinds of people from its inception. As classical scholar E. R. Dodds wrote:

Christianity was open to all. In principle, it made no social distinctions; it accepted the manual worker, the slave, the outcast, the ex-criminal; and though in the course of our period it developed a strong hierarchic struc- ture, its hierarchy offered an open career to talent.[2]

To use Dodds's phrase, early Christianity represented "an army of the disinherited" from every social and religious caste.

So the evangelical worldview naturally stimulates feelings of both humility and confident self-acceptance. These are essential character traits of the effective Christian. The personal relationship with God only intensifies such a view. When combined with the evangelical's heavy emphasis on the emotional, relational, holistic, and egalitarian aspects of social interaction, this worldview has a natural fit with the recent calls for a kinder, gentler workplace.

For the CEO, evangelical or not, who wants to adopt the premises and style of the new leadership that is being advocated in business journals today, there is much to be learned from this worldview. In this chapter we will explore how the evangelical outlook shapes the interviewees' attitudes toward personal success, since it is clear that these attitudes, which are essentially statements about personal ego, are a key factor in making their philosophy of caring actually work.

What we will see is a constant balancing of contradictory factors that I mentioned earlier, and great pressure from the current business culture to throw these values out of whack. Of all the tensions reported, this is the one that is the least likely to be dominated by generalist or justifier denials of conflict. All the interviewees said that they were aware of the dangers of ego in their positions, and that they deliberately sought guidance from their faith and from Christian colleagues on this matter.

Areas of Conflict

The interviewees repeatedly mentioned three areas of conflict in connection with the ambiguities of success: wealth, power, and self-reliance. All three have the potential of being the foundation or result of effective leadership as well as a distraction from one's relationship with God. The first conflict is discussed in Chapter 9, "Charity and Wealth," while the other two are considered in the following subsections.

Power

Tom Jones, former CEO of Epsilon, was not alone in his awareness of the ego massage that accompanies the office of chief executive:

Everything is built to reinforce the ego of the CEO. The wallet full of platinum cards, the "other" entrance to the building. Everything implies you're more important than everyone else. You get to believe it.

What may be surprising is Jones's resistance. By most accounts, the engines of capitalism are driven essentially by a longing for money and power.[3] Drexel's Michael Milken, for example, is said to have begun each of his junk-bond conferences by doing a rough calculation of the total buying power of his guests in the room. At a 1983 fund-raiser, for example, he is said to have announced, "Our total access (buying power) in this room is one hundred billion dollars."[4] The implication was clear: The name of the game is money, and winning the game is the measure of the person. He must have been on to something. Lots of people put up the cash to buy in.

Nowhere is the almighty dollar of more obvious importance than in the chairman's suite. So pervasive is the stereotype of the Beverly Hills mogul and the J. R. Ewing standard of success-to-excess that some people actually feel that anything less than extreme power and influence is tantamount to total failure.

And so two types of managers have emerged since the 1980s: the driven and the withered. The driven find that no amount of money or power gives them satisfaction, and yet the only compensatory action they can imagine is to search for more of the same. The withered suffer from what Douglas Coupland, in a perceptive book titled *Generation X*, calls a condition of "fame-induced apathy," by which he means that "no activity is worth pursuing unless one can become very famous pursuing it."[5]

Given the extreme visibility of the CEO's position and the size of major corporations, such overpersonalizations and megalomaniacal conceptions of success are no surprise. The culture of the top office is essentially a culture of power, and Lord Acton's warning that "power tends to corrupt and absolute power corrupts absolutely" is to the point.

In a corporation, the first corruption is of a CEO's own judgment and perspective. No CEO's power is truly absolute, but corporate employees often work hard to create the illusion that this is so. Most reminders of personal limitation or equality are weeded out for the sake of enhancing the power of the top office as much as the person in it. In some companies there are only two classes of people: the CEO and all other employees. A culture of flattery prevails. All favorable results are attributed to the CEO; bad events are deflected from the seat of power.

Elmer Johnson, former Executive Vice President of General Motors, was very frank about the seductiveness of power for top executives. It comes with the territory, and in today's marketplace the power relations have escalated dramatically as the corporation's governmental relations have increased. No top executive of a large firm is able to be effective these days without having an ongoing personal acquaintance with top officials in local, state, and national governments. For companies in international settings, the CEO even becomes a kind of ambassador. He or she is graciously received by heads of state and is given access to senators, governors, and other prominent legislators. Without such "pull," the executive could never garner the political strength to profitably tackle such issues as, say, environmental cleanup or plant relocations.

Cultivating this kind of relationship, however, is both necessary and dangerous, because it places the CEO in touch with a world of extremely heavy perks and a great deal of status, without any of the normal checks and balances of the electoral process to help keep him or her accountable. As Johnson said:

> [In the 1960s and 1970s,] CEOs made increasingly frequent trips to Washington. In general, they spent more time on external affairs: giving speeches, meeting with senators, making acquisitions. Not surprisingly, CEOs often lost touch with their customers, products, and the technical leadership of their organizations.

Even a person's good deeds are vulnerable to ego. The chief executive is often granted great discretionary power over the corporate contribution program, and potential recipients frequently rely on flattery for the patronage. Fred Smith noted how one Dallas CEO was bragging that he'd done so many good things for the community, including donating a few million dollars to a civic project. Smith reminded him, "That's embezzlement. You got the credit for giving away the stockholders' money." The man laughed and agreed. Explained Smith, "He was drunk enough to be honest."

Then there are the material perks, which not only feed the CEO's ego but further isolate him or her from the uncomfortable commonplaces of human existence. As Bob Dylan once said, "Even the President of the United States sometimes has to stand naked." The corporate CEO rarely has to stand naked in material terms. Immune from the economic vulnerability of most Americans, the CEO is also given endless helpers for even the smallest personal task such as sharpening a pencil, buying a present for his or her own spouse, or picking out his or her own clothes. Such perks create an illusion of invulnerability that real life has a way of piercing. At the trivial level, chief officers end up with little "street sense" on which to proceed when the cushion of perks occasionally collapses. More than one CEO has been embarrassed out of proportion by having no change to make a phone call or to use public transportation.

As I have already noted, the evangelical sharply contrasts his or her understanding of the Christian worldview with the prevailing highlights of the secular culture. Ego was a favorite point for comparison among those I interviewed. As participants see it, the secular humanist is particularly vulnerable to ego because of his or her human-centered point of view. The evangelical, in contrast, has a built-in corrective device to ego by having adopted a God-centered point of view. He rejects individual gratification as the ultimate motivator and guide for decision making. The possibility of a mistake is not only real; it is inevitable, given the fallen nature of man.

But while interviewees felt that the secular humanist was more likely than the Christian to fall prey to ego, they also acknowledged that no one was immune to its forces. Commented Fred Roach:

> Virtually everyone in business faces the problems of ego, of success and wealth, all the time, and in funny ways. For whenever you are a success in business, your ego is given further play.

Frank Butler recalled that even the leaders in the Bible were vulnerable:

> I think of my reading. Look at the Hebrew people in the monarchical period. David was in a limited kingship, but Solomon was the first to get it

by birthright—and the whole arrogance and the seductiveness that come with being at the top.

Tom Jones understood Butler's point: "Yeah, that's the dark side of it."

The leader often falls by depending too heavily on his own former competency. For the evangelical, only faith, not rational calculation or morality in human terms, can overcome the temptation of ego. So there is a tremendous association of ego with ungodly behavior, and the interviewees were fearful of the temptations.

Jack Willome noted that power is a fundamental human defense mechanism:

> Everyone has a tendency to think that to be accepted they have to project something that they aren't. Not one of us can handle power.

He felt that in one sense this tendency could be a keen motivator of economic growth, but that it could also mislead a businessperson into mistaking growth and bigness for truly legitimate business goals.

Christian ethics are very clear on this kind of self-inflation; it goes against divine order. No human-based social or economic system can outweigh God and his order. In fact, the New Testament frequently turns human social systems upside down to describe God's power: "Even Solomon in all his glory was not arrayed like one of [the lilies of the field]" (Matt. 6:29). "The last will be first, and the first last" (Matt. 20:16). "Blessed are you poor,/ for yours is the kingdom of God" (Luke 6:20). Paul wrote in his letter to the Galatians:

> For if anyone thinks himself to be something, when he is nothing, he deceives himself. But let each one examine his own work, and then he will have rejoicing in himself alone, and not in another. (Gal. 6:3-4)

Such words are particularly challenging if we consider the typical condition of being a chief executive officer. The position itself is a favorable power statement: "chief." The CEO is "on top"—the one with the highest salary and the final say-so. He or she represents the corporate culture, millions or billions of dollars in financial assets, and a collection of many people. The CEO is larger than life. To recall Ralph Waldo Emerson's comment, "An institution is but the lengthened shadow of one man."

It is no surprise, then, that the CEO's position carries disturbing temptations from an evangelical point of view. The seeker's response to these temptations, however, is not a simple matter of avoiding ego altogether. Ego is complex, and it is actually a *dilemma* of leadership; a person needs a certain amount of ego, or self-confidence, in order to have the necessary stability, decisiveness, ambition, and independence of mind to be an effective leader.

Many of the interviewees have invested great time and effort in helping to cultivate healthy egos not only in themselves but also in their managers and employees. Zig Ziglar, whose motivational work is known to millions, is basically helping people learn to love themselves in order to be more effective in leading others. Although his personal source of belief is strongly Christ-centered, Ziglar—like the late Reverend Norman Vincent Peale—has generalized the message of self-respect for millions. When Ziglar wants you to believe that "*You* are a winner!" (his emphasis), he is attempting to tease out the productive aspects of your self-confidence and self-respect.

So the problem with ego is not with *having* an ego, but with losing one's proper perspective. This problem can be expressed in quantitative terms of excess—thinking *too much* of one's own abilities—or it can be expressed in terms of relationships. Hyperinflated self-regard contributes to broken relationships with God and with one's neighbor.

The interviewees had several common responses to ego. One response was to cultivate a folksy, deliberately modest style that frequently contrasts with these men's intelligence and strategic skills. The charges of hypocrisy from outsiders, of disguised charlatanism, may be explained in part by this gap between style and substance. People expect to get what they see, and feel deceived when the evangelical proves to be a smart businessperson.

But the folksiness is not all put on. Many interviewees were in fact first-generation financial successes, so that the unpretentious, common-sense style may have come more easily. Keeping that style, however, is a somewhat self-conscious act. Elmer Johnson, who left his home in Denver to go to Yale on a scholarship, said this:

> I wouldn't hit it off too well with the urban sophisticate. You get the feeling they're saying, "How do I look?" I'm not interested in that.

Believers also remind the business community at large of the dangers of ego, and they often share these thoughts with each other at fellowship gatherings. Max De Pree, for example, has written extensively on the leader's need to remain open to his or her own vulnerability and connectedness with the rest of the world. De Pree has also spoken eloquently and frankly on these themes at evangelical gatherings.

At the 1990 National Prayer Breakfast, former Secretary of State Jim Baker sounded the same warning about the dangers of becoming egotistical:

> Someone asked me what was the most important thing that I had learned since being in Washington. I replied that it was the fact that temporal power is fleeting.

He recalled driving through the White House gates and noticing a man walking alone down Pennsylvania Avenue. Baker recognized him; he had held Baker's position in a previous administration.

> There he was, alone—no reporters, no security, no adoring public, no trappings of power. Just one solitary man alone with his thoughts.
>   And that mental picture continually serves to remind me of the impermanence of power and the impermanence of place.

Baker went on to say that power had many bright sides: It brought excitement and a sense of satisfaction when things went well. But positions of power also have their very prosaic, human costs: an exhausting schedule, lots of conflict, and headaches.

Self-reliance

Like a snake biting its tail, even the headaches themselves can become a source of overinflated ego. The more responsibility that a CEO takes on in good conscience and succeeds with, the more evidence the CEO sees of his or her own abilities. The person of responsibility can be very well intended and self-satisfying, but also overly self-reliant, which is hard to recognize in oneself. This is particularly true for the CEOs with a heavily patriarchal approach, who may in their willingness to take on a heavy leadership role forget to develop the strengths of others.

On the one hand, self-reliance, like power, is a plus in that it helps CEOs to set and accomplish their economic objectives, to be innovative, and to channel the commitment of others to a common purpose in the organization. Furthermore, the evangelical's strong sense of being personally accepted by God clearly supports a self-reliant outlook, even when it gets lonely and scary at the top. It helps the leader take risks.

On the other hand, self-reliance can also tempt CEOs to be too confident of their own judgment. They can fail to consult others, or they can be reluctant to admit their own mistakes. In seeing themselves as separate from the crowd, self-reliant CEOs can also see themselves as being above it. In that case, not only do they forget their commonality with God's children, but they can forget their dependence on God's grace as well.

While this kind of self-reliance is sinful, it also has bad business effects. Tom Phillips, former chairman of Raytheon, identified ego (in the sense of unquestioning self-confidence) as the number-one ethical problem for CEOs. He also saw ego as the number-one cause of business mistakes, thereby illustrating how the evangelical worldview puts Christian values and economic values in the same hopper. Phillips used takeovers as an example:

> In most takeover situations, the CEO goes to the board initially with incomplete information—by necessity. They recommend an offer, and only then are all the financials available. At that point it is almost impossible for a CEO to change his recommendation. His ego's on the line. It was his project. And yet that's precisely the point when a good leader must have the ability to say, "This was not such a good idea after all."

Former Borg-Warner chairman Jim Beré agreed. Beré's self-reliant ability to produce needed change was described in the previous chapters with regard to his introduction of a much more egalitarian

and communicative corporate culture. But even Beré was vulnerable
to ego. He felt that the most serious ego mistake he ever made was
in becoming too isolated about his evaluation of a proposed merger.
It was only after a good friend on his board, who had never disagreed
with him before, took Beré aside and gave him an honest reading of
his own view of the problem that Beré backed off. Everyone on the
board, including Beré himself, later agreed that they had made the
right decision.

Several interviewees, in commenting on the dark side of the
leader's self-reliance, pointed out that the evangelical is particularly
vulnerable to this problem from a psychological standpoint. As one
said:

> There seems to be a presumption among my peers that Christians are in
> some way "different," which makes them immune from problems some-
> one else might feel. It seems to me that a Christian businessman is never
> immune from the problems that every other businessperson faces.

One way of fighting the delusions of ego was to have a firm
sense of accountability. Fred Smith was particularly clear about the
need for CEOs—and even for all managers—to remember that they
did not own the business. Jack Willome commented as follows:

> The only safeguard for trusting any one of us to hold power is for that per-
> son to grant permission to be held accountable. To the extent that I avoid
> accountability, I'm going to get zapped, because I will inevitably abuse
> whatever power is given me, if left to my own devices.

This is a startling statement in light of the resistance of many
CEOs to questioning even from their own board of directors. Kenneth Wessner of ServiceMaster also felt that it was crucial to build
accountability into every position in the organization and to create
evaluation systems that accurately reflect the contribution that each
person makes.

Fred Smith, a business consultant, added that it helped to
remember that the ultimate accountability is not on this earth but in
the next life. This larger perspective—on one's whole life now and
in the hereafter—was supported by biblical references to heaven and
the relative insignificance of earthly pursuits. To use Peter Berger's

term, religion provides a "reality potential" that helps the CEO interpret and understand his or her own accomplishments in light of larger truths.[6]

Dick Crowell, formerly of The Boston Company, drew on a long-term perspective to summarize the delicate balance that every evangelical must maintain in order to be an effective manager and a true Christian. He described this balance in paradoxical terms of self-confidence and gratitude, ego and humility:

> We are made in the image of God. We are able to do things like work, make deals, do constructive things.
>   At the same time, we are fallen from that nature, so we can do incredibly terrible things.
>   So I guess I feel that when something that has been accomplished that you have been part of occurs, you feel a sense of accomplishment, and a sense of thankfulness that you're able to participate. You must realize that your whole life is hanging by a thread. . . . We're dependent on the grace of God for the gift of breath. We have to have a sense of accomplishment and thankfulness that we're here.

The transitory nature of human existence that Crowell described was evident in several other interviews. One lay minister who advised CEOs felt strongly that Christians, in acknowledging God's love, must also accept the idea of their own mortality. For such people, the presence of death is very real, and it plays a large role in their understanding of their own significance. This particular interviewee himself recalled an evening's walk when he suddenly became overwhelmed with the thought of the resurrection and the hereafter:

> I was ready. I really was. I said, "God, hey, take me now, if you want me. I know you'll take care of my wife and children." And since I've felt that way, I've loved life so much more. It's incredible, the love God has for us.

While few interviewees were as focused on the hereafter as this person, many drew on biblical time frames and a life-after-death perspective to explain their sense of distance from everyday accomplishments. As Fred Smith said, referring to his own business success:

> This is just the practice. The real game is played in the hereafter.

Does this kind of mind-set prevent the megalomania and depression that plague many leaders? Several interviewees thought so. Tom Phillips thought that the eternal view would help prevent fantasies of unlimited risk taking. The eternal view also keeps at bay personal feelings of total devastation when risks appear to be failing. I met with a number of associates of the interviewees, and almost every one of them said that his or her CEO had an extraordinary calmness when the rest of the organization was panicked. Henry David Thoreau said that calmness came from wisdom. If so, the detachment of the evangelical CEO is a wisdom of biblical proportions.

Tom Jones of Epsilon was very explicit about the eternal instability of success and the need to take a long-term view:

> I remember Richard Ferris, former president of United Airlines, saying that the major failure you make is when you feel success is achieved.
>
> Tom Peters mentions this frequently: If it ain't broke it soon will be. If you create the myth in your mind that you've created a success, you will fail. Success needs to be continually achieved.
>
> I don't know exactly how you measure success. For me, in this company, my success would be to have left three legacies: One, someone to replace me so that the company is not at risk; two, a solid value system that will transcend both them and me in terms of what the company stands for; and three, economic soundness and stability.
>
> Money? I've already made more money than I thought I ever would if I were a success. But the others, especially the second one, that'll take the longest. But it's probably the one you'll feel best about ten or fifteen years out.

The Role of Outside Forces

Given the group's general sense of limited personal power, it is important to understand the role of other factors in their explanations or theories of success. No one ignored the importance of being competent in business basics, and they deplored evangelicals who minimize that importance and who instead resort to wishful thinking. But they agreed that success is not solely a result of technique. All the CEOs recognized outside forces that are beyond their intellectual or strategical control. This acknowledgment in itself suggests a slightly modified sense of ego from the self-congratulatory attitudes so rampant today. Are these outside forces divine intervention, luck, or just environment?

The interviewees did not agree in their interpretations of divine intervention in business. The concept of God dealing in the affairs of humans is, of course, consistent with the evangelical worldview. To interpret even a minor business victory as an indication of the larger presence of God in the world is just another example of the evangelical's view of a personal God. But not all participants understand God's presence in the same way.

In its most naive form, the idea of God in business is a very mechanical sense of divine intervention—God helps me get parking spaces and customers. Most of the interviewees extend the context of God's intervention to character formation—God gives me that strength and acuity *to find* parking spaces and customers.

They are divided, however, on how actively they feel that God wants their businesses to succeed. Reading God's handwriting was not an easy task, and it never justified suspending sound business analysis. A businessperson could choose to take a loss for what seemed to be the higher cause—say no to certain products, for example—but never suspend analytical insights. So on divine intervention, as on many other aspects of business and faith, the evangelical's religious belief is not *replacing* business skills but rather *supplementing* them.

Some interviewees had a sense of direct assistance from God. For example, Tom Gerendas, of Temptronic, decided not to expand his liquid-controls business in 1975, when the market was unforeseeably about to suffer a sudden and severe turnaround. He attributed his decision to "the fortunate resisting of temptation," and described the orders that he received during those hard times as "'accidentally' coming in" (quotations his). In Gerendas's explanation of events, we can see how divine intervention plays into the evangelical CEO's sense of balancing ego between personal modesty and self-confidence:

> I believe that God—in whatever way, we will once understand—has an interest in our job and in our decisions. Not because they are crucial compared to major events but because He has interest in the lives of every individual.

I often wonder what decision to make next and do not feel awkward to pray for God's guidance. Then I use whatever talents and energy He gave me, and try to do my best to implement the decisions wisely. When I win, the glory is His. When I lose, the fault is ours.

I sincerely believe that we would have had far less chance of success if God hadn't blessed our efforts. What has been achieved is certainly more than what was expected, based solely on our backgrounds and talents.

Although all of the interviewees would have agreed that their success is "with God's grace," several said that this very expression of faith contained the seeds of a sinful ego. It is all too easy for the faithful to confuse their own will with God's. As Dick Crowell said:

My pet peeve, and I think this is the ultimate sin, is for the individual to say, "I am God." You do find people in business, including evangelicals, who for one reason or another are believing they are God, that they can do no wrong. This is not just a factor of being a CEO. You can find people in low-level jobs who have the same problem.

Commented another:

It's hard to take a mundane aspect of life and say that's the word of God, but it is. But you also have to look at what you're doing and ask, "Is this just my ego or self-interest at stake?"

When two people disagree at a meeting, and you say your view is right because you're doing this for the glory of God, that's wrong. It's a huge leap of logic to say that here's what God wants, and what I want, and therefore I'm right.

The interviewees saw these tendencies coming out particularly in connection with incidents of misuse of funds by some churches and Christian organizations. Fred Smith recalled how one televangelist had solicited money:

He told me to send him a dollar and the Lord would send me sevenfold in return. I wrote back and said, "If that's the case, why don't you send *me* the dollar and then your organization will be all the richer?" I even sent him my vacation address so he could start getting those returns right away! (emphasis his)

Despite the jokes and cynicism, there remains for the evangelical leader, as a partner with Christ in a personal relationship, a constant need for self-imposed discipline and a sense of obedience. Charles Babcock, now chairman of King Charter Company in Miami, explained how the Christian's sense of ego contributes to these disciplines, with good business results:

> People who accept bribes and the like have an ego quite dependent on status, and it makes them morally vulnerable.
>
> The followers of Christ have kind of thought about themselves a bit more, about the problem of their own self, and whether their self is God. They've already wrestled with the question of whether self is the greatest thing in the world or whether He is—the Father.
>
> And since they've thought about that process, they are more likely not to have an ego problem, and not be susceptible to stealing or cheating.

Prayer

In discussing the evangelical's sense of immediacy about God's intervention, an important question arises concerning a person's appeals for God's help. How does the evangelical CEO's sense of ego affect his or her prayers concerning business? Many evangelicals pray in a highly specific, contractual manner: "Lord, help me win this deal." At my interviews, many of the CEOs included a prayer for the success of this book in the grace before the meal. Are such prayers an acknowledgment of God's help and of the person's own insignificance, or are they an unconscious bid to God for favoritism because of the partnership? Would one attitude be more legitimately "Christian" from a biblical standpoint than another?

The interviewees were divided on this issue. Some balked at the idea of asking God's help on a business deal. Commented Fred Smith, "I personally can't believe that Jesus died for my balance sheet." So, too, when Jack Willome asked his prayer group to pray for his victory in the lawsuit against him (see Chapter 3), a member responded, "I can't pray for that. All I can pray for is that you be treated fairly and that the truth come out."

Others were quite explicit about the correctness of asking God to take a direct interest in the outcome of their dealings. Said one CEO who had bravely and with great conscience fought a court case that involved charges of pornography, "I thought we were doing the right thing, and you can bet I prayed to win!" This topic was not raised by many interviewees. It seems that prayer is such a culturally defined phenomenon that you simply tend to do what others do. Though it is personal, it is filled with sacred ritual expressions that tend to resemble the formulations of the person's own denomination. So it is not particularly surprising that few interviewees had questioned what it meant to "pray to win." It is an indication of how meaningful prayer life is to this group, however, that when I raised the topic among a group of about a hundred evangelical CEOs, it generated intense discussion and debate.

What they agreed upon was that *equating* one's personal ambitions for the business with God's willed order was an egotistical attitude. "Thy will be done" is a prayer that is never taken lightly. As retired wood merchant and ServiceMaster executive Allan Emery said:

> We must always remember that it's very hard to read God's handwriting. We do not have the mind of God.

However, Emery is keenly sensitive to the role of God's intervention on earth and to its invitation to human humility. Several interviewees quoted a line from his book: "When I see a turtle on a fencepost, I know it didn't get there by itself."[7]

Motivation

We might expect that such sentiments would impede effective business behavior. And yet, for the obviously successful men I interviewed, God's will did not seem to justify the sacrifice of economic rationales. I asked several interviewees about this phenomenon. How could they on the one hand deliberately see their activities as personally less important, and on the other hand be highly motivated and decisive in a competitive arena? In light of what Jesus said about the lilies of the field—that without any effort of their own they exceed Solomon in his glory—how can these CEOs fire themselves up?

Few of those interviewed saw this as a true dilemma. You work hard just because you do. You see yourself and your success as "nothing," and you attribute all good things to God simply because it is right to do so. Hard work, effort, self-discipline, methodical behavior—the old Protestant work ethic—is still taken as part of the discipline of being a person of Christ. As one interviewee put it, "Bloom where you're planted."

Another CEO from Dallas replied:

> The Bible is fairly precise about our stewardship of all our resources—not only money, or spreading the word, or being a help to another person, but also in utilizing your talents to the fullest. You have this talent; it's a privilege to have it and to use it to the fullest. You just can't take yourself too seriously.

Bob Buford, the well-known cable television executive/owner described in Chapter 4, said with some amusement that he himself had adopted two very distinct modes of thinking, and that he was always moving between the two. When it came to achievement and competition, he acted automatically:

> It's just like a tennis match. When I play, I play my best. I just do. I don't see it in light of eternity.

However, Buford is keenly aware of the transitory nature of success in this world. His only son, as mentioned earlier, had died as a young adult. The event caused Buford to reassess his career goals. Mindful of Proverbs 13:22—"A good man leaves an inheritance to his children's children, / But the wealth of the sinner is stored up for the righteous"—Buford was motivated to build his business partly by a desire to create an inheritance for his son. He substantially withdrew from the management of his cable television business in order to pursue nonprofit projects with Peter Drucker to help nonprofit organizations, especially churches, build better management supports. Buford's long-term view is tied very strongly to his son's death:

> How do you measure your life? I figure what's happening here and now is just a few decades. My relationship with my son was only twenty-four years. But we will be together till eternity in heaven. If eternity is one million years long, then I spent twenty-four one millionths of Ross's life with

him here on earth. We will probably be separated for thirty years then together again for the balance.

And yet Buford continues to be an effective, innovative leader
in his new project. The fact that he is doing so "out of a primary
commitment to Jesus" only fires him up more.

The competitive drive to accomplish something excellent *in this
world* comes so automatically to most of these CEOs that they failed
to see their double perspective as remarkable. As Fred Smith said,
"It's not a paradox at all."

The evangelical CEO's extremely strong emphasis on hard
work and achievement bears a striking resemblance to the workaholic practices of the typical so-called secular humanists, the Wall
Street yuppies. Is there any difference here?

Certainly there are similarities. Michael Milken, for example,
was hard-working, methodical, and extremely egalitarian with employees (no titles, no limos). The distinguishing feature between
Milken and the CEOs described in this book, however, is their
understanding of power. Milken's egalitarian relationship with his
employees, while unusually self-effacing, was rationalized not in
terms of the basic oneness of humankind, but out of a belief that this
attitude could do more for the business. And if religion is about
ultimate purposes, business was the religion. Everything was directed at the acquisition of more money and power. Milken himself
worked twenty-hour days, sometimes to his physical collapse. He
expected the same work schedule of his coworkers, to their physical
and mental collapse. He is commonly reported to have been ruthless
in his ability to intimidate and cajole others for the sake of the deal.
In such behavior there is no concept of temperance. As it was with
Samuel Gompers, the only motivational banner is "More!"

By contrast, not only is the evangelical CEO's motivational
purpose (value creation and service) different, but also he places less
value on material success and financial clout. For convicted felon
Milken, the desire for power appeared to be limitless, causing him
to place no constraints on either his ambitions for growth or the
means of achieving growth. For the evangelical, earthly power is
always suspect, no matter how much is accomplished. With the

temptation of limitless ambition reduced, so is the ethical temptation to do "anything" for the deal. When these things get out of whack, the CEO's ego needs are frequently at the source.

Failure

The equanimity that many interviewees seemed to have toward success also has been evident in the face of mistakes. The harmony of God's order includes human fallibility and failure, two concepts that the philosophy of the ego finds unacceptable.

Gary Ginter, whose futures market-making firm had outstanding success, found it acceptable—even mandatory—to have some failures in his traders' track record. Instead of making excuses to avoid losing face, a good trader or CEO should willingly acknowledge mistakes. Ginter sees this ability as directly tied to the state of the person's ego:

> It takes a very unusual person to succeed in this business. You have to be willing to take risks, and some of these will result in losing trades. You also have to be able to handle success, because a single trade can make a lot of money in a matter of minutes.
>   It all boils down to a trader's ego. He can't have too big an ego. And he's got to be able to put everything in perspective.

Tom Gerendas saw failure itself as a very human-centered notion:

> When we fail in spite of doing our best, it could turn out to be a step towards better things we cannot see at the time of apparent failure. I could recite scores of cases. Sometimes, the loss of an order allowed us to work on more important things we would have sacrifiiced for a quick return. Once the failure of a product woke me up to look for better engineering leadership, which had excellent effects on our competitive position.

Similarly, Patrick Morley of Orlando described a downturn in his real estate business by saying, "God wanted to get my attention." He attributed his need for God's discipline to misguided ego inflation over his own success: "All men tend to become satisfied and forget who God is and what He has done for us."[8]

Even those who did not see God's hand directly steering the

outcome of every transaction in their businesses attributed their
ability to tolerate mistakes to their faith and their Christian perspective. Many felt that this ability was unusual in business, where success
is idolized and failure is unthinkable. Tom Phillips's comments,
reported earlier in this chapter, about the average CEO's unwilling-
ness to voluntarily back out of a proposed merger are a good example.
Tom Gerendas faces the prospect of occasional failure as an inevita-
bility that must be taken in stride:

> We have to get used to the fact that traveling through the green pastures
> and calm seas of the past decades has changed into a bumpy journey
> through rumbling and storm-tossed waters. We may object to it, but this
> is the reality and even it has merits: it keeps us humble and fit, and teaches
> us to do the most with little.
>   In fact, we may end up feeling more secure and have an even better sys-
> tem of values. I have no concerns about our future in this place as long as
> we try to do our very best in all aspects of our job.

Boston's Richard Crowell compared the attitude of evangelical business leaders he knew with the stereotypical MBAs from
well-known liberal institutions. Crowell, too, mentioned their
inability to accept failure, and attributed this in large part to
overinflated ideas of their own career goals:

> I'm not sure you're going to like this, given your background. But it
> seems to be that MBA graduates [from an unnamed source] are some of
> the most unhappy people in the world. They're training to be CEOs, and
> in the first year most of them don't make it. And still not making it in the
> second year. Their expectations have built in a high level of success, and
> rapidly. The good side is that it can encourage you to think about how to
> do it a better way. But the bad side is that they can't tolerate partial failure.
>   And in so doing, they fail to acknowledge their own success. If we al-
> low the goal of growing 100 percent and then only grow 90 percent, how
> can we say that's a failure?

Crowell's observation combines the same themes already identified: self-confidence (in this case to set one's own goals or to back
out of a bad decision rather than to jump to the external expectations
of the financial markets), a constrained set of personal career expectations, the toleration of failure, and the acknowledgment of accomplishment. A related notion is that earthly goals in themselves are

never a final completion of what's really important. As Jack Willome said:

> God makes things right for us, then he makes us right. He saves us the way we are. I think that's what happened with me and will continue to happen. The Christian journey is moving from being self-centered to being God-centered. That doesn't happen to anybody overnight; it's a lifetime process.

Alberto Fernandez, the CEO of PYOSA, a pigment manufacturing firm in Monterrey, Mexico, agreed:

> Yes. You end up dying and still, whatever day you die, you did something toward that goal. It's not something that finishes.

Jack Feldballe also stressed the ongoing nature of the Christian's life journey:

> We have so many obligations as leaders: to get a fair price for our products or services, to help employees, to help developing nations. What do you do? Ship production offshore and shut down a plant here? How do you make such decisions? We always have to wrestle with the dilemmas, even if someone is inevitably going to be hurt.

Vester Hughes, who served in an advisory role to the tax and economic councils of several administrations and congressional committees, said that the "instant mentality" also contributed to our inability to confront the full implications of unsound financial decisions. He thought that the lack of awareness of a long-term view was behind most of the economic problems in this country:

> When people had to spread news by horse, they were able to think things out. Now everything is instant, and it does terrible things. The ultimate example of the by-product is Michael Milken.

Hughes backs up this sentiment with concrete commitments. He would like to see the nation solve its national debt crisis by making a large, short-term sacrifice for the sake of the long-term health of the nation. He retains his fresh perspective partly by studying history:

History tells us a lot. I like to read history. What's left of Karakorum, home of Genghis Khan? There's a six-foot stone turtle there; that's all that's left. When he lived, he was undoubtedly the most powerful man in the world. When I am trying to balance my perspective, I think of that turtle. I think of that and then of Christ: which of them affected people through the centuries?

Friendship

Not surprisingly, but quite unlike the business norm, the interviewees relied strongly on personal relationships to help restore their proper sense of self and service. Family relationships were one example, and are discussed in the next chapter. Friendship was another. Even though the interviewees did not always consciously connect the delusions of ego and an anecdote about friendship, the two often appear in tandem in their remarks. Take this passage from Jim Baker's speech at the 1991 National Prayer Breakfast:

> The fleeting aspect of power, I think, causes us to understand the importance of lasting personal relationships—friendships. Ralph Waldo Emerson said, "God evidently does not intend all of us to be rich, or to be powerful, or to be great, but he intends all of us to be friends."
> The Scriptures—both Old and New—affirm this reality by speaking about our relationships to God and our relationships to each other. The first and greatest commandment, of course, is to "Love the Lord your God with all your heart, with all your soul, with all your strength, and with all your mind. And the second is to love others as yourself."

In this spirit, Baker has joined a fellowship group of about ten to twenty-five top politicians who meet once a week for prayer. The group is nondenominational and has members from both political parties. They talk openly about problems they are encountering, especially personal problems that are often aggravated by their positions of leadership. As friends, they pursue faith through friendship. Part of the service they provide each other was described as follows:

> To remind our[selves], frequently, that we, who would be leaders, must first be servants. That we, who have large egos and great ambitions, should remember that the kingdom of heaven is promised to those who are "humble and are poor in spirit."

Such fellowship networks are quite common among evangeli-
cals and frequently form the basis of lasting friendships. Some of the
CEO groups are worldwide, operating through conference calls.
Other groups are more mentor-oriented: one senior executive meets
with several younger managers of like faith for prayer and counseling.
There are national groups such as the Christian Businessmen's
Committee, and many local prayer gatherings offered by churches
or initiated by laypeople.

Over a decade ago, Raytheon's Tom Phillips, Harvard Medical
School professor Armand Nicholi, and Nate Hubley, former president of Carter, Inc., started a monthly breakfast group for CEOs and
other top leaders in the Boston area, called the First Tuesday group.
The purpose is to help reaffirm each other's faith and to discuss
common problems of leadership. In order to ensure a sense of trust
and camaraderie, the group is limited to people of similar economic
and organizational standing. As Phillips explained:

> Being a CEO is the loneliest position in the world. And you have to have
> someone you trust to whom you can talk and compare notes. We restrict
> membership because we want people who share the same kinds of prob-
> lems.

So, too, Arnold Bandstra, spiritual counselor to several prayer
or Bible-study groups in the Chicago area, felt that it was best to
group people who are in similar business positions. Others said that
when they had participated in more diverse groups, they tended to
get "hit up" by some member who was looking for career advancement. Fred Smith commented in his book *You and Your Network,* that
"unfortunately, as we mature and our friends come into power, they
find that they are very limited in the new friends they can trust, and
so they must stick to the old ones."[9]

The fact that these men make such deliberate space for personal
time is itself unusual. The 1980s have marked a transition in the
personal style of the leader that began to place great value on workaholic patterns of behavior. Mike Milken's famous faint on the trading
floor is only one of many examples of how extreme the macho work
ethic can be: it is reported that when Milken fainted, his brother,

Lowell, came over, saw that he was recovering, and ordered every-one, including himself, back to work. Underlying this ethic is the metaphysical assumption that corporate man is man at his best—es-pecially if the meals are catered.

The corporate culture refined this ethic to its extreme in recent years. Material amenities such as special meals, laundry and car service, or exercise facilities became a regular part of the world of the corporate elite. Casual chores are taken care of, and meals are not eaten outside the company of other workers. Leisure is devoted to sports—now a highly materialistic endeavor—to keep the old cor-porate machine in top form. Social gatherings are restricted to benefits or meetings among potential clients, so that charity and pleasure are now combined with business.

But all these amenities are designed to keep the executive at work longer, and they actually exclude relationships with family and friends. Friendships and time for reflection are not part of the new idea of leisure. Dr. Robert S. Weiss, a psychiatrist who has studied the social choices of executives, reports that friendship is an ex-tremely wide discretionary area for the successful executive. Many executives take no time at all for friendship, or they see this area of their lives as "totally optional."[10] In *The Organization Man,* William Whyte notes that the average manager's friendships were formed through the neighborhood, and served primarily social functions, forcing the manager to become outgoing, to belong to a group of conforming taste and occupations, and to keep up parenting organi-zation functions such as little league or PTA.[11]

The evangelical CEO has a different kind of friendship—far more relational, even intimate, and often carrying a religious func-tional role. He uses words like "brother" or "brethren" to describe his cronies, and takes pleasure in sharing intimacies with them about family life as well as sharing business problems. In short, relation-ships are not optional; they are a crucial way of enriching his faith and his personal capacity to be an effective executive and family man.

In these habits we can see once again a resemblance between the evangelical worldview and a more typically feminized, domesti-cated approach to life. Overall, women are much more likely to seek out and value intimate friendships. The importance of friendships and intimacy in these men's lives, and the personal nature of their discussions among friends, not only resemble a more feminine ideal of relationships, but they are a way of living out the nurturing values that the evangelical holds to be an important part of Christian leadership and stewardship.

However, the prayer network route to friendship is not terribly spontaneous. The evangelical has an obligation to "share the good news" to "work for the coming of the kingdom of Heaven on earth." These sacred purposes are not separate from friendship. Christianity is relational, and relations are not separate from Christianity. Friendship is intimate, and Christian purpose is a significant part of the evangelical self. Naturally, the evangelical would share this with friends.

In a secular society, such a coupling of friendship and religion can seem at best insincere and at worst exploitative of another person's gift of intimacy. Many nonevangelicals resent the evangelical friend who suggests an introduction to Christ. Normally, friendships are fairly spontaneous relationships, especially in the United States, and the test of friendship is, if anything, the preservation of individual choice, religious privacy, and informality. If you formalize friendship as a religious expression of brotherliness, its claims of intimacy become suspect. The friendship seems artificial, inauthentic.

For the evangelical this is simply not the correct interpretation of the friendship. A faith that emphasizes loving each other only profits from the formalized gathering of friends in prayer. Furthermore, the evangelical is not typically private about his or her faith. Whereas many friends in a pluralistic society deliberately avoid discussing religion out of fear of offending each other or of seeming censorious, "wearing it on your sleeve" is normal for the evangelical. Sharing with others strengthens it.

The interviewees' claims of great friendship and personal support from their prayer networks should be taken seriously. And to the degree that these networks offer acceptance of the inner person, bring constant reminders of the person's proper relationship with God, warn of the dangers of taking oneself too seriously, and provide the support of ego in times of trouble, then it is plausible to see such a network as a significant and effective factor in the evangelical CEO's ability to maintain a balanced perspective at work.

The fellowship networks, according to the interviewees, help repair the vertical and horizontal relationships of the evangelical CEO, especially when the brokenness is attributable to ego. The networks remind him of the right priorities, a longer-term perspective, and the role of servant leader. An example of the kind of discussion held came from Jack Willome:

> How much profit is right? How do you get growth and success without getting off track? Profits are necessary to survive, but they're not the object. Growth is the same.
>
> There's not a formula or prescription or book you can read to tell what is the right profit. Unfortunately, the stuff we're going through you have to learn from experience. And that's the value of fellowship meetings—so I can learn from the experiences of others. There are very few places where you can speak and learn and share in others' feelings.

Fellowship networks help participants sort out such questions as these, especially on delicate topics. Chicago's Herbert Hanson, retired CEO of Bradley Printing, reported that there were times when the fellowship group had to deal with its own disappointment over the behavior of other believers. As he put it, "Sometimes believing people do things it is hard to reconcile in the privacy of our own believing fellowship." At these times, the privacy and trust of a prayer network are all important.

Why are the groups all male? The decision is controversial to outsiders. Some of these groups have been strongly criticized by outsiders for their gender exclusivity. They have been accused especially of perpetuating a system that leaves women out of the "power loop."

Clearly, these criticisms, though ignoring the validity of other rationales for a single-gender gathering, have some validity. The gender attitudes of the interviewees are discussed in greater detail in the next chapter, but I want to mention here two rationales for the segregated nature of these groups. One is the freedom to unself-consciously discuss what are commonly called "the problems of men." The term implies not only sexual issues but also the psychological problems and responsibilities of professional positions.

In an interview with Chicago executives George Kohl, Jeff Semenchuck, and George Kubricht, the topic of counselling from friends was widely discussed. These men found it very important to have the opportunity to counsel each other in fellowship about very intimate aspects of their lives. As one of them said:

> If you are working sixteen hours a day, and never seeing your family, a friend can say, "Hey, you're obviously running from something. Let's talk about it."

Other interviewees reported that their counselling sessions with trusted friends who were also executives provided a major vehicle for bringing faith to their personal problems. Former Citibank president John Ream was mentioned by a number of executives as an especially valuable counsellor. Ream himself noted that his fellowship networks were especially important in helping him assimilate quickly when he moved to a new business community.

The second rationale for all-male groups is that there is a general reluctance among evangelicals to duplicate social settings that are associated with adultery. Intimate discussions with women outside the context of marriage groups makes many of them uneasy, though it is not at all unusual for a member of one of these men's groups to also belong to a couples Bible study.

This issue was one that I found very difficult to pursue in my research for obvious reasons. Any serious probing on my side was particularly subject to misinterpretation. Was I trying to build a conspiracy theory? I was assured there was no conspiracy. Did I not see that having women in the group would change the dynamics? I admitted it would. The question I could not get at, however, was why that change would be bad. The general touchiness of this subject led to a restraint among many interviewees about sharing any details of such groups.

What little I did learn, however, shed some light on how these groups counteract the delusions of ego. The groups generally tend to stress that the male ego is fragile and that it can do terribly arrogant and destructive things to marital relationships, and working relationships. The prayer networks are about supporting the ego through faith and fellowship. They remind the successful businessman of the

relatively fleeting nature of success and of his more important relationship with God. They also give support to those who are in
trouble, and they help rebuild self-esteem in hard times. They even
involve a kind of down-home marriage-counseling service about the
perceptions that women have of their husbands.

Such networks fit well with the relational orientation of the
evangelical and also echo the gathering of disciples in Jesus' name.
What is ironic, however, is that their composition is perhaps the least
reflective of their otherwise egalitarian preferences, which operate
so strongly in many aspects of their businesses, from their choice of
nonhierarchical corporate cultures to their covenantal approach to
business purpose.

Many of those interviewed reported that they valued these
networks as much as or more than their formal church experiences,
where they sometimes found that the clergy did not understand their
problems. Several interviewees emphasized the sense of security and
acceptance they felt from being with fellow believers. One of these
was "Joe Beck" (disguised name):

> We're all a family, and we're going to have to live together for eons, so we
> better start learning to like each other right now. I've never seen a better
> way of demonstrating our love of Christ, who said "Love one another as I
> have loved you." Friends like to be with one another; they bring friends to
> meet other friends. Any friend of Jim's is a friend of mine. So I think
> there is a security in that.

Tom Jones found a further benefit:

> I rely on these people in my support groups on a regular basis, to get in
> touch with the social justice issues.

Frank Butler, who is in one of Jones's groups, agreed:

> The problems CEOs face is what the monarchs faced. We don't handle
> success well. Christianity is no more sure than anything else. You need a
> support group, someone who keeps reminding us that Yahweh is the one
> who led us out of bondage; it was his gracious act. And Christianity has to
> do with doing justice, love and mercy. That's the heart of the whole issue.

Most of the discussions that take place when these groups meet appear to be just that: discussions. But occasionally specific business comes directly out of the networks. One interviewee told of an occasion when a fellow member reported that an annuity board was withholding approval on an investment for a large pension fund for preachers. The interviewee immediately intervened to get the deal done.

More often the networks result in a changed *attitude* that in turn changes the CEO's behavior and ultimately the business. Jack Willome's dramatic change in attitude toward the citizens who were suing him (see Chapter 3) took place after a prayer discussion by phone. A similar story came from Frank Butler, who told of a time when he came into a prayer breakfast "just steaming." He was angry at a local official who had been uncooperative about Eastman Gelatine's sewer taxes. The leader of the group listened and then suggested that they pray together for the official. According to Butler, it completely changed his attitude toward the official, and enabled him to respect the man when the two of them met again. They eventually settled the dispute to their mutual satisfaction.

Summary

It seems that the problems of ego, as they apply to the evangelical CEO's business thinking, are generally regarded as problems of perspective. The role of faith is to reestablish the proper perspective, but that perspective is itself full of paradoxical viewpoints that combine a deep sense of the immediate with a calm sense of distance. Life is measured in eternal terms and yet demands spiritual interpretation of even the relatively insignificant immediate event.

Such a view seems to invite a self-confident, secure attitude, but also one that is humble and that is able to accept moral and economic limits. The believer CEO has the decisiveness and courage to act, and yet chooses to lead according to more relational, participatory input.

The comments on ego that were made by the interviewees point to a very different kind of attitude about self than is frequently seen among top leaders. This attitude leads to an interpretation of personal accomplishment in business that is distinct from the egotistic norm of today's "If you've got it, flaunt it" ethos. Far from equating a completed business deal with sound judgment, these leaders are constantly aware of their own limitations of judgment and power, and they are suspicious of flattery. Whereas many a CEO seems to unhesitatingly impose his will as explosively as possible, the evangelical business leader favors soft-spoken calmness and a listening attitude.

The paradoxical concepts of Christian faith—that in death there is life, that the first shall be last, that in the acknowledgment of sin there is salvation, that faith is a combination of fear, dread, joy, and love—clearly shape the evangelical's quest to understand his or her own value and power. The evangelical wants to achieve, to excel, to see himself or herself as part of a divine order, and yet wants to be self-effacing, calm, and detached. As Dick Capen said in his prayer at the 1991 National Prayer Breakfast in Washington:

> Many here are blessed with incredible talent and enormous influence, yet each is here to humbly express absolute dependence on you.

If we superficially combine the statements of humility with the effort expended in achieving wealth and power, it is easy to misinterpret the evangelical CEO as hypocritical—as many church people and outsiders have done. We must understand the evangelical CEO's statements about success in the context of the paradoxes I just mentioned. For the seekers, too, the interpretation of their own activities and selves requires a constant reminder of this context. Keeping these paradoxes in tension is what keeps the ego in check, and yet it creates the self-confidence to take risks, handle failures, accept short-term sacrifice for long-term value.

This change in the understanding of personal power results also in a very different understanding of the purpose of business and ways of judging results. Economic success is not a target to be achieved once; it is a process. This view may be more suited to the future economic environment than does the more familiar attitude of being "successful." Several interviewees described the growth of their businesses in biblical metaphors reminiscent of Ecclesiastes. As one CEO said:

There will always be failures, and backtracking. These are a part of God's order. There's a time for harvest and time for fields to lie fallow. It's the maintenance of relationships and a healthy sense of self which pull you through.

Of course, it's easier to claim that wealth is nothing when you are a CEO and are established than it is when you are a struggling junior executive with a new family. Certainly several interviewees acknowledged that they were more "driven" by the business problems and the rewards in the earlier stages of their careers. But unlike the insatiable ambition and greed that are obvious in many executive egos, the attitudes of those I interviewed have been modified over time. These men see their changes in attitude as a function of faith, not of experience. As Dick Crowell said:

> If I had $100 million, I'd still be working the same job. I like doing it. I work with good people. I have good clients. There are problems you can help solve. Everybody wins: we're better off; they're better off.

Frank Butler commented:

> I don't feel I'm called to be successful. I'm called to be obedient.

To maintain this kind of understanding, the ego must be kept in check. Once the ego is kept in check, the very definition of business changes. It returns to the covenantal purposes of providing value and service to others in such a way as to keep the economic entity going. Said Butler:

> I do have responsibilities as a CEO to have some kind of measurable goals of success. A key one is selection of a successor.

These altered visions of success are especially noteworthy in light of the idolatry of self-aggrandizement that seems to dominate the coverage of business today. As Max De Pree of Herman Miller commented:

> If you are able, and you are lucky, and the market is right, you can serve

God and be successful in business. But if things do not go well—say you
bought a company for $2 million, and eight years later it's at $2.1 million,
and you and your wife are sole owners, a lot of people would not say you
were successful. On the other hand, if in those eight years you maintained
the same number of employees—fifteen jobs—you are a success, and
you're also being faithful.

But this is not what makes it in the eyes of the majority. We get away
from the fundamentals of capitalism in our search for what's media wor-
thy, in our search to create megaheroes. It would almost be banal for
Forbes to write articles on the basics. The basis of the capitalist system is a
job. The basis of the social system is the family. We have people in business who don't see that the making of a job is some kind of calling. Perhaps the media ought to spend a bit more time celebrating the people who
do the basics.

As one who makes a living in part by trying to publish what I
write on business people, I would heartily agree with De Pree. There
is a tremendous distortion in the media to create a cult of the ego
instead of sound business advice.

In my own research, one of the chief ways I bump into executive ego is in asking for an executive's time. As one business person
advised me on another project, "the only way you'll get anyone to
participate is to guarantee they'll be in the company of someone who
they feel is more important. If there's status, they'll help you; otherwise, not."

On many other occasions when I have interviewed business
leaders this formula has been true: no status, no access. It was clearly
not true with the evangelical CEOs I interviewed. Although there
were few ways in which I could substantiate the comments of my
interviewees with observable fact, I can say that on the ego issue, the
value many participants placed on Christian humility was lived out.
Participants met with me even though there was no status involved.
They gave their time to a total stranger because a friend had suggested
it. Even though in some cases meeting with me was an expression of
friendship, it was no ego trip.

CHAPTER

8

Tension 5: Family and Work

> Men's work is necessary as a foundation for their lives, but their families have an ultimate, irreducible emotional importance to them that their work cannot have. Nevertheless, among the paradoxes with which men live is that their work may demand most of their time and energy.
> —Robert Weiss[1]

The family has always had great significance within the Christian tradition, as it has had in other religions. In Genesis, marriage and child bearing are the first step in the social order imposed by God after the Fall. Biblical metaphors often rest on family associations: Christ and the church are the bridegroom and his bride; God is often referred to as "the Father."

No one who is listening to political campaigning today is unaware of the primary place that family has in the social agenda of the conservative right, especially the evangelical right. And nowhere are family and religion more inextricably related than in evangelical thinking today. As sociologist James Hunter notes:

It is curious that the significance of the family has achieved dimensions perhaps never before seen. . . . The family has become a symbol to Evangelicals, a symbol of social stability and traditional moral virtue. As a symbol, it is commonly reduced to a slogan.[2]

It would be impossible to fully analyze the evangelical position on family in one chapter. Instead, I will confine this chapter to what the interviewees had to say about family *as it related to their integration of faith and economic life.* Even this more limited topic, however, is extremely difficult to analyze, for I found that the interviewees in general offered fewer responses on the topic of family than in almost any other area of our discussion. Though they felt that family was a

197

hallmark of evangelical culture, the details of how family life related to their faith and work remained, for the most part, elusive.

Several explanations are possible. One is that both I and the interviewees avoided this topic as a function of etiquette. As a working mother, I represent a set of choices that many of those interviewed deplore. Politeness and a desire to keep the conversation productive may have inspired them and me—consciously or otherwise—to steer clear of this controversial topic. Also, several confessed to having been treated very rudely by "feminists" in the past, so perhaps they feared a rude response from me as well. Or perhaps they feared that they would later want to turn a cold shoulder to my entire project.

A second explanation could be that there is no real connection between family, faith, and work. Though the interviewees would *like* to think that they hold family to be an essential, when it comes down to the work-family balance, family has been terminally put on hold by the successful executive devoted to his business.

But this explanation, while carrying an element of truth for every committed executive, does not seem to be the full story here. The general statements that the interviewees *did* make about family indicated a potentially profound integration of family considerations in their decision making. They attributed family values squarely to their Christianity, and, like their faith, family was not up for redefinition by the prevailing secular culture.

A third possible explanation for the lack of detail on family in these interviews is that to some degree the family is by definition the perfect topic for a generalist approach. Taken for granted and assumed to be universal, the problems, the joys, the daily routines, the *meaning* of family is lived rather than recounted.

So in the following comments you may find, as I did, a great deal of meaning without much concreteness that requires us to make rather large leaps of interpretation. Nevertheless, the interviewees shared a number of common reflections about the forces that they must contend with as fathers, CEOs, husbands, and individual Christians.

Models of Family

Just what does the evangelical CEO mean by *family*? Is there a single model to which most of the interviewees subscribe? Absolutely not. Though the majority favored a "traditional" family organized on the nuclear structure, with children and nonworking wives, and also with grandparents, the wives of many of the interviewees were working, especially the wives of the younger CEOs. Many older couples were working together on new, often socially responsible, business projects following a cutback in the CEO's earlier business activities. A few were divorced, though most were strongly in favor of a life-long marriage. None of them openly advocated either premarital sex or adultery. Of those who mentioned the moral education of their children or their own strengthening of faith, the family was the focal point for teaching and living the values of the Bible.

"Traditional" family authority structures were subject to redefinition. But the nineteenth-century ideal of the distant father—all wise, all powerful, the ultimate decision maker for the family—had its appeal to many interviewees. As one CEO put it:

> Every organization has to have one head. You cannot get anywhere if you try to have two heads. This includes family organization.

And yet the attitudes of evangelicals toward family have undergone some definite changes. Nowhere was this more obvious in the interviewees' remarks than in the discussions of their relationships with their spouses and children. Parenthood and marriage have become somewhat sentimentalized. Both males and females expect more sensitivity, involvement, and emotional sustenance from males than in the past. Many interviewees expressed strong commitments to improving the ways they "nurtured" their wives, and they focused on their children's welfare in making career decisions.

Such attitudes and actions reflect a change in the formerly rigid role distinctions that traditional family models supported. James Hunter noted a similar shift in his interviews. He found that evangelical college students expected "softer," more personalized characteristics for the male head of a household: he must be nurturing, sensitive, even personally involved in his children's upbringing.[3] For the most part, however, such shifts in models were not extended to the economic role that each partner plays: among participants in this study, males were still seen as the chief bread winners, and married women who worked were suspected of harming the family. One interviewee even argued that it was a small step from child-care centers to gay couples adopting children.

The Effects of Family Relationships

Once again in these interviews, family was best understood in relational terms. The real question for participants is not so much who works and how long, but what benefits and responsibilities does the family relationship pose for the evangelical CEO in relation to his working life and his faith as a whole?

First of all, the family is clearly a chief source of spiritual sustenance for these men. More than a few interviewees attributed the strength of their faith to their spouses. In fact, the few wives I did meet mentioned their husbands' spiritual needs, but did not provide many details for public consumption. A typical comment of a CEO about his wife's role in his faith was as follows:

> X is really more religious than I am. She led me to Christ, and it was a struggle. But she just kept being patient, and prayed for me. It was the strength of her faith that helped bring me to Jesus.

In *The Unchurched American*, George Gallup reports that women were considerably more likely than men to say that religion is "very important" in their lives (61 percent, compared to 47 percent males).[4] While the interviewees are universally committed to the idea of religion being important in their lives, the women are often the leaders for their husbands' spiritual health. As Dennis Sheehan said:

> I give a lot of credit to my wife for helping me keep faith alive in this environment. She is a devout person, a different religion than I, and extremely active in it, and well read.[5] We regularly went to three churches on Sunday in the summers: Catholic Mass at 8 [Sheehan is Roman Catholic], Episcopal Eucharist at 11, and a Baptist service at 3. The kids used to joke they got a lot of religion in those days. We never felt it was an obligation— just something we thought important and enjoyed doing.

If the family strengthens a CEO's faith, one of the chief parental obligations of the CEO is to see that the children are raised in a biblical environment. Jack Turpin expressed the connection between love, family, faith, and business in the following comment:

> I've seen in my life how as you mature you move from fear to love. And that's how your relationship with Jesus matures. It's harder to trace it in business, but it's there too. I guess you can see it best with the wife and family. We've been married over forty years, and during our kids' childhood I was always in church on Sunday, raising the kids. I'm not very pleased with the lack of attention I paid in church, but at least we were there.
>
> God is very patient. Eventually, you know, things started to have more meaning, in the raising of the sons. And I concluded that it's a task almost too big for a parent, and I became—my wife and I became—dependent on God. Part of my background is to pray every day. And that dependency is very important.

Wives also facilitate an integration of faith and business, again by contributing to the spiritual activities of their spouses. As Jim Baker recalled:

> I remember, particularly, a situation a few years ago when I was really struggling with a particular problem. No matter how hard I tried, I couldn't figure it out, but I found strength in being able to talk it over and to pray about it with my wife, Susan. And as we did, a truth from the book of Proverbs finally crystalized our thinking: "Trust in the LORD with all your heart; lean not unto your own understanding. In all of your ways acknowledge him, and he will direct your path."
>
> Susan helped me to see that I really needed to stop trying to play God and really turn the matter over to him. Without this kind of partnership, I am quite convinced that I would never have resolved that problem.

Tom Jones, formerly of Epsilon, directly credited his wife with helping him to keep perspective in the face of extreme contradictory pressures from the business world. She was instrumental, for example, in his decision not to do business with the tobacco industry. Commented Jones:

> I'm married to somebody who is a whistle-blower from day one.
> *Nash:* So your wife helped you to question your position?
> *Jones (with great affection in his voice):* I'm not so sure I'd refer to this attrib-

ute as being "help" so much as a cross that I bear. She cannot handle emotionally at the most gut level anything that would tend to inflate my ego. And anything that touches on social justice issues sends up a flag. And we wrestle with this constantly.

Such partnerships are often acknowledged to be really a three-way partnership between the CEO, his family, and God. The triad often provides the stability and direction for these men's major career decisions. Ed Yates, owner of Highland Park Cafeterias in the Dallas area, described his purchase in 1981 of the business from the rest of his family—a business that he and his wife were already involved in. With three kids in college, they borrowed at a 21 percent interest rate. The risks and the work were back-breaking. Said Yates:

> That was the hardest time I ever had, just to go to work. It took everything my wife and I had in terms of spiritual phenomena just to get through.

Yates is the first to acknowledge that his strong marriage played a major role in his ability to launch the business, but he ultimately attributes his success to God:

> As a believer, I've come to have confidence that the Lord truly does provide, not only money, but the inward strength. That's what counts. When you have the real crises, it doesn't matter how much money you have in the bank. It's what you have inside you. And you know, the ego difficulties were extreme—a lot of ego bruises at the time. [*He pulls himself up and says cheerfully.*] But you get through times like that. Things smooth out.

Jack Turpin of Hall-Mark Electronics Corp. does not directly credit family strength for his ability to take business risks. Nevertheless, the subject of family creeps into his explanation of his decision to leave a Fortune 200 company when the opportunity for advancement and a move to the northeastern headquarters was proposed:

> I had no money of my own, so there really wasn't that much risk. My friends helped with the financial backing. And the opportunity seemed excellent to succeed. I didn't really think much about it. Youth, I guess. And I really did not want to leave the [Dallas] area. I was an engineer, had been exposed to large corporate life, and I didn't particularly like what I saw. I wanted freedom of time.

When you start your own business, there is no time, but freedom to ar-
range your time.

My grandmother helped raise me; she was a strong, devout Christian
lady. Mother was also a Christian lady. So I was exposed to what I call an
Old Testament Christianity. I depended on God during that period. At
times I felt it was all I had.

As I dug deeper, it turned out that even Turpin's understanding
of his role in God's order and of his chances of success with God's
help was based on events in his family. Biblical authority helped link
them:

The Bible says, "A man reaps what he sows." I thought my family was
reaping what my dad had sown [a broken family]. I had sided with my
mother. So God has a plan and a purpose. Now looking back, I can see the
blessing and learning of what you reap you sow. . . . And so I was keenly
motivated to achievement. No one had gone to college in our family.

Turpin's remarks, almost circular in content, are typical of the
way in which the interviewees discussed family, faith, and business
success in the same arena. We can see how the stability and support
of family and faith allow for greater risk taking and for the ability to
say no to expected career paths.

So, too, family bonds that go beyond material connections allow
for support when times are bad. I was particularly moved by a wife
whose husband was facing bankruptcy. A former widower, the man
had been married to this woman only a year when it became clear
that his business was going to fail. Her friends urged her to divorce
him fast, before the bankruptcy was official, so that she could get a
better alimony settlement. She was appalled, and stuck by her husband. Running into her two years later at another gathering of
evangelical CEOs, I asked her how things were going. Despite the
bankruptcy, she and her husband had begun building another business together.

Jim Carreker is perhaps the most eloquent speaker on the topic
of family, faith, and business success, and he has been asked to tell
his story all over the southern United States. When Carreker was
made president of the Burdines department store, he moved to the
Miami area from Texas. The new position excited him for several

reasons. Burdines was one of the most profitable of Federated stores. Miami was, in his words, "such a non-Bible Belt area" that the move gave him tremendous opportunity for evangelism. He spoke at many programs, deliberately using his position as "president of Burdines" to arouse people's curiosity and then "talk about things more important than business success."

Carreker's position drew people in, but it was a family experience shortly after his move to Florida that really provided the vehicle for his witness. Carreker had just bought an all-glass house, and one day, before moving in, he and his four-year-old son went to see it. The house, which was twenty-six years old, turned out to be built of paned glass, and his son went right through a window. The boy was cut from head to foot, and both legs were slashed, one down to the bone. His throat was cut, and he could hardly breathe. Carreker recounts what happened with tears in his eyes:

> To make a very long story short, through a series of miracles it worked out. The house had been vacant a year and a half, and the phone still worked. If I hadn't been able to call, he would have died. The police came first, and we all grabbed a leg to keep him from bleeding to death. He survived, though he continues to need operations on his leg.
>
> After I got past my disbelief, I sat there watching him trying to breathe, his fingernails black, and I knew I was losing him. For the first time in my life, I was willing to step in his place. Up until that point, even though I was a Christian, I had logically come up with the reason Christ had to die, but it was that personal experience and willingness to step into the son's place. I understood how Jesus stepped into our place and bore our sins.
>
> The accident became very well known in Burdines. People hurt with me. A lot of people changed their perceptions of why Christ had to die on the cross from that one accident.
>
> I think men especially need logic. That's the way I came into my faith. . . . It made sense to me. But being a parent is a great experience [for understanding] the message. Being selfless is not a human trait; being a parent is the closest thing. Anyway, God used me that way. So I went on the trail.

Carreker's interpretation of his experience is an example of how the love of family is closely linked in many interviewees' minds to the love of God. Metaphors are traded easily in both directions. The fatherhood of God and fatherhood of man are the most obvious associations, but so, too, the symbols and language of courtship find an easy exchange between faith and family. Many interviewees used dating language to describe their conversion experiences and their evangelizing, and they discussed having "introduced someone to Jesus" almost as if he were a blind date. Several CEOs described their own dating of their wives as a very formative experience, and they relished the details. Many of them, no matter which generation they represented, had a special fondness for the romantic rituals of court-ship. Some of the youngest spoke of their "brides" with as much sentiment as the most aged. All of them saw their investments in their family's emotional health as well returned; the stability and support of a loving family are a key factor in helping these men to be effective business leaders.

Zig Ziglar, for example, speaks affectionately of his wife, and challenges men to consider the beneficial effects of an exciting marriage. In one of his books, he cites statistics from a West German insurance company indicating that men who *really* kiss their wives good-bye each day live 5.6 years longer than the men who neglect to include "this pleasant little interlude" in their daily lives. "Not only that," adds Ziglar, "these men earn from 20 to 30 percent more money than do the men who leave home under their own power."[6]

Ziglar tells many stories of the connection between family stability and business performance. The experience of the chairman of another company sums it up. After a period of extreme estrange-ment from his teenage kids, this man was motivated by Ziglar and another counselor to consider what it would be like if everyone he loved were taken completely out of the picture. The man made time that week for a long outing with his son to the baseball park. He took his daughter out to dinner "at one of the fancy places I take my important clients." This was more time with his children than he'd spent in the previous six months. The problems weren't solved instantly, but as he put it, "the walls began to crumble." His conclu-sion, according to Ziglar:

> When I leave home every day I know all I have to concentrate on is my job. I'm convinced I am currently the chairman of the board because of the fact that my family situation has straightened up so much. I can com-mit all my creative energy to my job when I'm on the job because I know everything is fine on the home front.[7]

It would be misleading to conclude from such remarks that the family is seen only as a means to an economic or spiritual end. Family also demands responsibility, but it ends up being a support for major career risks. Jim Carreker, for example, had left Burdine's by the time of our interview. Though his tenure at the department store was very successful, he had decided to leave in order to return to the Dallas area. He had failed to convince the rest of his family to move to Miami, and so he moved back to Dallas:

> I wanted my children to have the family going to church together, playing at the table together. I needed to come back, even though Burdine's was still very successful at the time.

Carreker joined Trammell Crow's Wyndham Hotels division as its new president. Trammell Crow is a company whose own culture boasts several nationally admired evangelical executives, including its chairman, Don Williams. Carreker, who was made president of Trammell Crow in 1994, acknowledges the risk of his decision, which was not without moments of struggle:

> It was hard going to a very small company. I have to say it was traumatic for me. Technically, I took a salary cut to one-fifth of what I'd been making, but there was ownership, so if I make it work, then it can be what it was before.
>   It's hard to describe how much I enjoyed Burdine's, the city, the blessings of sharing my faith all over the state. I made the decision over a time of prayer. Having the peace after enough prayer that it was God's will. I don't think I could have made that decision without my faith. I would not have had the courage.

It is hard to "prove" that prayer and family have a significant influence on such life decisions, but obviously they provide the key to a CEO's *self-understanding* related to his success and business activity. "Joe Beck" said that his family and faith caused him to make a major revision in his value system. Beck had transferred to a very large executive recruiting firm in the U.S., a move that had brought him terrific financial success and status. A series of encounters with his family and his Christian colleagues, however, caught him up short.

First, he was on a retreat when a Lutheran minister posed a question: Was today's executive mortgaging his faith in return for a paycheck? Beck's innermost thought was, "Of course, you dummy!" But somehow the question lingered. Then, on a vacation back to his native Brazil, his daughter confronted him during a walk on the beach. In a very emotional speech, she told him that he had changed. "You've become a mean, old you-know-what!" she said. Beck realized she was speaking the truth. As he put it:

> I had blood all over me. I'd become one of the better players in the executive suite. I was building an organization within the organization and my boys were rewarded. And I had my business plan, my ego to be fed, my bank account to build; life had to be taken care of. How does a Christian fit into that?

He called the chairman of his company after his conversation with his daughter, and quit his job. Because he was not a U.S. citizen, he immediately had to leave the country. He called a Protestant minister and reported that he felt naked and scared, with no image. The man replied that the Lord would take care of him, and that Beck was very important. Beck responded by committing himself to God publicly at that moment. According to Beck, he had made the commitment then, but it really took almost six years to feel reconciled. The biggest relief, he reports, was in not being allowed to straddle the fence any longer.

His family continues to be a support to him, and he attributes his Christian commitment to that support:

> We love ourselves more. There's nothing threatening our marriage. My job used to be the most important thing in the world. I felt I had to provide expensive things. That was just an excuse to justify my act. I didn't have time to think of sin.
>
> Maybe I should have stopped in the middle of the day to pray like Jim [Kubik, another interviewee], but I know that the minute a client called and said can you do this for us and the price is so much, I would have had to interrupt my prayer and say, "Lord, I'll be with you in a minute!"

The Conflicts

On the whole, the interviewees expressed a belief in a positive relationship between career and family. As Zig Ziglar writes:

> One tragic myth which permeates our society is the belief that you can't be a hard-charging, successful businessman *and* a loving, caring husband and father. (his emphasis)[8]

Ziglar cites an article in *U.S. News and World Report* that says that a survey of millionaires showed that 80 percent were from middle- or working-class families, and had lasting marriages, often to their high school or college sweethearts.[9] But while the interviewees felt a profound connection between family, faith, and business, they also knew that the evangelical understanding of family carries the possibility for conflicts with modern secular society, including business society.

Family Time versus Work Time

The most obvious conflict is the competition for a chief executive's time that family and business represent. The observation is almost so universal as to seem trivial, but it is significant that the interviewees expressed concern in this area; they were aware of the competitions and often were concerned about how well they had struck the balance.

But how do executives with responsibility for a whole company take seriously the time needs of the family? Psychiatrist Robert Weiss suggests that part of the problem is in seeing family time as a residual commodity, a kind of "left-over" after everything essentially is completed. He believes that men ought to treat their marriages as "partnerships that are fundamental to everything else."[10]

Many of the evangelicals interviewed for this book would agree. The priority of family means consulting ahead of time with spouses about the time commitments that the family requires. The late Jim Beré, then chairman of Borg-Warner, fondly told me that when his children became teenagers, his wife suggested that they make a commitment to be home every Friday evening in order to be able to host their kids' social hour. Having made the commitment, Beré told me that he'd had a surprisingly good time with his teenagers.

As a result of such thinking, CEOs tend to be clearer about setting limits on the demands of work, but also are likely to take extreme risks with their careers, knowing the necessary family stability is there. By investing this kind of time in parental roles, these CEOs may be better able to avoid some of the lessening of importance that modern life has attached to male heads of households.

Antoine Prost, in *Riddle of Identity in Modern Times,* suggests that, in the past the man had a multifaceted status in his household—his professional status as tradesman, farmer, or whatever, as well as his position as head of household. But the man's identity today, says Prost, is much simpler: His status is based largely on how much money he brings home. Men have become "monetarized."[11]

I would go further and say that the rest of the family has undergone this same devaluing to materialistic terms, so that family and work appear to be more like each other but not necessarily to an improved quality of life. Whereas the evangelical is more likely to see his or her business as being like a family, it is the families in most households that are becoming more like businesses—especially in broken households. Children are either assets or costs—property to be assigned by the court—and all members can be bought or sold out of the corporation.

However, for the evangelical who is bent on integrating family, faith, and work, the meaning of *parent* has the potential for becoming a richer concept, and the time spent in parenting is invaluable. Frito-Lay president Steve Reinemund, who was formerly head of Pizza Hut, is a strong advocate of family values and is not shy about discussing his parenting. One memorable story is that he asked his boys where they wanted to go for dinner on a night when his wife was out. They replied they'd like to cook dinner together. Steve agreed and bravely offered to help them cook anything they'd like. Of course, they chose homemade pizza. Certain situations were especially difficult for the interviewees in terms of the balance of work and family. As Fred Smith quipped, "People say you got success at the cost of your family, but I say you invested your family in your success." The early years of these CEOs' careers were the worst, just at a time when parenting needs are often highest. Some ended up with extremely broken relationships with their children that were mended only in the advanced stages of their careers. Others managed to swing through. Jack Feldballe, whose married daughter and grandchildren live within a short distance and have formed a business with his wife, had no insight into what had made it work:

> I'm sure my wife and family have a different perspective. I really enjoy my work. I'd get home at night dead tired, and I couldn't wait to get to bed to get to sleep to get up and go to work. Yet I believe you have to respond, to take responsibility to take corrective action if your family tells you you've got it out of balance. I tried to achieve balance. But I went to night school for seventeen years, and I was out at work all day. I had to do it. My kids have turned out. They have the skills needed for life and work, self-reliance, responsibility, and a religious faith.

We could speculate that evangelical women, many of whom express a great capacity to accept a submissive and supportive role, may have eased the family demands for time in ways that these CEOs were only partially aware of. Some interviewees seemed less than sensitive to the typical tensions with family because they'd never been made aware by their spouses. One interviewee noted that the family

> ... just accepts what time you'll give them. You want to be at work and see what people need, how they're doing. But you shouldn't forget that your family needs the same thing.

Another CEO remarked with apparent satisfaction:

> I get up early, get home at seven, work on weekends—all the things you're supposed to do. I'm not driven by it. I could walk away from it, but I thoroughly enjoy it. It's all I've done for thirty years.

Others were more self-critical. Dick Crowell remarked that the corporate culture often encouraged executives to think that the sixty-hour work week is inevitable. Crowell, who has a very strong sense of family, added:

That's just ego. You tend to get trapped at the office, and most people are really less important at an office than they think they are.

Another interviewee agreed:

This is a choice. If you have an hour lunch, and an hour exercise, and then get home at 8:00 P.M. and say you have no time for family, you've chosen not to make time.

The Parental Role versus the Business Leader Role

An even greater tension than time is the change of roles required in being a successful executive and a good parent. At the office the CEO is the boss, the leader of the pack, which at upper levels of management tends to be all male, and fairly rational and controlled. At home there are demands for emotional support and for egalitarian actions that may be hard to meet with simple logic.

For the evangelicals, whose relational, egalitarian tendencies we have already discussed, these transitions in role are real, but the differences in venue may be a contrast. Ironically, their business lives are more like the relational nurturing of the family, and their families may tend to be more hierarchical and authoritarian than average. Pat Morley, of Morley Properties in Orlando, told a story that was repeated with many variations among the interviewees, and that was often even told by their wives. Morley's daughter came home upset over a disagreement with another child. He asked her what had happened, and then quickly fired off a four-point solution to her problem. She burst into tears and asked him not to say anything "logical" from now on when she was upset.[12]

The late Colman Mockler's wife, Joanna Mockler, tells a similar story with gentle humor of how her husband had sat down with one of their teenage children to have a good talk. For about thirty minutes she could hear the deep tone of her husband's voice, and almost no high responses. When Mockler came out, he reported with great satisfaction how healthy it was to have a good dialogue with your children. "Dialogue!" responded his wife. "You did all the talking, and she did all the listening!"

Such encounters, which are humorous in retrospect, point to the extreme difficulties that most successful working parents have in making the transition to family roles. The more successful the career and the higher one's position, the harder such transitions from "boss" and "problem solver" to "parent" or "spouse" can be. Interviewees' business philosophy could either help or hinder this process. Those who saw themselves in very paternalistic stewardship roles tended to have trouble adopting an egalitarian attitude at home. Like Morley in his "logical" approach, they tended to problem-solve for others rather than listen.

Even the nonworking wives have found that their role as CEO spouse can present great conflicts with the family. The ideal evangelical wife stays home with the children. In most of corporate America, the ideal CEO wife travels to exotic places with her husband to schmooze on weekends. She attends endless benefits in the name of community service.

Pat Morley was eloquent in describing this process. He said that once his business began to take off, he and his wife received countless social or civic invitations, and at first they accepted them all without discrimination. They soon realized, however, that although these occasions were the generally accepted culture of the successful CEO's social life, the family itself—and specifically time with their kids—was being sacrificed. Morley and his wife, Patsy, found many of these events superficial and materialistic, and at Patsy Morley's urging they deliberately set some limits on their social lives. With a characteristically evangelical long-term view, they asked themselves, "Why not prioritize everything we do on the basis of who's going to cry at our funeral?" Family came out on top.

Family Values versus the Social Environment

The world of work in which a CEO operates can also become a source of pressure on the evangelical emphasis on family. Family values and sexual standards have been undergoing dramatic change, much of which is anathema to the interviewees. The two tensions that came up most frequently were freer sexual standards and working mothers.

For the majority of the interviewees who discussed this topic, there was the implication that mothers who work are abandoning their children's spiritual and emotional needs. The results are the degeneration of the child and of society as a whole. Many of today's social ills can be traced to the disintegration of the traditional family support in which the mother is at home. In this attitude, many evangelicals are less ambivalent and more able to commit to hard choices than are many Americans. This commitment may, however, go against employee expectations or challenge other Christian values such as egalitarianism.

Daniel Yankelovich notes from his survey data that the majority of Americans long for "the old days" of stable family life, but they are not in favor of a return to old sexual standards, spic-and-span housekeeping norms, or a male monopoly on working outside the home. Yankelovich concludes from these attitudes that there is a longing for the warmth and closeness that people associate with traditional family life, but not a longing for the rigid hierarchies and "old rules" that governed family structures.[13]

The interviewees agreed with the general desire for the traditional warmth and intimacy of family, but that is where they drew the line. They saw the traditional family structure as the only way to get there, and traditional Christian education as a chief way of supporting the functions of family. Any other family or sexual arrangement is simply unbiblical. Furthermore, it will destroy the moral foundations of America. As one speaker at an evangelical conference put it:

> The feminists just don't want to hear that. They are rewriting the textbooks in order to avoid facing up to this.

What about male responsibility to the family? Harvard psychiatrist Armand Nicholi, a strong counselor to many conservative Protestant groups of successful men, has gathered data suggesting that the absence of the father is particularly damaging to sons, who may not display any ill effects until late in their teen years. When confronted with such data, do evangelical CEOs acknowledge a conflict with the sixty-hour work week and extensive travel? Some do, as I reported earlier.

What is even more obvious, however, is a change in *attitude* among younger evangelicals about the dual responsibilities of par-

enting. In James Hunter's surveys, 97 to 99 percent of male and
female students in evangelical colleges and seminaries agreed that
"both father and mother have the responsibility to care for small
children."[14] Surprisingly, this statistic stands in sharp contrast to the
supposedly more liberal attitudes toward dual gender roles among
the general population. When Yankelovich asked the same question
to a broader population, his affirmative response rate was only 56
percent.

Clearly there are some generational distinctions to be drawn
here. James Hunter's survey material suggests that new evangelical
entrants into the workforce may not be as convinced that a working
mother does irreparable harm. When comparing younger evangelicals with older evangelicals, there was a substantial difference on such
issues as whether "a preschool child is likely to suffer if his or her
mother works."[15]

So, too, the interviewees who were the most comfortable with
the idea of working parents either were in the youngest age group
(35-42) and had wives who worked or had friends whose wives
worked, or were older parents whose daughters were pursuing
business careers and were about to start families. Though not en-
dorsing working motherhood, these interviewees were clearly rethinking the traditional assumptions of the husband being the sole
breadwinner and the wife working only out of financial desperation.

Far less generation-bound were attitudes about sex. For the
evangelical, "free sex" is not only a personal sin; it has also been
responsible for many of the antifamily attitudes in America today.
These attitudes—ranging from the casual acceptance of divorce to
the apparent lack of concern about the number of unwed mothers—
ultimately harm children. Not surprisingly, the interviewees feel
responsible not only for their own sexual health but also for that of
their fellow believers. Sexual topics and marriage counseling are a
frequent subject for discussion in prayer groups or in serious conversation. My impression was that among some groups the talk is
fairly wide-ranging and that the desire to discuss each other's sex lives
is strong. One person I was interviewing cautioned me privately
about the group I was meeting with:

I have real reservations about your study. You see, I know that one of the people you are interviewing is considering having an affair. I've been counseling him on this, but I know he's having a hard time.

Two other people in that group also privately told me that X was already having an affair. These comments were entirely unsolicited.

How do I interpret such conversations? The information gained here is too incomplete for me to make any definitive statements. What we can see, however, is a strong pattern of holistic thinking in operation. Sex is often related to sin, it is related also to family health, and both sex and family health are concerns based on a biblical orientation. Other Judeo-Christian ethics such as honesty (such as to one's spouse and to interviewers) and self-restraint quickly surface as subthemes, making it imperative for the caring believer to be concerned about sexual norms.

The responses of some of the interviewees to the "free sex" morality of today's secular society were particularly rigid, but there was little direct discussion about how this affected worklife. Other interviewees had found an easier mix of their own conservatism with the business environment. Max De Pree, for example, reported that several associates were razzing him prior to our meeting because he had met an unfamiliar woman for dinner (the woman was a book agent), then gave a speech to about five hundred people at lunch, and then met me—also a stranger at the time—in the afternoon. Max had responded to them:

This is your problem. My wife and I don't need to mistrust each other. You'll have to live with your imaginations, because it's a lot better!

Other interviewees were not as lighthearted. Several interviewees would not be seen in public alone with another woman, lest they give the church a bad name,[16] and they also wanted to avoid temptation. One man asked his family along to lunch after we had spent the morning alone in his office conducting interviews. Another apologized for not being able to take me to lunch; all the women who might have accompanied us were out that day.

Hierarchical Structures at Work versus at Home

The attitudes I have just described imply a hierarchy of authority based on gender that is bound to pose problems for the evangelical CEO who prefers egalitarianism and informality in communicating with other employees. However much the evangelical may celebrate the intrinsic worth of women and may mourn the loss of respect for motherhood, if he carries his gender distinctions to work, he runs the risk of creating a discriminatory hierarchy of power. This kind of structure is not only illegal in the workplace, it is also a contradiction of his attitude toward empowerment. At the personal level, several of those interviewed felt that Paul, in Ephesians 5:22, is right—"Wives, submit to your husbands, as to the Lord"—but that his command places an obligation on the husband to act like Christ, by treating the wife with love. As Pat Morley said, "If the wife's role is to submit and operate under an authority structure, then the husband's responsibility is to create an environment for good relationships."[17]

In some cases, both spouses welcomed a hierarchical family structure and saw it as biblically based; as one interviewee put it, a home, like an army, can have only one leader. The wife must obey. Love must govern them both. We could easily imagine these men having problems with working mothers at their own workplaces. However, *none of those who advocated a strongly hierarchical view of authority at home expressed any sense of difficulty in relating to career mothers or parenting fathers at the office.* Was this an example of justifier or generalist thinking? This was clearly an area of extreme discomfort for me as an interviewer, voting with my suitcase, as it were, and I found it very difficult to probe this issue. Here is a typical exchange:

> *Nash:* If you feel strongly that mothers should stay home and that they should support their husband's career over their own, it must be difficult to be supportive of mothers who work in your office place. Aren't there tensions between your religious disapproval of their family choices and your ability to work well together?
> *Interviewee:* Not really. I treat all my employees the same.

I'm not sure I would have made much progress in getting a clarification of the potential tensions here whatever my own gender.

The strength of the tendency to generalize about family may make this area one of the hardest to probe for contradictions or tensions between Christian ethics and workplace habits, whether the issue is working mothers or the sixty-hour week and extensive travel for top managers.

Obviously there is great tension here with regard to the workplace. To the degree that a person supports facilities and policies that cater to working mothers, does that person contribute to sin? Some interviewees said yes. One reported that his church had discussed the possibility of having a child-care center on-site. They had the room, and the facilities were not being used during the week. They decided, however, not to have one, because they did not want to encourage mothers to work. The only ethical issue, in this man's opinion, was that by making this decision the church was losing opportunities to draw new members.

The law says that there must be equal opportunity for power, and that the choice of whether to work or not belongs to the parent, not to the employer. So how does the evangelical CEO obey the law and still be true to Christian values? Is he actually encouraging sinful behavior by employing working mothers?

Very few felt that they were. Most of them directed their attitudes about family and sexuality toward ways in which they could *support* family rather than impose on people's personal choices. Ken Wessner of ServiceMaster told of an annual session held for the top performing executives to which spouses were invited. One part of the program included a speech by a noted marriage counselor or child expert.

Jack Turpin tries to establish a personalized relationship with employees' families. One annual custom is to send a personal letter to their homes at Thanksgiving. He also tries to support policies that are family sensitive, such as no hard alcohol at company functions. Whereas many companies seem to have no problem with requiring week-long travel at the drop of a dime, Hall-Mark tried to ensure that its managers did not travel extensively:

> Philosophically we are directly involved with the employee's family. We operate thirty-five plants around the U.S.—fourteen hundred people. The

corporate direction is that family comes before the career. My personal
feeling is that God comes before the family.

Similarly, Tom Gerendas does not allow company activities to
be scheduled on Sundays, and tries to protect employee privacy.
During working hours, however, he expects his people to "do the
most and the best." But, as Turpin said: "If you wish to strive for
productivity, it's very difficult if the family scene is not intact." Once
again, the evangelical ethic has its economic rationale.

There are, however, some hard and fast lines that these CEOs
are *not* willing to cross over, even though their own personal values
would argue a different standard of behavior. Hiring decisions were
the chief area. Several interviewees explicitly stated that they did not
allow marital status (divorce or unwed cohabitation) or gender to
influence hiring and promotion decisions. Some, however, were
uncomfortable with this stand, and acutely felt the tension between
what the law says is right and what their hearts say is best. Working
mothers were given a chance, although in some cases these CEOs
offered special mentoring in order to compel a woman to consider
in advance the sacrifices of family that a top-management job would
demand. Such advice was not necessarily given to men.

The "Juggling Act"

Obviously, the lines get blurry when the daily business environment is so radically but subtly different from the values of one's
religious culture. How far the evangelical CEO should extend his
own family ethos to the workplace is truly one of those gray areas of
decision making. The generalists prefer not to think about it, and in
this the culture actually supports them: many nonbelieving executives are also content to "look the other way" in response to the
pressing tensions between family and work demands.

For the seekers, however, there seems to be a very real integration of their own family in the rest of their lives—an integration that
has existential implications. Family is not just one more factor in a
busy schedule, qualitatively equal to other demands on time. Barbara
Whitehead, in summarizing her study of working parents' attitudes
toward family, makes the important observation that the "juggling

act" metaphor for the work-family relationship is not really appropriate. The parents she interviewed didn't identify with this metaphor, because it implies that all the demands are qualitatively indistinguishable. As Whitehead said:

> This metaphor suggests that today's families must learn to keep more balls in the air, more plates spinning. . . . The balancing metaphor defines the challenge facing parents as primarily technical. It says that parents can keep all the plates spinning if only they learn to be more nimble, better coordinated, more efficient and organized. Thus, the metaphor is morally neutral. It doesn't draw distinctions among all the balls and plates.[18]

The "juggling act" metaphor helps us to classify three contradictory understandings of the role of work and family. The first is the *married-to-the-job* strategy. Underlying this familiar stereotype is the assumption that work and family are important but that they both demand essentially the same kind of personal skills and life goals for their success. With this view, it is most likely that the family will become more like a business, with the focus being property rights and time management. In all likelihood this is a setup for failure; using business skills will not suffice, and by cultivating a business persona, the successful executive increases his chances of being co-opted by the job and unable to have a strong relationship with his family.

The second understanding of work and family is the *total segregation* strategy; all the work-family balls are seen as completely different—unequal in weight and incapable of being coordinated by one person. This is the working father/nonworking mother household strategy, which carries tremendous efficiency advantages and is backed up by traditional authority structures in the Bible. But it also runs the risk of monetarizing the father and, like the first strategy, it deprives him of any identity beyond token authority as a parent. If the CEO who is a believer thinks of "traditional family" merely as a slogan, he is likely to be co-opted by the demands of the business. In the early years the devoted mother will be so good at her job, and apparently so suited to it, that it is easy for the father to leave the parenting to her so that he can meet the needs of the business. To many, this seems an inevitable "price" to pay. As many interviewees suggested, however, this strategy tends to diminish rather than enhance the significance of family for the CEO. It may even destroy it, but the harsh tragedy of a disenfranchised child may not be apparent until that child is well into the teen years.

A third understanding of family rejects the juggling metaphor but also rejects the idea of the complete compartmentalization of roles. This is the *integrating* strategy, and like the other creative tensions, it has proved to be at the heart of the seekers' approach to business and to life. In the integrating strategy, the successful executive takes the time and invests the emotional effort to assume a hands-on, nurturing parental role. A result of this approach is that work and family become more similar, but work becomes more like family than the other way around.

The carryovers from family to work were apparent among those interviewed: a more nurturing approach to employee relations, à la Max De Pree; an awareness of how advertising and product choices can be family friendly or can contribute to the general devaluation of family in our society, à la Steve Reinemund or Charles Olcott; and most widespread, a sensitivity to the family needs of employees, which a great number of interviewees expressed. At a personal success level, the integrator CEO helps to keep his family stable, but in many cases this stability and enhanced character gives him the perspective and skills to take risks and to face business problems with a level head, as was seen in Paul Kuck's decision to start a new business or Jim Carreker's move to a new job in Dallas.

This kind of strategy suggests that the seeker CEO has integrated his family into his very identity. For him, the family is specifically part of his identity as a Christian. It has a sacred quality. As such, both the role of CEO and the role of spouse and parent are reshaped. The successful chief executive is not one who has managed a hat trick—married to the firm while espousing a devotion to family—but rather is a person of many facets, all of which contribute to his effective leadership.

9

Tension 6: Charity and Wealth

We have a choice: either we seek God and live by the laws of his Kingdom as Jesus taught in the beatitudes or else we worship money and live for consumption and the creation of a personal fortune.
—Brian Griffiths[1]

In 1991 the average CEO compensation in the Fortune 200 was $2.8 million, not including perquisites and fringe benefits.[2] Meanwhile the gap between the top and bottom income levels in corporate America has widened so significantly that a full-time employed worker can legally be paid what amounts to a below-poverty level income for a family of four.

Personal wealth is a fact of life for most chief executives, including the evangelical CEO. Not surprisingly, this fact is greeted with varying degrees of concern. The Bible itself provides ambivalent statements about the role of material possessions. Though it may be difficult for the rich man to enter the kingdom of heaven, and though the man who foolishly spends his time building larger storehouses may have forgotten that he could die before he has had time to enjoy his wealth, God did promise a land flowing with milk and honey. Two passages from the same book of the Old Testament convey a sense of the ambiguity that is attached to material enjoyment: "He who loves pleasure will be a poor man; / He who loves wine and oil will not be rich" (Prov. 21:17) and "There is desirable treasure, / And oil in the dwelling of the wise, / But a foolish man squanders it" (Prov. 21:20).

Even in the New Testament, where celebrations of the poor are more abundant, material dependence is accepted as part of life. In the parable of the talents, economic reward is built into stewardship.

Not surprisingly, nearly every imaginable philosophy of materialism and wealth has already been expounded in the doctrine of
some arm of the church. Though clearly not wealthy themselves,
Jesus and his twelve disciples engaged in a communal sharing that
depended in part on contributions from the wealth of others. Early
prominent Christians such as St. Anthony opted for complete non-
materialism, adopting what would today be described as a masochis-
tic asceticism. The Calvinists sought to put a strong upper limit on
worldly wealth, which created its own ambivalence by providing the
basis for even more wealth accumulation. In contrast, all sense of
limit was abandoned in the popular prosperity gospels of the 1980s.

For the successful evangelical there are strong incentives to look
the other way to avoid the potential problems of faith that are
associated with being wealthy. First, it comes with the territory.
Wealth accumulation is one prize of the capitalistic game that the
evangelical CEO supports. This system also provides the best vehicle
for serving others. Second, financial success has its obvious advantages: family financial security, self-reliance, and the influence to
have things done according to preference.

The Generalist's and Justifier's Views

None of the benefits I've just described are necessarily wrong
from a biblical standpoint. In fact, they are hallmarks of the evangelical culture, as we have seen from earlier parts of this discussion.
Furthermore, the local church is dependent on its wealthy parish-
ioners. Though many clergy might emphasize charity to the implied
condemnation of wealth accumulation, few would actively condemn
wealth to the point of drying up the well.

And finally, there is ironically a strong potential for tolerating
wealth in the nonmaterialistic ethics of evangelical thought. If your
ultimate vertical relationship is what really counts, what does money
matter—whether you have a little or a lot? As one interviewee put it
(not with any sense of having struggled to find this position):

> It's not what you have; it's who you are. You have to have the right atti-
> tude, and that's what counts.

Another stated with conviction:

You *can* be rich and be a believer.

With typical generalist aplomb, both CEOs declined to offer any guidelines for distinguishing between a believer whose riches were okay from a spiritual standpoint and one whose riches might make it very difficult to enter the kingdom of heaven.

Underlying the generalist's view is the assumption that wealth and position are morally neutral things and that one's attitude is independent of such externals. One can be a humble millionaire. One can take luxury yacht trips and still care about the poor whom Jesus, at the end of the parable of the talents, commanded us to care for. One can live in exclusive suburbs and still not *feel* superior to those in working-class neighborhoods. This view is theoretically possible and practically implausible. In practice, the generalist has no specific sense of limit as to what is an acceptable distancing from the nonelites of the world. Like all perceptions of wealth and poverty, his baseline is relative. So what seems simple from the point of view of the generalist is simple only when judged within the narrow cultural context of other CEOs' lifestyles. Without being deliberately hypocritical, the generalist is unaware of how privileged and exclusive his choice of neighborhoods and associates really is. Joining the right country club, driving a luxury car, assuming his spouse would automatically have financial stability in the event of death, and living in an impressive house have all become automatic.

Philosophical disputes over lifestyle aside, this laissez-faire attitude toward wealth has a potentially schizoid element to it. The same man who expresses strongly egalitarian views on the social environment at work ends up, by his very lack of concern about wealth, sharply delineating his private life along status lines. Money then *separates* him from the human family whether he intends it to do so or not.

Some interviewees took a justifier approach to their own condition of wealth. They saw this kind of lifestyle and choice of associates as a way of reinforcing the capitalistic system in the minds of other people. Playing the luxury game is also good for business and ultimately for employees. An exclusive lifestyle helps guard against being exploited by the less fortunate and also contributes to one's ability to bear witness among other CEOs. The cultural assumptions in the last two justifications are intriguing, and they point to a less egalitarian attitude than some justifiers would like to believe they support. Is there not just as great a potential to be exploited by another CEO looking for business or for a directorship as there is by a junior executive looking for contact with a higher-up? Why would other CEOs and other wealthy people be the primary focus of one's witness?

Despite the generalist's and justifier's seeming lack of concern over questions about wealth, there appears to be much ground for tension over faith and financial success. Jesus' statements about the camel passing through the eye of a needle suggest that wealth does indeed present problems of faith. Furthermore, the extreme materialism of the 1980s is credited by many as the chief symptom of a spiritually diseased society—a statement that many evangelicals would agree with. Too close an alignment with the cultural environment should give any evangelical pause for second thought. As evangelical and free-market advocate Brian Griffiths writes:

> To allow wealth creation legitimacy is not to endow it with autonomy. To allow economic life independence and place no bounds on wealth creation would be to justify a philosophy of materialism.[3]

The concept of limit is important to Griffiths's discussion, as is the attitude of the successful businessperson from a Christian point of view. The questions of how much and of what value, as well as for what purpose, need to be answered. Pursuit of profit can easily corrupt personal goals so that the accumulation of gain eventually becomes the only goal.

We can see these tendencies not only in the experiences of nonevangelicals on Wall Street but among justifiers in the group. The justifiers take on the topic of wealth and success with relish. They interpret wealth and position as a legitimate and appropriate *reward,* with little thought of its future impact on their own behavior and spiritual journey. When simplistically applied, however, the view that the reward is for doing what's right (creating wealth and creating dignifying jobs) can be confused with the view that the reward itself is the intrinsic spiritual goal of business (make money and you must be doing what is spiritually right).

This latter viewpoint, kept within reasonable bounds, fits well with the ethical basics of capitalism as outlined in the covenantal ethic; but given half a chance, it invites personal covetousness, or a name-it-and-claim-it prosperity gospel. Several interviewees were frank on the topic and confessed to feeling suspicious that some of their brothers were too preoccupied with the power of the almighty dollar. The record of certain televangelists did nothing to reassure them on this score.

The Seeker's View

Most of those I interviewed, however, would be categorized as seekers with regard to their attitudes about wealth. (I was not in the position to observe much of their actual lifestyle.) The questions raised earlier—how much, what personal value, and for what purpose—were questions that they struggled with. Despite their roles as captains of industry, they see money as a significant source of tension for the Christian businessperson. As Clayton Brown, head of Clayton Brown Associates in Chicago and a friend of several participants in my interviews, wrote:

> In general, Christian businessmen face the same kind of temptations as anyone: the lust of the flesh, the lust of the eyes, and the pride of life. However, there is one other special temptation: to measure everything in dollars.[4]

Similarly, Elmer Johnson wrote early in his career:

> The worldly man is highly ambitious for personal advancement and material gain. This strong drive in a business organization is the cause of great friction. In contrast, while the Christian pursues personal excellence, he regards his own material gain as much less important.[5]

Commented Boston money manager Richard Crowell:

> If you read Exodus, the time between the Red Sea and the golden calf was

three months. My experience is that crisis comes, affects us, and then we
quickly forget the lesson.

Dallas CEO Ed Yates, head of Highland Park Cafeterias,
pointed to antimaterialism as one of the chief differences that an
outsider might observe in a business run by a Christian. Said Yates:

> I think you *should* find, certainly, in the Christian's office a lesser emphasis
> on material things as a sign of success. (his emphasis)

Some interviewees associated their spiritual conversion with a
direct change in attitude toward the importance of money. "Joe
Beck," who had been a top officer in a leading executive search and
compensation firm, said that money was just about his only motivation before his conversion:

> I joined a man to form a company. His design, though he didn't say it,
> was, "I'm going to make you every bit as rich as I am, Joe." And I didn't
> see anything wrong with that; I had ambitions for money. The only thing
> that kept me honest was that I was in an environment where I could estab-
> lish my own rules. But I was extremely well rewarded, and I really liked
> that.

As described in the previous chapter, Beck subsequently had a
conversion experience that caused him to withdraw from his old
business and to take a deliberate cut in salary and lifestyle. He said
that he felt that this helped him to become the type of person whose
life and attitudes could conform more closely to the Christian ideal.
He was honest enough to report that the familiar incentives to seek
position and power, however, were a repeated temptation for him as
his business once again picked up.

Like Beck, most of the seekers acknowledged that material
reward is a definite motivator and a part of the economic system that
they support. Those in financial services seemed to feel this most
keenly. Jim Kubik, of Griffin, Kubik, Stephens, and Thompson, in
Chicago noted that in his business money is an inescapable incentive:

> I am *paid* to think about money. That's my responsibility to the client.
> How can I not value it and stay responsible as a businessperson? That's a
> particularly hard dilemma in my industry. It would be a lot easier if I were

in manufacturing. If you nail some boards up and put up a house, there's a lot of satisfaction just in doing that job. But for me, the carrot is the significant factor, and keeping that in balance with your faith is not easy. (his emphasis)

Another man who was a spiritual counselor to Christian businessmen, expressed some of the ambivalence that the concept of money carries for those he counsels:

> Money isn't totally bad, but it carries great temptations. Look at the men in the Bible whom God used. You see Abraham, a wealthy person; King David, a shepherd boy who became aide to the king, then became king himself. And then he screwed up his life because he had a thing with sex. Then there was Daniel. He was like a cabinet minister.
>
> So I don't think wealth is bad, but . . . many of my friends are multimillionaires, and I wouldn't trade places with one of them. You can only take one thing with you: your relationship with God. And the next life is so much richer than this.

Tom Jones, who was in a very prosperous business, described a different attitude toward wealth—one that combined the conservative Protestant value of frugality with a more modern acceptance of wealth:

> My father's father made a lot of money in coal. My father probably gave away more than he sold during the Depression, but I saw his admiration for his father, and that signaled that it [wealth] was okay.
>
> I've been able to understand that the having of money is not the real motivation for me, it's the having of options. Doing well financially provides me with a series of options that if I hadn't gone through this experience, the options wouldn't be mine—the people I meet, the experiences I have, the things I can cause to happen. [Note the order.] That's the underlying motivation for being involved in this business.

Jones's comments were typical of the group. Their understanding of wealth was alternatively a means to other ends or a logical offshoot of respectable business activity. At the same time, they were mindful of the ego and lifestyle temptations that a high income can bring. Given this awareness and the ever-present potential to experience great wealth, how does the seeker CEO keep a Christian perspective in the face of inevitable status rewards for his business success?

Today's seeker is materially better off than any early Calvinist would have liked. Some seekers—such as boat manufacturer Paul Kuck, Cadillac dealer Ed Williamson, luxury resort manager Jim Carreker, and upscale real estate developer Jack Feldballe—even sell material luxuries to others. Nevertheless, the question of degree is an important one. Many interviewees displayed a strong sense of conservative protestant frugality in little but very personalized ways such as in their choices of clothes or restaurants, while also participating in the normal rituals of wealth that accompany their positions: membership in exclusive clubs, upscale homes and second homes, and widespread travel. Ironically, they assume an egalitarian attitude and adopt a semi-egalitarian lifestyle, but are nevertheless quite wealthy in fact.

Sam Walton was indeed a "man of the people," who never failed to rub shoulders with the customer and the employees. He set himself a relatively meager salary of under half a million dollars when other CEOs in his industry were receiving four or five times more. But Walton was also reportedly the richest man in America, according to the annual *Forbes* magazine estimates of the richest people in the world, based on his personal assets from the company. Today's top executives at WalMart still receive relatively low salaries in their industry but extremely handsome performance incentives.

Many of the evangelicals interviewed for this book display the same combination of stylistic folksiness or frugality as Walton while maintaining significant personal assets and the privacy that only extreme wealth can buy. Even though they may have very upscale houses, they deliberately set limits on the material possessions that their workers might see, choosing, for example, to drive a midsize Buick or Maxima rather than an upscale car. They shun obvious status symbols such as limousines, separate building entrances, or remote and elaborate offices.

One participant, for example, told of a fellowship gathering he'd attended in Washington, D.C. All the participants were highly successful businessmen and their spouses. They had chosen the topic of social justice, particularly as it related to money, as a focal point for their discussion of faith. During the meeting there was a strong consensus among the group that they needed to be more in touch with Third World issues.

As they left the facility, a stretch limo pulled up for the CEO. He had rented a midsize car that was supposed to be delivered to him. Seeing his specially marked charge card (a common "courtesy" to a CEO whose company does business with a particular firm), the rental place had automatically sent along a limo. As the other participants watched in amusement, he tried to explain why he didn't want the car and that he hadn't ordered it.

The incident, of course, was minor, but the discomfort he felt and the general notice it brought are common indications of the less pretentious attitude that this group has about material things. When, for example, this interviewee told the story later that evening, another evangelical confessed he had flown first class to the same meeting, had thoroughly enjoyed it, and now felt guilty. Their conclusion: It is very important for the evangelical CEO to remove himself from the cultural context of the wealthy, not just for reasons of its secularity, but for its debilitating effect on his awareness of the less advantaged. Remarked one participant:

> You can feel comfortable with something in one context, and when the reality of the social justice questions really comes into focus, it's hard to deal with that special treatment. It really is. It's hard to make sense out of the use of resources to do this sort of thing.

Dick Crowell, of The Boston Company, expressed a similar understanding of the relative nature of poverty and wealth:

> I think there's a rolling scale here. Even if I went from the top income bracket to welfare, I would still be incredibly wealthy in comparison to people at other periods of history.
>
> I don't deny myself worldly things, but I try to moderate. I try to find a more efficient way, more Christian way, of accomplishing what I need to accomplish. Many in my industry [financial services] drive upscale cars. I drive a Maxima. I have a boat; it was my father's. I spend $2,000 a year fixing it versus the $25K many people spend on maintaining a boat. I bought a condo on a lake because a house would have been more expensive.

What is striking in Crowell's remarks and in the approaches of other interviewees to issues of wealth is how they automatically combine Christian sanctions with economic rationales. As Crowell said: "That doesn't necessarily make me more righteous, but it does seem a more logical way to go about it." Translate "logical" as "efficiency" and you have all the elements of conservative protestant frugality.

Such choices, however, cannot be applied categorically to all the interviewees. Differences in lifestyle—from cars to housing to vacations—were among the most extreme variables in this group. Some of these men, such as Tom Gerendas, drove ten-year-old cars and set out paper plates for our luncheon at the plant. Other interviewees sported Mercedes 560s, boats costing upward of $400,000, penthouses, and exclusive vacation homes. Some of these men were also the most generous philanthropists in their communities.

There is, however, widespread agreement among those with the most upscale lifestyles and those with the leanest lifestyles that the church's traditional criticism of wealth and capitalism is misplaced. Though it appears that the church's anticapitalism has been rapidly changing as a result of the events in Eastern Europe and in the former Soviet Union, it has been very much a part of these interviewees' own experiences. Jack Feldballe, who lived in a mixed-income neighborhood in Chicago for ten years and drives a Buick, nonetheless found the anticapitalist sentiments of the clergy disturbing:

> I'm flabbergasted by the high degree of abnormal criticism and suspicion of wealth you see among clergy of all faiths. They think that because an individual is wealthy it was ill-gotten gain at someone's expense. Capitalism has created the wherewithal, the jobs.

Feldballe does not use being misunderstood, however, as an excuse for not thinking about the meaning of wealth at all. In the same conversation, he paraphrased Matthew 6:21 to make a further point:

> Where your focus is, there your heart is. I really believe that materialism can separate you from your God. We are a very materialistic society.

Dennis Sheehan responded:

If you look inside yourself, you will find that your anxieties will increase in proportion to your net assets. And these anxieties are manifestations of possible differences between the inner self, the articulation, and the action. The very fact that you increase your assets increases the tension between the three.

The Importance of Giving

A very important Christian response to the tension that Sheehan described—and which interviewees said they identified with to greater or lesser degrees—is to strongly emphasize giving, as does the Bible. Said Sheehan, "In my own case, in all candor, I wonder if wealth doesn't impart a mission to benefit a broader segment of society."

For the evangelical CEOs I interviewed, giving is a very significant concept. Many of them take seriously the biblical command to tithe, even though the tithe—one-tenth of their yearly income—is about ten times larger than the average personal charitable contribution in America. No one expressed resentment about giving.

When I asked one interviewee if he really tithed, he hesitated and then replied that he did. At first I was afraid he'd hesitated because he thought I was going to ask him for a contribution to my research project. Then I wondered if he was telling the truth. Seeing my confusion, he enlightened me. He tithed on pretax income, he said, thereby receiving the tax credit, and he had wondered whether I would count this as really tithing!

While participants' general assumption that they are obligated to give something back is admirable but not unusual among evangelicals, they have a special understanding of the concept of charity itself. Most important, they see charity as being opposed to consumption, which is a hallmark of secular society today. Spending is the getting for oneself; charity is the giving to others.

The traditional economic rationales that influence other aspects of the evangelical's understanding of faith also influence the attitude toward giving. Very few of the interviewees simply "give money away." Many of them focus their giving on things that they hope will be productive. So they understand charity to be an *investment* rather than a generous throwaway. Their giving, just like their approach to business, is touched by the stewardship desire to create value.

For example, they favor projects that encourage self-help. Their evangelical biblical worldview, with its particular economic and spiritual characteristics, resolves some of the conflicts between acquiring wealth and caring for the oppressed. Whether it is an investment in efforts to bring others to Jesus as the first step in self-help, or seed money for start-up businesses in minority communities, these CEOs want their giving to have productive power. However, their sense of Christian oneness with the disadvantaged carries over not only into their egalitarian policies at work but to their giving as well.

The interviewees generally preferred to contribute to two kinds of activities: (1) those that bring others (especially fellow executives) to Jesus, and (2) those that materially help the disadvantaged to help themselves. The first kind is an investment in people's spiritual well-being, the second in their physical well-being. Historically, these two categories have reflected differences of biblical interpretation of Christian duty that separated liberal social gospel advocates and fundamentalist groups. Participation in both kinds of giving is one more indication that the evangelicals I interviewed are more eclectic than other Protestants on either side of the giving fence.

There is, however, a definite preference here. The majority of interviewees (with some notable exceptions) appeared to dedicate a much larger proportion of their giving to the first kind of activity. Activities that seek to introduce spiritual "seekers" to Jesus are particularly attractive, from the Washington prayer breakfast to Campus Crusade for Christ to InterVarsity Christian Fellowship to the Christian Businessmen's Association. There are evangelism groups that work among professional athletes, prison inmates, Eastern Europeans, people in underdeveloped countries, and senators in Washington. Similarly, personal spiritual counselors, whose living is essentially provided by a group of businessmen, receive widespread support.

This tradition of business leaders funding the evangelists is firmly imbedded in the history of evangelism. The fundamentalist movement itself was spawned in 1910 with the aid of two oil magnates, the Steward brothers, who backed the distribution of a religious tract. Dwight L. Moody, the great revivalist, began as a shoe salesman but wanted to use his talents to convert others. His evangelism was launched when a group of business barons backed him financially. This group included Cyrus McCormick, J. Pierpont Morgan, John Wanamaker, and William Dodge. John D. Rockefeller was a benefactor and personal confidant of the evangelist and social reformer Walter Rauschenbusch.[6]

In this kind of activity there are several common assumptions about advancing social good. The first is that nothing on earth is as important as personal redemption. The second is that until a person is saved, no lasting change in personal welfare is possible. The third is that social change will occur only when many people have been saved. This reasoning rests on the belief that the adoption of a Christian point of view will most likely result in better chances of economic self-reliance.

Charles Colson's extraordinary Prison Fellowship group, which ministers to inmates around the world, sometimes under extremely dangerous conditions, is a good example. Its first mission is to share the good news, to bring joy and hope of salvation to those in the darkest of situations. (It is widely known that Colson himself became a committed Christian after a personal visit from Tom Phillips while Colson was still in prison following the Watergate conviction.) Colson's real concern lies in the moral education of society, which he feels can be accomplished only through family, faith, and fellowship. Representatives of Prison Fellowship visit inmates to tell them the gospel, to help them in their spiritual journeys, and to give them hope. At the same time, a commitment to Christ implies a commitment to strong values about work and self-discipline. These representatives provide concrete assistance to the families of inmates, and they teach the inmates job skills. Project Angel Tree, another Prison Fellowship program, provides Christmas gifts for the children of inmates and for other needy families. This action is linked, however, to getting these people involved in local churches and to providing "friendship and models of Christian love."

As Colson's group demonstrates, the relational aspect of this kind of charity is strong. Money and material goods are not the only donations; a relationship with the receiver is formed with the specific view to conversion. Similarly, Doug Holladay's One-on-One group in Washington provides mentoring by businesspeople to inner city youths to provide practical advice for daily living but more importantly to bring them eventually to Jesus.

Although spiritual counseling is the first goal, several economic results occur, as the donors well know. Bringing someone to Jesus, they believe, is the best first step toward personal economic improvement. Self-esteem and the discipline of faith have their obvious practical effects: cleanliness, the abandonment of drunken or abusive behavior, and self-reliance. Chuck Colson, for example, reports visiting the notorious Lurigancho prison in Peru just days after a riot. Known as the largest prison in the world, the place was a hell hole, with cell blocks six stories high and open sewers. Colson came across a fellow wildly gesticulating and grinning as he pointed to a graduation certificate from a Prison Fellowship seminar. "We grabbed one another in a fierce hug of Christian fellowship," Colson writes. As a side note, Colson mentions that the fellow's cell stood out as being clean and neatly swept.[7]

A story from the 4-Way Test Association is another good example of how the evangelical tries to help create both a community of shared values and a community of shared wealth. The 4-Way Test Association was established to further the efforts of evangelical businessman Herbert Taylor, who authored the 4-Way Test (later adopted by the Rotary Club). The association created 4-Way Test Campaigns in which local Rotary businesses launched a massive publicity campaign to communicate their commitment to the principles of the 4-Way Test. The first campaign occurred in Daytona Beach, Florida, in late 1955 in response to rising crime rates, juvenile delinquency, and a group of four hundred motels whose records for violence were giving the city a bad name among tourists. Ministers, chamber of commerce members, newspapers, and others plastered the community with the 4-Way Test. In the words of the association's document:

> As the principles inherent in the 4-Way Test began to work, the atmosphere of the community changed. Motel owners agreed to try a central clearinghouse for visitors. . . . As one doubter put it, [describes his change of attitude and the fact that he now passes on business that he can't han-

dle] "There is a give-and-take in applying the 4-Way Test that I never
knew could exist in the business world." By the end of 1965 due to 4-Way
Test programs, traffic injuries were down by 20 percent and juvenile delinquency down by 50 percent in the Daytona Beach area.

While such analyses may seem naive in the face of the complex,
continuing decay of urban areas, they point to a fundamental social
assumption that is represented by the contributions of evangelicals
to evangelizing organizations—namely, that economic and quality-
of-life improvements should follow from religious commitment.

Many interviewees, however, also expend much of their time
and financial resources on more direct financial projects for the less
fortunate. One retired builder-developer took on what he saw as
"three full-time nonpaying jobs." His chief commitment was to a
four-year African-American college. He and three other businesspeople took on the job of instituting proper business practices at
the college. They raised $2.3 million in ninety days from corpora-
tions in the area to make up the budget deficit.

This man reported that raising money to cover a deficit was an
especially challenging task, in spite of his reputation as a leading fund
raiser in the area (this came from several other interviewees who
proudly mentioned his name as an outstanding example of an evangelical business leader, especially in his work with a certain national
charitable organization). His goal was to create a financially sound
organization to provide special assistance to African-Americans in
the area. His sense of need was frank and compassionate:

> I would hope that we wouldn't need to have a so-called black college in
> twenty or forty years. But there is a need for a special niche by race at this
> point in time. Unfortunately, many blacks in this city become drop-outs.
> They do not appear likely to complete their education unless they get spe-
> cial attention in a special environment, which this school gives.

This interviewee's philanthropy was ever mindful of the relationship between education and the creation of economic skills. He
hoped to start a small business school at the aforementioned college
and also a seminary. This commitment comes partly out of past
failures: he had been a strong supporter of a large community
development project, but he discovered a frustrating lack of qualified

candidates with sufficient educational skills to fill the jobs that he had hoped would be created in that area.

Such efforts at financial improvement of the less advantaged in society fly in the face of the stereotypes that portray evangelicals as being indifferent toward the poor. Such examples were frequent among the interviewees. Several mentioned supporting a group in Chicago called Opportunity International, formerly headed by Dave Hardin of the Chicago Sunday Evening Club until he died in early 1994, and now headed by Erick Thrum, a former business partner of Jack Feldballe's. Opportunity International provides loans for small micro-enterprise economic development projects in less developed countries. Gary Ginter has helped a number of start-ups in communities of need in various parts of the world. Jack Feldballe is funding a project that develops innovative new materials and programs to combat adult illiteracy. As Feldballe said, "Until people can read they will not have the capability to perform jobs." Dennis Sheehan provides three scholarships for advanced education to employees.

Evangelicals have often been accused of being indifferent to poverty. But the new donation patterns of the evangelical CEO, based on all the information I could gather, point to a much keener sense of responsibility about improving the material conditions of the poor than in the past. And much of this new direction can be traced, I think, to the fact that the evangelical CEO tends to combine his business persona with his mission role.

Some interviewees apply the same combination of business sense and mission work to the business of the church itself, specifically in solving the problems of managing the religious institution. Max De Pree works closely with Fuller Theological Seminary in this regard, both on management issues and on rethinking the way that it ultimately serves the business community. Robert Buford decided to withdraw from the majority of his cable television business activities in order to devote his time and resources to helping leaders of large churches. Working closely with Peter Drucker, Buford helped produce a series of audio tapes on the topic, and is continuing to support conferences, newsletters, training events, and a variety of projects in this area. Buford states his life mission as "to work on transforming the latent energy of American Christianity into active energy."

Many of these activities end up combining spiritual counseling and social activism, just like Colson's Prison Fellowship did. Howard Butt's Laity Lodge Foundation sponsors an intensive three-day retreat for leading evangelical CEOs and other interested seekers. The sessions, which are by invitation only and are attended by extremely thoughtful business leaders, are focused primarily on ministering to those attending the event. But speakers such as builder-developer Jim Rouse spark a strong commitment to social action when they talk of their own activities. Rouse's Enterprise Trust Foundation is dedicated to finding solutions to the urban housing problem based on Rouse's past successes in revitalizing downtown marketplaces. The dedication of Jim Rouse and his wife, Pat Rouse, to the needs of the disadvantaged is something that no one encounters with indifference.

Several other interviewees have also turned their resources toward ministering to their own flocks. Tom Phillips has been instrumental in forming the First Tuesday breakfasts in Boston, which invite CEOs to share in a reflective spiritual event once a month. Miami realtor W. Allen Morris and his wife host several upscale evening events a year. They invite a wide range of Miami businesspeople to hear a well-known person speak about his or her career and personal spiritual journey. Commented another interviewee:

> Sometimes you do more good by adopting a style similar to the average CEO. I can do more in terms of bringing people to Jesus if I am comfortable in their social setting.

What about the next generation of business leaders? Jerry Dempsey, for one, is very concerned about passing on the double emphasis on work and Christianity. He has helped start a career development program for young people through the pastor of a major church in the Chicago area. His commitment to this program is, in its own way, an investment in the future. Similarly, Dempsey has set aside an annual donation to a fund at Clemson University to develop careers in engineering.

Summary

We have seen in this chapter that many evangelical business leaders feel a common tension and responsibility about wealth and the distribution of wealth despite their wholehearted involvement in profit-making enterprises. Many of the comments about charitable donations and mission work returned time and again to the issue of attitude. In the end, attitude is the secret to faithfully resolving the inevitable tensions of having financial success. As financial advisor Jim Kubik warned adamantly, wealth can be put to good use, but the temptations of "that big carrot" are real and need to be addressed. If wealth preoccupies a person's mind and distracts that person from maintaining a relationship with God, then indeed it is easier for a camel to pass through the eye of a needle than for that person to enter the kingdom of heaven. But as one interviewee pointed out, a life of extreme poverty may also cause a person to become preoccupied with money.

Doug Sherman and William Hendricks, in their book *Your Work Matters to God,* point out that one of the practical benefits of work is that it allows a Christian a concrete way of serving others. In discussing this idea they suggest that the qualitative, character-forming aspect of giving is of ultimate value:

> So giving some portion of your income away is a discipline and a privilege taught by Scripture.[8]

The evangelical connection between faith and charity is relationships, not money, and yet the optimism that the poor who put their faith in God will see an improvement in their quality of life is fundamental to this belief. While this response may seem inadequate to the crying needs of the poor, and has been criticized by the minority in the evangelical left, it remains true to the worldview of evangelicalism as described in Chapter 1. Some comments by President George Bush at the 1990 National Prayer Breakfast illustrate how deeply this viewpoint is ingrained in the political agenda of conservative Protestant leaders today:

A truly religious nation is also a giving nation. A close friend of mine sent me a poem recently which eloquently embodies this spirit of giving:

> "I sought my soul, but my soul I could not see.
> I sought my God, but my God eluded me.
> I sought my brother, and found all three."

> Thousands of Americans are finding their soul, finding their God, by reaching out to their brothers and sisters in need. You have heard me talk about a thousand points of light across the country. Americans are working through their places of worship, through community programs, on their own, to help the hungry, the homeless, to teach the unskilled, to bring the words of men and the Word of God to those who cannot even read. And so, I believe that this democracy of ours is once again proving, as it has throughout our history, that when people are free, they use that freedom to serve the greater good and indeed a higher truth.

As with so many other aspects of their business ethic, the evangelical CEOs approached the opportunities and temptations of wealth from a personal, relational standpoint. Although they did not suggest systemic changes in national or state policy that might result in increased standards of living for the poor, they contributed generously to charitable causes that were hoped to accomplish this result. Their holistic approach did not stop at the threshold of philanthropy. Most brought a "business attitude" to their giving, a hope that their donations would be made in such a way as to multiply in productiveness. At the same time, whether the issue was their own wealth or the poverty of others, these men were absolutely certain that no change was as important as the change for the better in one's relationship with God. Get that right and all else follows.

10
Tension 7:
Faithful Witness
in the Secular
City

[There has been] a severe rupture of the traditional task of religion, which was precisely the establishment of an integrated set of definitions of reality that could serve as a common universe of meaning for the members of a society. The world-building potency of religion is thus restricted to the construction of sub-worlds, of fragmented universes of meaning, the plausibility structure of which may in some cases be no larger than the nuclear family.
—Peter L. Berger[1]

In the eighteenth century the average New Englander heard seven thousand sermons in his or her lifetime. Abraham Lincoln regularly used the phrase "this Christian nation" in his speeches, and as political commentator Garry Wills notes, this was not a code for *Judeo-Christian heritage* but rather a universalized term for conservative Protestantism.[2]

Today not only is Jesus banned from public discussion, but even the word *God* has been excised from the vocabulary of institutional belief as well. What was once taken for granted is now seen as offensive and old-fashioned. Nowhere is this more true than in American business.[3]

The extreme secularization of the American business culture in the second half of the twentieth century raises severe cultural and moral conflict for the CEOs I interviewed. They do not generally advocate a return to preindustrialism or to pre-Darwinism, but they are angry and dismayed at the extreme secularity of today's mainstream. Terms like "dark ages," "paganism," and "a cultural civil war" circulate frequently in evangelical circles to describe their disaffection.

As effective leaders in a culture better known for conformity than for cultural rebellion, evangelical CEOs constantly encounter the opportunity or even pressure to participate in cultural practices that go directly against their faith. As a result, many intellectually and culturally sophisticated evangelicals are put into a paradoxical position. They are torn by a dual identity: They are both part of the modern culture and yet not of it. As CEOs, they must be "insiders" in the corporate culture while maintaining their "outsider" identity as committed Christians.

Add to this paradox the evangelical obligation to bear witness to one's faith, and the conflicts became even more apparent. The Puritan minister Increase Mather was able to describe himself as "God's agent on earth." The evangelical CEO may believe his identity as lay minister to be much like Mather's, but few would say so openly among a group of nonbelievers from their office or among their clientele. In the company of believers, however, these same men adopt a language that is heavily steeped in sacred and ritualistic vocabularies, testaments of faith, and interpretations of God's presence on earth.

The Two Cultures

Given the conflicts I have just mentioned, the evangelical CEO faces two intensely disturbing pressures in his or her role as CEO: (1) how much and in what ways to assimilate into the moral attitudes of the general business culture, and (2) how to ensure that his or her faith is an active and relevant part of the daily experiences of business.

As Peter Berger points out in the passage quoted at the beginning of this chapter, the only coping device for many believers working in the secular society is to relegate religious life to the private sphere, thereby fragmenting the meaning of life between sacred and secular contexts. But such a fragmentation and compartmentalization of religion goes deeply against the grain of the evangelical worldview. The holistic and emotionally intensifying aspects of the evangelical view do not tolerate being "a little bit secular"—at least not in theory.

Today's evangelical may be fully sophisticated in terms of education and comfort with modern materialism and science. And yet his or her religious identity is substantially grounded in the fundamentalist experience of an earlier era.4 These dual interpretations of reality and their accompanying social assumptions put many intellectually and culturally sophisticated evangelicals in an ironic position, especially with regard to business culture. A scientific technological orientation often makes good business sense and contributes to the stewardship that is valued by evangelical concepts of work. The sociocultural foundations of scientific knowledge, however, are dominated by secular humanists. So any nonfundamentalist evangelical chief executive of a large business is going to experience a cultural civil war right in the office place—if not in his or her own mind! And so the seventh tension is defined: faithful witness in the secular city. The CEO cannot resolve the conflicting forces of modern values and religious values simply by saying no to narcissistic, sexually liberated hedonism.

Wrestling with the tension of being religiously conservative in a pluralistic culture was a topic of intense interest to most interviewees. As with the other six tensions, there wasn't a universally held approach to this question. Also, the obligation to bear witness raised important ethical questions about coercion and the abuse of power, which invited lively discussion and a wide range of views among this group. Finally, interviewees contended to varying degrees with the political labels generally attached to being associated with evangelicalism. This last topic, though important, is not addressed here in order to focus on the business arena.

The Choice of Associates

One of the main choices that the interviewees wrestled with was the choice of business associates. Can and should the evangelical be exclusive in order to be culturally consistent with his or her beliefs? Should the evangelical accept the democratic ideal of pluralism, even if it results in creating a work culture that dilutes his or her faith beyond recognition? The *legal* answers are no to the first question and yes to the second. The norms, however, give far greater latitude to the concept of equal opportunity, and they are backed by historical practice.

A large number of evangelicals, though certainly a very small part of this interviewee group, try to limit their exposure to the social values of the secular society. They restrict their business associations as much as possible to those who share the same values. There is, for example, a Christian Yellow Pages in most major cities for those who would like to favor suppliers with allegedly similar religious commitments. Few of the interviewees in this group, however, support such an effort, citing business reasons as frequently as ethical concerns about unfair exclusivity.

More pervasive and problematic was the question of peer associations, especially in terms of seeking professional advice from boards, legal representatives, or just other friends in similar positions. To start with, no one advocated or unwittingly betrayed a conspiracy of believers. If this group has within itself any dark webs of interlocking business relations that lead to unfair competitive advantages in bidding on contracts or the like, I couldn't find them. Of course, what are commonly called *interlocking directorates* exist among the believers, but board membership within the publicly held companies is fully disclosed, and the companies that I knew of also had nonevangelicals on their boards.

Herman Miller's board, like the company itself, is a diverse group. To quote Max De Pree, its composition is

> half confessing Christians, one Jew, one fairly atheist. But over the years they know where I come from.

Ed Yates was also unapologetic about the composition of his board, which he justified in terms of business judgment and the ability to probe:

> One board member is one of my closest friends, one is a theologian, but they are all good businessmen. My friends are very hard on me. I need people around me who are smarter than I am, and these people are very smart.

The existence of prayer groups also raises the question of exclusivity and unfair competitive advantage. Those charges have been repeated regularly by the press—as in "the businesses that pray together, play together." I saw no indication that interviewees channeled prayer-group memberships into transactional relationships. They overtly participate in various fellowship groups, from Doug Coe's annual National Prayer Breakfast in Washington, D.C., to informal national phone fellowships, such as the one that so profoundly influenced Jack in the situation reported in Chapter 3. Some of these groups hope to collectively shift the balance of cultural forces back toward a religious America (see the previous chapter), but the fellowships are primarily support groups, an important way of keeping faith alive. Their influence is to remind each other of their spiritual duty, to gather together in Christ's name, and to assert a Christian perspective. It is *not* to establish an inside connection to bring in more business.

These groups do, however, offer each other business advice, and to this degree they provide an alternative to a completely secular perspective on business problems. You may recall that when Jack faced a legal crisis in his firm, he eventually consulted with his phone group for spiritual aid. Their input directly influenced his decision to change his strategy about the lawsuit, which had tremendous financial implications.

Some executives find such behavior offensively exclusive and against the objective responsibilities of a good manager. Shouldn't a CEO consult an independent board on such matters? But others, not all of them believers, have responded to this example with less indignation. Don't *most* CEOs have an informal circle of peers with whom they bounce off problems in a confidential setting? Aren't their formal choices of advisers based on shared values and an ability to establish good relationships?

Decisions about Hiring

While outsiders have frequently charged that such groups give believers unfair access to power, the interviewees drew a sharp distinction between their private associations and their employment policies. While their private associations definitely gravitate toward exclusivity, the employee pools are not restricted. We could reasonably conclude that it would be unrealistic to expect them to say anything else. Admitting such a policy would be hardly likely since in publicly held organizations they would be legally jeopardized.

But several interviewees backed up these assertions of open hiring with a personal philosophy of diversity in the workplace. Max De Pree's support of a racially diverse population outside Zeeland, Michigan, was mentioned in Chapter 6. Jim Carreker, president of Wyndham Hotels, also made an explicit commitment to a diversified employee group. He explained in this way:

> I've never hired someone based on whether or not someone was a Christian. I have hired based on efficiency, capability, and ethical standards.
>
> As Christians we're called to step into society. Totally Christian-filled companies are not the ministry they can be if they embrace other people.

I asked Carreker if he wasn't being somewhat simplistic to look for common ethical standards among believers and nonbelievers. Characteristically, he gave what amounted to a very integrated set of concerns that included his faith, common economic sense, and his employee relations philosophy:

> I chose the business, retailing, before I was firm in my faith. My boss was successful and a man of faith, so there was consistency there. Trammell Crow [his current boss] is a person with strong ethics and is known for that. So it's easy for me to embrace these values in a business context.
>
> And I don't think it's a denomination. It's a philosophy, not a strategy. And I'm fairly convinced you can't be schizophrenic in this regard. If you're going to be ethical with your employees, you'll probably be ethical with your vendors and customers.
>
> Having been a Christian, I couldn't work at a place that didn't share a common value system. From a selfish standpoint, I want to work with people I can trust, respect, and learn from. I believe this is good for business.

The Secularization of Corporate Ethical Beliefs

Carreker's comments are fairly typical of the interviewees' awareness that there are good management reasons for trying to stay consistent with the shared values of a firm. His comments also indicate a widespread belief among the interviewees that in the U.S. there is a common ethical heritage that is not exclusively "Christian" but Christian-dominated. As such, "American" values were expected to present no real conflicts with their own religious values. Among some CEOs this was clearly naïveté. They lived in cities where the dominant culture was strongly colored by Southern Baptist or Methodist traditions, and having started their own businesses, they had never encountered a situation in which an organization's culture was sharply distinguishable from their own personal values. They *were* the organizational culture.

Many interviewees, however, represented very large and diverse corporate populations, and for these the questions of diversity were more pressing. Several interviewees, for example, raised the topic of anti-Semitism, acknowledging its presence among some groups of believers and condemning it.

Though exclusivity was not a major preoccupation, the interviewees did talk about having an obligation to "secularize" Christian ethics in the large corporation. By this they seemed to mean generally suppressing religious language while keeping the essential moral stance of their faith. Tom Phillips, for example, felt that at Raytheon he was obligated to "secularize" the values that are part of his understanding of a Judeo-Christian heritage. Phillips is adamant about not imposing on people's religious choices at work, but he is also adamant about "doing the right thing" as he understands it. To achieve that goal, the company has created a series of videos and ethics seminars about contracting and other dilemmas of the defense business. Religion is not mentioned in these presentations, but ethical principles are.

Similarly, Jim Beré, while chairman of Borg-Warner, established a consistent set of ethical commitments in secularized form. Called "The Beliefs of Borg-Warner," this document, like Johnson & Johnson's Credo, outlines a complex set of commitments to ethical values. Beré told me that he saw this document as a focal point in his push toward less hierarchical (translate *less bullying*) and more accountable management practices. He credited the source of the beliefs to his own Christian belief, but also felt that they were appropriate for a diverse organization for two reasons: (1) they did not use religious language, and (2) they held up to sound management analysis. (Note: In 1979 Johnson & Johnson removed the phrase "with God's grace" from its own Credo.)

For the majority of interviewees, the secularized or privatized assimilation of Christian culture into the business environment is an ongoing concern. CEO Jack Turpin says this:

> I am still learning how to handle my convictions in my own company. It's wrong to impose my Christianity on the whole firm. If I want to say something, they've got to listen, so essentially I've tried just to live it, and not take advantage of my position.
>
> I don't think anyone in the company realized our basic management philosophy was derived from the Bible. Well, the people close to me know it. I call them "the guys down the hall." This is the executive team which really runs the company, and has been with me an average of seventeen years. They know where I'm coming from, no question.

Pat Morley, who does use overtly Christian language in his mission statement (such as a reference to Jesus' command to carry someone's load a second mile), also creates generalized rituals that are quite similar to Christian rituals but that do not directly impose religious practice on employees. For example, he established an enforced "quiet time" between 2:00 and 3:00 P.M. daily in his Orlando office. During that time, staff members at Morley Properties can make and receive phone calls, but they can't talk to each other. The ritual was established as a way of providing time out from the intensely interactive office culture, and came out of a planning retreat. It is obviously similar to a devotional or meditative hour. Offending employees are fined (department heads being the most frequent offenders), and the money collected funds a monthly party. At that event Morley also hands out one hundred dollars to each of three outstanding employees, nominated by their peers for "going the second mile."

So Morley's evangelical orientation to Christian ritual, balanced with the wider diversity of his office place, has a concrete business carryover that makes great sense and that reinforces the economic mission of the company.

So, too, the evangelical CEO's willingness to listen, which in practice often plays a major part on the road to sharing the good news or introducing someone to Jesus, generally reinforces the skills of participative management and an employee relations philosophy of teamwork.

Most interviewees responded to the ethical dilemma of being unjustly exclusive versus maintaining a culture consistent with Christian values not by agonizing over fairness toward others, but rather by focusing on their *own* choices about where to work and how to deal with diversity in their own relationships. This interviewee's comments reflected the approach of many when he spoke of creating a consistent *values environment* through his own character and leadership:

> I've always worked in an ethical place. I've always been willing to lose a battle if I thought the cost of winning too high. What happens is, pretty soon people understand you and you don't get placed into a predicament. You have to send a signal and then people respect it.
>
> More often than not, if you run up against severe ethical tests from the people around you, you've put yourself there, and you can correct it.

Max De Pree also understood diversity to have an environmental aspect, which he described in spacial terms. Diversity is not so much a matter of adopting the values of others as it is of giving them space to be who they are. Characteristically, the concept of giving space to others was integrated into De Pree's private faith, his family life, and his employee relations:

> I suggest managers should learn how in their own minds and in the way they practice their relationships to understand what it means to give another person space to be who they are. We are different in many other ways besides Christian and non-Christian.
>
> Years ago I read Henri Nouwen's *Clowning in Rome,* and I was particularly struck by his discussion of the celibacy of the priesthood. I grew up isolated in a Protestant town, and I had always understood celibacy as simply sexual restraint. But Nouwen talks about celibacy really being about giving space to God in your life.
>
> So you also have to give God space. Then I got to thinking, Doesn't that apply to leadership? It applies very clearly; it is one of a whole series of gifts that leaders owe.
>
> When I think, What do I need in the secular environment of business?, I need people to give me space as a Christian in a secular environment. So

if I need that, then I owe it as well. That would be one of the things to work at, how to give people space for who they are.

Then you have a right to expect it for yourself too.

I asked De Pree if he had ever worked for "secular people" and if that was relevant to his understanding of space. He harkened back to his experiences in the army, when he was quite young: "I wasn't given the space to be a Christian lots of the time."

Three Ways of Witnessing

De Pree's comments introduce one of the most difficult responsibilities of the seeking CEO: the obligation to bear witness. As Dietrich Bonhoeffer wrote in his famous letter from prison, "How do we speak of God without religion? . . . How do we speak of God in a secular fashion?"[5] The evangelical takes witnessing very seriously, and the speaking of God quite literally. Jesus said, "Whoever acknowledges me before men, I will also acknowledge him before my Father in heaven" (Matt. 10:32, NIV).

Where and how should such acknowledgment take place? What level of overt witnessing is appropriate in the space of an office? When does Christian commitment from the chief executive constitute an unfair use of space, and when is it a duty not to be denied simply because the business culture frowns on it?

All the interviewees felt that they bore witness in some way in their working life, but the ways in which they deliberately affected the business culture fell into three categories of responses:

1. Overt, institutionalized witnessing through the use of the language, rituals, and symbols of Christianity
2. Overt but personalized witnessing
3. Indirect or passive witnessing

Response 1: Overt Witnessing

The first type of response, overt witnessing, was represented by a small but powerful minority of interviewees. ServiceMaster, whose very name speaks of religious commitment, would be the most frequently cited representative. ServiceMaster offers employees many opportunities to participate in Christian rituals, from attendance at an on-site chapel to sponsoring morning prayer sessions during Lent. Needless to say, these choices are controversial. Some interviewees were very concerned that such sponsorship impinged on employees' constitutionally guaranteed religious freedom. They felt that even though the practices were voluntary, the fact that top management sponsored them put undo pressure on employees to conform.

What was not in doubt, however, was top management's intention. (Ken Wessner, ServiceMaster's former chairman, was frequently suggested to me as the "perfect" person to interview—a pillar of the evangelical business community.) Moreover, the location of the firm—very near to Wheaton College in Illinois—sets it in a strongly evangelical community. As ServiceMaster moves into other cities, such as Boston, the name stays the same, the commitment to service stays the same, but employees may be less exposed to the Christian connection.

Interestingly, several interviewees were very hard on believers who were overt about their Christianity during business *transactions*. Several suggested that there was an inverse relationship between religiosity and honesty in business, as illustrated in Mark Twain's comment, "When you encounter a man who advertises his honesty, keep your hands on your wallet!" Said one interviewee:

> I'm nervous about people who wear their faith on their sleeves. In general, my experience with those people has been so bad.
> But you shouldn't generalize. Maybe they've been so wounded and scarred up that they're desperate to know Christ, and so they push it.

This kind of suspicion reflects a larger belief that true Christianity brings a calmness of character, a belief that has already been expressed several times in this book. Said one interviewee concerning the "pushy" Christian businessperson:

> You have to be more at ease. Christ was so balanced. He was never off

guard or ill at ease. Standing before Pontius Pilate and never even answering the charges. It drove [Pilate] nuts.

Some believers feel the need to be very overt about their commitment in order to make a dent in the secular orientation of the business culture. One CEO, whose name is disguised here, considered putting an add in *Fortune* that would run like this:

> Does Bill Jones only care about business?
> No. He's committed to Jesus.

"Jones" reported that all of his friends advised against this tactic on the grounds that it would be offensive—perhaps even to Jesus. He still regrets, however, that he listened to them.

Assimilation with the business culture has historically occurred most easily when the economy is booming. In times of rapid economic growth, justifiers have a field day with the claim that "religion pays." (So do junk-bond sellers, visioning trainers, and a variety of other evangelists.)

While complete assimilation—or co-option—of the concept of Jesus into the business culture may seem ridiculous today, a certain metaphor was adopted by several companies: God is chairman of the board. Though not legally binding, the cultural power of this image is immense. It also incites great controversy among interviewees. For those who use such a phrase in their business literature, the image stands for commitment to the nonfinancial goals of Christianity as well as to financial purposes. Others see it as an exploitative suggestion of endorsement. Scoffed one:

> Lots of people are going into business for God. That's ridiculous. No one says God ran my business when it goes bankrupt.
> I remember someone telling me that the SEC [Securities and Exchange Commission] ought to investigate him. God was on his board and that gave him unfair advantage. That man's stock went from 60 to 1. Now God must have missed a meeting or two. That is pure superstition. It's bribing God.

Another interviewee objected to holding devotions at the office:

There are a lot of kooks out there. And they're most militant about their Christian culture. They tithe and put up verses out of superstition.

Take devotions. You should not allow devotions on the premises until you've proved your business is better than average, and then it's a perk, a badge of honor.

One interviewee suggested that some managers hid behind religious language and symbols to make up for a lack of preparation. In defense of devotions, however, Ed Yates reports that his employees themselves instigated the practice of having a devotional for five minutes every morning. Yates welcomed the suggestion but insisted that it be a true devotional, which included the word of God and "not just a pretty story." He also gave all of his managers Fred Smith's book, *You and Your Network,*[6] which he described as "a book that makes good business sense . . . a good common sense book." The book is indeed a wonderful compendium of anecdotes about choices that successful businesspeople have made—especially Smith's own mentor, Maxey Jarman, head of Genesco. The book also pays ample attention to prayer and religious faith.

Yates decorates his place of business with some religious symbols. A crèche is put up in the cafeterias at Christmas, but not a cross at Easter, although resurrection lilies are displayed. Verses from the Bible also appear, and according to Yates, he has received very little criticism, because "we don't jam it down their throats; we present it as an option." What particularly incenses him, however, are the secularizations of Christian holidays in which most businesses engage for commercial purposes. Easter bunnies and eggs are never part of the decor.

Interestingly, some familiar traditions in Christian culture are not applied at work by anyone. No one, for example, absolutely forbade doing business on Sunday. Some offices were closed, but managers were allowed to travel on Sundays to business destinations. Yates confessed that early in his business he closed the cafeterias on Sunday so that he could teach Sunday school, but as he came to realize that Sunday was not the original Sabbath, he changed his practice. Other interviewees said that they tried to avoid having people work on Sundays but that they frequently found their managers having to travel on the Sabbath. At the same time, special meetings held on weekends—such as management retreats—featured some short lay service on Sunday morning.

As I reviewed the reports of these decisions, it became apparent that interviewees frame their choices about assimilating Christian ritual into work in terms of whether or not to *include* Christian practices. The choice of *excluding* business practices on the basis of religious rituals is less articulated.

"Joe Beck" also heads a company overtly dedicated to Christ. The company was founded on Romans 12:11: "Not lagging in diligence, fervent in spirit, serving the Lord." The verse is posted on the walls throughout the office. Beck feels it is "easier" to be among people who share the same beliefs, and would extend the same choice to all businesspeople:

> If I was a Jewish company, and I felt I could relate better to Jews, I don't think there's anything wrong with it. I don't think there's anything wrong with being selective, pursuing certain ideals in keeping with your church. So long as individual rights aren't infringed: female, black, that sort of thing.

While Beck has been isolated so far from criticisms of infringing on other people's rights, he is finding that as his business grows, diversity inevitably creeps in and it is harder now to feel comfortable about a completely overt Christian culture. His solution has been to "keep it low key" —in his eyes.

Response 2: Personalized Witnessing

For those interviewees who were disturbed by the ethical implications of the unfair use of power to influence employees' religious choices, or whose companies are simply too large to remain isolated from mainstream cultural forces, the obligation to bear witness is more often relegated to the personal arena. Ironically, though this second kind of response is meant to accommodate religious diversity, in many ways it can seem more coercive to employees who are not expecting the Christian orientation of their boss. I vividly remember an embittered executive who, when he heard of this study, railed against all evangelical CEOs because his own boss had, on several occasions, taken the opportunity of "selling" his evangelicalism during a moment when they were working particularly closely together on a business project. The man was a devout Roman Catholic and interpreted such witnessing as a personal criticism of his own religion. He resented the fact that he could say little in response without jeopardizing his job.

Participants tend to "disguise" their Christianity to varying degrees, especially depending on the context. Several who are very active in the evangelical community said that they are not even known by their own employees to be evangelical. Many interviewees try to keep their witness "low key" by creating passive opportunities to express their faith. Some keep Bibles on their desks or have religious pictures in their private offices but said they would speak about their faith only if asked.

Many of the religious symbols at the office place— the Bible on the desk, or a pin showing support for a Christian organization—are passive ways of inviting questions. A key feature of being a witness is the willingness to explain how one's faith works and to share personal experiences. Being prepared is important. Asserted former Secretary of State Jim Baker at the 1991 National Prayer Breakfast:

> I really do believe that those of us who are put in positions of public trust really shouldn't be hesitant to speak about spiritual values. In fact, I happen to believe that spiritual values are important in the pursuit of world peace.

Baker's assertion poses a very real quandary for nonexclusionary evangelical CEOs. On the one hand, their Christian duty clearly calls them to bear witness, and as leaders, they have the social status to make that witness a powerful statement. On the other hand, if they direct such witness at their employees, they may be unfairly exploiting their power. Reasoning from a "Do unto others" point of view, several interviewees acknowledged that they would find it extremely uncomfortable if they were confronted with a statement of faith by a boss who was a fervent Zen Buddhist.

A frequent practice is the ritual of dedication for a CEO's private office. A lay preacher or pastor dedicates the space to the glory of God in a private prayer service. Such rituals serve as concrete reminders that the evangelical CEO's first priority is God, and as such they help the CEO to consciously assimilate a Christian perspective into his or her work life.

For the new evangelical, however, assimilation must work both ways. The orthodox retreat from modern life that characterizes more conservative sects is *not* embraced by this group. Several interviewees suggested that while the assimilation of Christian rituals at work is an important question for the evangelical, an equally important question is the assimilation of business reality into the church's language and perspective. Jack Feldballe, for example, felt himself very fortunate to know a member of the clergy who would actually visit his office from time to time: "He would take an interest, and actually visited my workplace and found out what I did, and had an understanding of what we're facing."

Tom Jones, former head of Epsilon, reflected on the CEO's power to shape values, and called it a luxury:

> There's a luxury involved in being at the top. I can send any signal I want. I can say it's OK to be Christian. People with less power in the organization have more trouble doing that. It might affect their position. But witnessing, however you choose to do it, is also a responsibility that comes with the position.

Jim Carreker, whose own evangelism is a strong part of his life, also appreciated the special power to bear witness that being a CEO gave him:

> When you're in a leadership position, people seek out your standards. You establish a kind of comfort zone.
>
> I probably would have made a terrible minister. I've counseled a lot of people not to go into ministry. Some people are just not going to hear the word from a paid professional. They need to hear it from somebody who shares their world.

While Carreker has a very active witness, he is much less overt and more "assimilated" with a pluralistic culture at work. Nonetheless, his Christian social beliefs pose a constant conflict with the larger culture and the basics of consumerism on which his business success is largely based:

Some people think it's hard to be strong in your faith and be in such a worldly job. Retailing is very contemporary. You have to be up to date with styles; it's your job to be an authority on the current materialism of the day. The hotel business is similar. You have to provide people with an experience that represents the current style of the day.

We always walk a fine line between staying in pace with style and not being offensive. For example, Burdine's sold all types of lingerie, but I never allowed it to get distasteful in print. Our catalogues and newspaper ads were tasteful.

If the consumerism of capitalism puts pressure on Carreker's social values, the tremendous diversity of capitalism's markets helps him find a business solution consistent with his values:

So we said we would be a family store, and we wanted to make a place that was comfortable for the whole family to shop. Now I saw that as good business. As a result, Burdine's had a good but not a great lingerie business; there were several competitors doing better. But in the whole context, I felt this was the right decision.

You have to interpret where you're comfortable in all the lifestyles.

Ed Elliott, president of Domain Communications, does not in his opinion run an "overtly Christian business." Domain's logo is a four-leaf flame, which remotely suggests a cross in the minds of the managers but is not recognizably a religious symbol to outsiders. Said Ed, "Our logo is not obviously a cross, but we wanted something that reflected who we were in terms of our faith, *and to give us the opportunity to talk about it from time to time.*"

Being prepared to talk about faith is an important part of the evangelical obligation, and the quiet symbols of personal faith are deliberately placed to invite questions. Many interviewees shared stories of troubled employees who asked about the Bible on the desk and subsequently were introduced to Jesus. Ed Yates told of how a female employee came to tell him she had a serious health problem. He responded by saying, "I'll certainly pray about that." Yates pointed out that his choice of words was very careful:

I could have said, "I think you should become a Christian." But saying "I'll pray for you" said something about my belief without infringing on her privacy. Maybe she will be interested in asking me about it. Maybe not.

Yates was extremely sensitive to the possibility of exploiting his position or the employee's helplessness to the cause of proselytizing. This is a constant tension for those who have overcome the normal taboos about never discussing one's private religious commitments at work.

Some of the examples most frequently given to me of "faith making a difference at work" involved counseling an employee about marriage troubles. Many interviewees, when asked how their faith affected their work, told of going out of their way to counsel a secretary or colleague on a family problem. Such events are a staple of the witnessing experience. CEO Bob Slocum comments on this practical side of evangelicalism in his book *Ordinary Christians in a High-Tech World:* "I give a high score to those who can get across exactly how their faith worked in such a practical way that I could understand and use it myself."[7]

Slocum reports how when he was at a large manufacturing company, the manufacturing manager of his department told him that he and his wife had separated the night before. Up until that time, Slocum had not even known that the fellow, Jim (not his real name), was married. He shut the door and listened to Jim pour out his story of a messed-up marriage. Slocum describes his response to Jim as follows:

> I got up my courage and finally said, "Jim, if you and Joan want to put this marriage back together, I believe there are spiritual and technical re-sources available to help you do it." Then I sat there in an awkward si-lence, wondering if Jim thought I was some kind of fool.
> He finally leaned forward and looked me in the eye. "I'm not a relig-ious person, but last night I got down on my knees and said, 'God, if you are out there and care, I could sure use some help.'"

Slocum put Jim and his wife in touch with a Christian marriage counselor, and they subsequently joined a small Bible group. After three weeks, Jim approached Slocum at work and asked him what he thought commitment to Christ meant. As they talked, Slocum realized that Jim felt he could not "commit" until he had identified all his problems and confessed his guilt and vowed to sin no more.

Said Slocum, "If you can do all that on your own, what do you need Christ for?" According to Slocum, "That night, Jim and Joan got on their knees together and committed their lives and their marriage to Jesus Christ." [8]

I found that such stories are more likely to occur in the Southern Baptist culture of Dallas than in Boston, but the willingness to overtly discuss one's personal commitment to Christ is strong in the Northeast as well. One of Tom Phillips's Raytheon associates, who is Jewish, happened to tell me the following story—a wonderful illustration of the perceived noninvasiveness of Phillips's approach:

> We were having a great deal of difficulty about a contract we were bidding for. It required many changes, and no one knew exactly how much we should put the company on the line. I was personally very worried about winning it. We were at a small meeting, discussing the contract, and Tom Phillips said quietly, "I prayed last night about this contract, and I feel good about it. I think we're doing the right thing. I think it's going to come out OK."
>
> Now I was really impressed, and really admired him for being honest about where he was coming from. You knew what he stood for.

The Christian obligation to be a faithful witness obviously has the potential for creating a kind of moral self-consciousness in the believer. Many interviewees spoke of how important it is to be a good role model and not give Christ a bad name. Commented Charles Olcott on his role as CEO:

> People are watching to see whether or not you are living a Christ-centered existence, in and out of the workplace.

Another interviewee, Dennis Sheehan, observed:

> What you say as CEO is like a lead shot. It drops right to the bottom of the organization. You have to be careful that you are not misinterpreted.

One group of interviewees suggested that image was an important part of witnessing. In their discussion of this theme, it became clear how far from a literal, longstanding biblical tradition the concept of Jesus has evolved to assimilate modern custom:

Paul said we are in the world but need to be transformed. It strikes me that you have to recognize that image is important to men. A good friend of mine is a governor, and he asked me to help him run for reelection. It's all image. To be successful you have to look successful. Jesus said be wise as a serpent and harmless as a dove.

Another interviewee reported that he had considered simplifying his lifestyle but had rejected the idea because his image of being part of the power elite reinforced his ability to witness among his peers.

I asked how passively or actively businesspeople should bring up their spiritual lives to nonbelievers. Would they, for example, mention the role of prayer in their decision making?

Some felt not, arguing they would be "natural" (unobtrusive) about it, but as the disciple Peter advised, they would always be ready to give an answer if someone asks.

Fred Smith, who was perhaps the interviewee who felt most strongly against overtly associating any normal part of business very closely with Christ, drew a sharp distinction between being a good Christian (Christ in you) and being an imitation of Christ in one's desire to be a role model:

> I could no more bring a model of Christ into the corporation than I could fly. I can bring the spirit of truth. I can take the scriptural principles. But when someone says, "What would Jesus do?" my imagination isn't that good.

The role of the model Christian is an important one to many of those interviewed, and once again the understanding of Christian mission has a beneficial economic side effect: clients trust the genuinely ethical businessperson. As one interviewee commented:

> Most of my clients are Jews. That's interesting. Why do they work with me? Because they think I'm really honest. I've found that in business, trying to be honest, having the Lord on your sleeve a bit, not showing off, you've got to watch it, but you get respect and it has never hurt business.

Charles Babcock of King Charter Company in Miami reported that wearing your Christian ethics on your sleeve in a different

business environment can be helpful in staving off temptations down
the road:

> You get to be known as the person who doesn't take bribes or give them.
> In all the years I've done real estate only one county commissioner asked
> me for a bribe, which is unusual. They know it won't work.

Response 3: Indirect or Passive Witnessing

For other CEOs, the whole question of *being* a moral person,
versus talking about it, is at the heart of the evangelical mission. When
a younger CEO asked Digital Equipment's Ken Olsen how to be
Christian, he is said to have responded, "Don't just do the right
things, do *the* right thing." (In keeping with his alleged belief in only
private acknowledgments of faith, Olsen would not agree to an
interview even though his name was recommended by at least 30
percent of those interviewed.)

Tom Jones draws a distinction between his private life, where
he feels he has more overt responsibilities as a Christian, and his role
as CEO. For him, management consultant Tom Peters's theories, as
put forth in *In Search of Excellence,*[9] provide the secular translation of
Christian values for the workplace:

> I'm excited because Peters gave me a mechanism that allowed that to hap-
> pen in this company. You don't see it spiraling toward something self-in-
> dulgent, but I see people doing something selfless, and they just feel it's
> right and know it's right. You motivate the feeling of rightness.

Such motivations come full circle for the evangelical CEO.
They make moral sense, and they make money.

Frank Butler worried aloud about the dangers of secularizing
the message, because he felt that it might water down the basic
message of Christianity:

> The problem is, you take a Tom Peters philosophy, and it's all very appeal-
> ing and makes sense—up to a certain point. But it doesn't cause people to
> share the tough things.
> All that is the warm fuzzy part. The tough part is, as I see it, that at the

core of my faith understanding, there is a dominant consciousness and cul-ture, and you try and live an alternative at a cost, at a price. The paradigm of Jesus' life is that he ended up on a cross. And we get into trouble when people have false expectations, if you leave it with the moral comforts of selflessness. We have to prepare people for the fact that there is broken-ness; we have to keep expectations real. There will be debts, failures, and other things, and in that paradigm these things aren't fatal. Failure is not terminal. That's the stuff of new life.

Threats of Co-option

While the choices of religious practice and the use of religious language at work are important ways of reinforcing the cultural context of Christian faith, these are only outward symbols. What is really at stake here is the secular culture's assault on the evangelical CEO's *inner* point of view—the very structure of his or her thought.

This is not just a case of sliding down the slippery slope of tolerated sins (first the mixed luncheon group, next the racy ad, and finally open adultery in the corporate headquarters). Nor is it a mere suppression of symbolic religious culture (not mentioning Jesus without embarrassment). Rather, it is the extent to which the ration-alized, scientific thought process of postindustrial society dilutes the evangelical's sense of the supernatural: the mystery, the miracle, the irreducible existence of God and the Trinity. You cannot boil these things down to a safe, neutral abstract expression such as *love,* without losing the force of faith.

On the other hand, many evangelicals are, of course, quite familiar with a scientific point of view. And far from rejecting it, they are often conversant with it. They seek to somehow integrate scientific reasoning without abandoning their sense of the supernatural or their emotions.

The common sense "show-me" empiricism of early modern thought is revealed in the attitudes of the interviewees toward business. Even with regard to Christian ways of thinking, several interviewees in my group may have been expressing the integrating viewpoint I have suggested when they talked about "the inescapable logic of Christ." All of them, by being highly educated, and by depending on sophisticated techniques of financial analysis, certainly reflect the scientific point of view in their own structure of thought, and yet they sustain a sense of the more intuitive, relational, and sacred aspects of work.

This integration, however, is not without conflict. For the evangelical CEO the paradoxical tension between economic rationality and instinctive spirituality can be as subtle as it is pervasive. Thinking like a businessperson is to think like both a Protestant and an atheist. The difference is not in rationality itself, but in the maintenance of a personal relationship with Christ. The latter rests on the nonrational aspects of the evangelical worldview. While these aspects have often stimulated evangelical CEOs to find creative solutions for employee and market problems, explicitly acknowledging the source of these faculties turns many businesspeople off. Therefore, the CEOs tend to disguise their faith in the rational language of business problem solving. In so doing, however, they can be easily co-opted into the secular culture.

Max De Pree was keenly aware of the subtlety of the co-option process that his ability to be successful in business unwillingly invited:

> One of the problems of going from being Christian to being in a secular context is there is a reasonable temptation to adopt a secular standard. It happens without thinking about it. Unless somebody articulates something different, you are going to adopt a secular standard without even thinking about it.
>
> Who gets to articulate what it is you're talking about? If you are talking to a group of Christians, the question is, To whom am I accountable in the end? Now that changes all your FASB [Federal Accounting Standards Board] rules and everything else. It changes your approach away from legal to human resources management.
>
> The question is not, Am I being successful? It is, Am I being faithful?

De Pree's remarks sound a clear warning: Unless you are on your guard, secularity will inevitably shift your thinking. As Charles Olcott reflected on leaving his position at Burger King:

> We have to keep reminding ourselves of these things [that it is important to pay attention to the moral tone of the culture around you]. We have to recharge our spiritual batteries regularly. You are never free from secular influence in the culture around you. You have a choice on how you will conduct yourself, every minute.
>
> I was surprised when I left Burger King to see, despite earnest efforts to

create a more Christ-centered lifestyle, how much a part of the culture I was trying to change.

Prayer

Prayer is the first and best bulwark of the faithful against the secularity of language and thought in business. Most if not all of the men I interviewed pray regularly and also belong to prayer groups. Jim Kubik commented on the importance of prayer:

> Keeping [faith and an ability to work effectively within a secular business culture] in balance is not easy at work. The only chance of keeping in balance is to have a victory a day. Somehow you must be able to be emotionally involved with God, spend some time with God.

Kubik reports that it took him three years to discipline himself to take this time and use it faithfully. A friend helped him learn to take "quiet time." Kubik still finds it very difficult to do this at the office, so he begins each day with a prayer. Jim bases his prayer time on that of Daniel, who stopped to pray three times a day. To keep his mind from drifting in prayer, he writes his thoughts down. Then he spends some time reading the Bible, using a "daily Bible," which selects passages for each day. Other interviewees said they are in the habit of reading one chapter of Proverbs each day (the book of Proverbs is divided into thirty-one chapters—one for each day of the month) or using a pocket Bible to study a variety of Scriptures.

For most evangelicals the study of Scripture is an important part of devotional time. So is the importance of participating in the fellowship of like-minded Christians, as I've already mentioned.

The crucial role of prayer and devotions serves not only to reinforce and revitalize the faith of evangelical CEOs. It also frequently helps them refocus their perspectives in ways that benefit their businesses. Dick Crowell, formerly at The Boston Company, reflected on how many times he had not known what to do at work, and was worried, but prayed about it "and something favorable happened." He does not explain this in terms of a prosperity gospel, but rather as regaining and reaffirming the right perspective:

> This is partly a reaffirmation of faith, partly a reaffirmation of the more di-

vine principle that one ought to have faith and not worry, and also it gives
you the attitude of service.

Crowell acknowledges that the service attitude has directly
benefited his relationships with clients.

Ed Williamson, president of Williamson Cadillac Company in
Miami, told this moving story of just how prayer affects his business
thinking:

> I have needs, too. And sometimes I get bored with the answers in church.
> My wife gets annoyed [with me]. But I do get more solutions [in church]
> about how to interact with people. . . . I get an awful lot of answers sitting
> in the pew. That's my main right-brain time.
>
> For example, a number of years ago there was a friend in this business,
> our nearest competitor, and he sold his company to a [hesitates]—a per-
> son with very poor business ethics.
>
> It made life frustrating for us. They were really shifting the balance, en-
> gaging in a number of unethical business practices. And they definitely
> took market share. They proceeded to do business in ways we thought
> were unethical, and it really made us mad.
>
> The problem was that anger was affecting the way I thought. It was
> making me start to think about changing the way *we* were doing business.
>
> Finally, over the course of a couple of Sundays sitting there [in
> church], I decided that I couldn't let that affect me that way. That prob-
> ably God wanted to make me think about the way *I* was doing business—
> maybe to set an example that I had forgotten, something to judge my
> business against. So he had given me in this other person's behavior exam-
> ples I could go to my people with.
>
> I told my employees, "Now tell our customers they really have some-
> thing to judge us by."

The late Steve Waters, former president of Miami Savings Bank,
was listening to this account, and nodded knowingly: "Well, that's
an attitude of love—turning the other cheek."

Williamson's story serves as a good example of how prayer helps
the evangelical CEO to integrate and creatively deal with tensions
between Christian ethics and some secular business practices. But it
does more than that. It also reveals how the evangelical's view of
business problems is intimately colored by a sense of God's involvement in the little details. Williamson's meditations did not just give
him an insight into Christian ethics, but created an awareness in him
of God's hand being directly in the marketplace. Peter Berger's

explanation of the traditional function of religion (quoted at the beginning of this chapter) is reaffirmed here: Williamson's faith has a "world-building potency" to affect not only a qualitative change of attitude but even his understanding of the basic ground rules of competitive behavior.

This faith once again stimulates a positive economic outcome even as it defies typical competitive norms—a paradoxical belief generally supported by the interviewees. Once faith changed Williamson's *attitude* it stimulated a rational competitive response: tell the customers about your competitive advantages instead of lowering your own business standards.

Elmer Johnson, former executive vice president of General Motors and senior partner of the Kirkland & Ellis law firm, in reflecting on the role of faith for the conservative Protestant actively engaged in business, repeated a familiar pattern of thought among interviewees: He stressed the utilitarian aspect of faith and then subordinated this aspect to Christianity's capacity to motivate personal virtue:

> When you talk to people running large organizations, they recognize early on that it [business] is not just utilitarian based. The best have very high ideals. So it's not hard for them to think about how to communicate these ideals so that others come to share their vision.
>
> Now not all the people that have this vision are highly religious, but I feel that being religious assures that you don't just rely on moral reasons [but] that your affections are driving you.

Johnson's observation led him back to the problem posed at the beginning of this chapter: the integration of faith by a professing Christian into the radically different cultural milieu of business. Does one become an insider, an outsider, or both?

In reflecting on this problem, Johnson highlighted yet another dilemma raised by the modern context in which the evangelical operates: The open displays of evangelicalism within our culture have themselves been so perverted by ministers of the mass media that any attempt to assimilate traditional evangelicalism is itself open to charges of bastardization and blasphemy. This is the final irony of the seventh tension—that neither the disguise and compartmentalization of one's faith nor a defiantly "different" religious attitude work as integrating solutions. Remarked Johnson:

> If you flaunt your religion, it has lost its power in your life. On the other hand, you don't really hide it, because it's too integral. It's the foundation of everything.

Clearly, the seekers, who by definition take both their business and their faith seriously, have more cultural negotiating ahead.

CHAPTER

11
Conclusions

T he question originally posed in
this book is profoundly simple:
Does faith make a difference in the successful evangelical's business thinking?

Pursuing this question and evaluat-
ing the interviewees' statements invites us
to reexplore the age-old question of the
relationship between spirituality and the
events of the real world. The findings reported in this book suggest that the evangelical business elites do indeed express a
profound connection between faith and
economic activity, but that in so doing they
are in a very delicate position. They must
maintain a traditional biblical view of the
world while participating in the modern

In Puritan religious
thought there was origi-
nally a dynamic equi-
poise between two
opposite thrusts, and
tension between an in-
ward, mystical, per-
sonal experience of
God's grace and the de-
mands for an outward,
sober, socially responsi-
ble ethic, the tension between faith and works,
between the essence of
religion and its outward
show. Tremendous en-
ergy went into sustain-
ing these polarities in
early years, but as the
original piety wanted, itself undermined by the
worldly success that
benefitted from the doc-
trine of the calling, the
synthesis split in two.
—John William Ward[1]

culture of the corporation. Rather than constructing an invisible wall
between the two, the evangelical's faith has the capacity to reconcile
these two factors and to make them applicable to each other.

However, they are still opposing forces rather than wholly
complementary ones—even though a justifier might call them
complementary. I believe that the resulting tensions have a powerful potential for creating economic and spiritual activity. It is as
if the new evangelical businessperson is poised on an energy point
that depends on his or her ability to maintain some distance—but
not too much distance—between the opposing forces of faith and
business.

To return to the analogy of the bow, if the evangelical's faith and economic thinking are too close, they will collapse on each other, and a secular, wholly rationalized mind-set will result. Too far apart, however—as in a completely privatized faith—and the bowstring becomes slack. Faith is no longer energetic in the economic world.

Throughout this book, I have tried to show that evangelicalism, *as represented by the worldviews and practices of the CEOs I interviewed,* is regularly the source of creative action as it stands poised between the tensions of the real world and spiritual commitment. The CEOs I interviewed represent a new elite among evangelicals: the business elite. They are well educated and are prepared for life outside the ministry; they are also successful in the material world.

Though it is beyond the capacity of this book to provide evidence that might fully explain the differences between their worldview and performance and those of most evangelicals, I would hazard a guess that the primary explanation lies in the recent growth of the evangelical community itself. Spanning more and more denominations, evangelicalism is drawing on new blood. The mind-set of this newer community is being influenced by a less traditional (and less rigid) *cultural* code, and yet the conservatism of evangelicalism—its biblical orientation and traditional social values—are being embraced by this group.

Do the CEOs really live up to their words? As I said at the beginning of this book, I conducted these interviews with the CEOs themselves. The factors of time and trust prevented firsthand observation within each company. But three other tests of reality were possible: (1) the ability of the interviewees to provide concrete, consistent examples, (2) the general reputations of their companies as reported in the media, and (3) the remarks of other businesspeople about the interviewees.

Two or three people were so extreme in their generalist views, or their company reputations were so controversial, that I did not include their remarks in this book. The absence of the name of an interviewee, however, does not indicate that he belongs to this group. Either that person requested anonymity or his comments were quite similar to those of another interviewee and were not included because of limitations on the length of the book.

My main concern here is not to explain every factor in interviewees' businesses or their overall economic performance. It has been to understand how evangelicalism influences these leaders in the ways they manage their businesses and in the ways they understand what it means to be a business leader. In tracing that connection between faith and work, I uncovered two important ironies.

The foremost irony is that the chief attributes of the Protestant ethic that Max Weber identified as significant factors in the rise of capitalism are *not the distinguishing features* of the seekers' approach to economics and management. Today the traditional values of the Protestant work ethic—frugality, discipline, the obligation to one's job, mental concentration, cool self-control, rational calculation, and planning—can be found among any workaholic group, whether it is atheist, Roman Catholic, Jewish, or liberal Protestant. As Weber himself predicted, once capitalism took off, the spiritual values would be easily secularized.[2]

What is even more ironic is that some of the main features of traditional conservative Protestantism would today be regarded as economically *counterproductive.* The old-style, highly standardized patriarchal techniques of early modern management, which are rigidly planned and executed, are ill suited to current economic environments. To the degree that the Protestant work culture supported rigid routine, authoritarianism, and inflexibly crafted planning, Protestant values are more likely to *restrain* competitiveness. Top-heavy, hierarchical management teams such as those in the American automobile industry in the 1950s to 1980s have proved to be unresponsive to changes in the marketplace. Similarly, extremely scientific, rational approaches to markets and to debt, as seen in the financial markets, have turned out in many cases to be poor predictors of what would truly be successful value creation in business.

There is no question that the traditional Protestant values remain an important part of the interviewees' general mind-set. They have not abandoned hard work, self-restraint, and discipline as business musts. However, these values have been radically modified and rearranged in the overall evangelical worldview. Nineteenth-century evangelicalism introduced a very un-Calvinistic intensity of emotion and relational outlook that has had a significant and productive influence on these men's approach to business. The new evangelical elite have not abandoned conservative Protestantism in their approach to business. They have, to a degree, abandoned Weber's Calvinstic Protestant ethic. But they have also abandoned the monklike withdrawal from earthly concerns that characterized early Baptist movements.

The new evangelicals in business are like neither the traditional Baptists nor the Calvinists. Their assimilation of classical conservative Protestant values with the emotional, personal aspects of evangelicalism has resulted in a new leadership framework for managing the corporation.

The Significance of the Evangelical Worldview

The sample of interviewees was too diverse and numerous to suggest a full blown "theory." But the common strand, their spiritual outlook, does provide a *worldview* that I have suggested influences their entire approach to business and to their own careers. Most significantly, this worldview seems to stimulate and provide support for the same business solutions that are being advocated as the most challenging concepts in management today: quality, spirit, relationships, the empowerment of all individuals, and the expectation of fluctuating performance over the long term. These are resounding themes in the latest management theories, from those of Charles Handy to those of Tom Peters. A passage from Peter Senge's popular book on learning organizations well summarizes many of the characteristics that I have identified in the interviewees' approach to management:

> What can leaders intent on fostering personal mastery do?
> They can work relentlessly to foster a climate in which the principles of personal mastery are practices in daily life. That means building an organization where it is safe for people to create visions, where inquiry and commitment to the truth are the norm, and where challenging the status quo is expected.[3]

Senge lists the following as the chief personal characteristics of successful leadership:

- the ability to integrate reason and intuition,

- the ability to see a connectedness with the world,
- compassion,
- a commitment to the whole,
- a commitment to personal mastery.

We have seen these themes in the interviewees' remarks throughout this book, and I have noted that they are well integrated into the evangelical worldview.

It is the relational, holistic side of the evangelical faith that seems to be the most influential and most distinctive aspect of the seekers' business leadership. They make space for the intuitive and the relational, not only in their personal activities, but in the ways that they encourage employees to relate to each other and to the market-place. This suggests a partial reversal effect—a movement away from the extreme impersonalization of business and its emphasis on technology, and back to the "softer," more domestic values of nurturing people.

So new conservative Protestantism is distinctive not so much for *prompting* entrepreneurism as for *taming it* in ways that still stimulate economic innovation and success. Many of the CEOs I interviewed would have been entrepreneurs no matter what their devotional lives were like. A number of them had committed their lives to Christ *after* achieving significant business success. What changed, however, was their understanding and ability to organize their activity and priorities toward a relational, stewardship approach to leadership.

This change in the Protestant work ethic comes at a time when the *context* for economic success is being radically revised. The change is not just a postindustrial phenomenon; it can be isolated to shifts in economic understanding over just the past several years. The intensely narcissistic pursuit of self-interest, and the rationally im-personal, fast-growth era of takeovers in the 1980s have collapsed. What appeared to be radically conservative ten years ago (manufac-turing, human services, hands-on management, investment in re-search and development, and personal attention to the customer) is now the cutting edge of management theory.

In short, the new configuration of Protestant values that is evident among the evangelicals I interviewed seems to have done a very good job of anticipating many aspects of the new economic order. It may have even larger ramifications for the *world* economic order. As David Martin's extensive study shows, conservative Protestantism has been growing at an explosive rate in Latin America, South Korea, and some parts of Africa.[4] Martin's preliminary work suggests a positive correlation between Protestantism and economic development at the local level. The evangelical CEOs interviewed for this book may be a small minority in mainstream U.S. corporations, but their business views may prove to be highly relevant to economic development overseas. In fact, Billy Graham and other evangelists are reported to be very active in tying their messages to economic development in Eastern Europe and Russia.

Having isolated the economically productive aspects of the evangelical worldview, however, I want to repeat that this ethic does not *automatically* provide the booster rocket to economic success. The operating word in this book has been *tension—creative tension—*and I have pointed out many potential conflicts between the evangelical's Christian values and the demands of business. We have seen that the claims of the spirit and of the bottom line frequently tug in opposing directions. It is only by creatively expanding the context in which such trade-offs are encountered or by reworking the process of value creation to take into account long-term fluctuations that a morally legitimate approach can be found.

A Backward Look at the Two Purposes of This Book

In the Preface of this book I said that I had two purposes. First, I hoped, by extensively interviewing the best of the best, to test the reality of the unproven stereotypes of evangelicals that permeate mass communications in America today. Second, I hoped to stimulate knowledgeable discussions about the role of faith and economics—particularly among Christians.

Testing the Stereotypes

While there are still many issues and contexts to be explored, the set of observations recorded in this book provide ample evidence to dispel the stereotypical image of the evangelical as an intolerant, knee-jerk, superstitious charlatan exploiting others in the name of religion. The evangelical elite described here reveal a depth of wisdom and effective leadership quite unlike the superstitious naïveté that many people assume to be behind the religious language and rituals practiced by evangelicals. While the language and social conservatism of this group tends to alienate some people, the temptation to dismiss this group is ill-considered. What may appear to be mere superstition or pietism is revealed by these interviewees to be a much deeper and more complex sense of the sacred in their daily lives. This awareness and the biblical foundations on which it rests have many practical implications for their business leadership.

The evangelicals can, therefore, claim that faith does indeed *make a difference* and *makes them different.* This raises an extremely problematic issue that can only be posed rather than proved one way or another here. How much does simply "being different" explain their economic performance? Is the evangelical's marginality—like that of many immigrant ethnic groups—the real reason for their economic success? Is it because they are outsiders that they are hard working and economically creative?

The comments in the previous chapter indicate a real self-consciousness about being "different" from the mainstream business culture, and also a desire—unlike many fundamentalists—*not* to be completely marginal. Many interviewees are very careful not to impose the religious view and language of the believer on their employees or to directly expose that view to their customers. Like other outsiders, they can "pass" for insiders, but if you scratch the surface, a very different set of norms emerges for family, for morality, and for their personal goals of business purpose.

This sense of difference is clearly a powerful defense in the struggle of evangelicals to resist what are perceived as immoral developments in modern culture. "Being prepared to talk about Jesus," praying, and voicing a belief in God's grace in connection with business decisions are in themselves acts of rejecting the prevailing culture. But while this outsider identity clearly strengthens their faith, does it contribute to their economic creativity?

My own conclusion is that the *primary* source of creative tension is not culture clash and a sense of belonging, but it is found in the very polarities of work and faith itself. It would be wrong to portray these CEOs as overly aware of having an outsider status. Furthermore, their own remarks identify so many moral tensions that insiders feel as well—work and family, people and profits, ego and personal limit, wealth and positive charity—and it is these that shape their business philosophy.

So I believe that the source of their moral compass, not the basic cultural tensions, makes the biggest difference. This religious outlook, more than the religious culture, gives them a profound sense of *distance* from many of the things on which other businesspeople place ultimate value: profit, steady growth, and personal status. This distance contributes greatly to their ability to take risks and to make rational judgments when the heat is on. They can afford to fail; they can protect themselves from getting too carried away with their own success.

Stimulating Discussion

As for the second purpose of this book, to stimulate discussion, I am equally torn between optimism and pessimism. It is relatively easy for action-oriented businesspeople to fall back on mental states that help deny the tensions described in this book. For the justifiers and generalists, life would indeed be more comfortable if questions about the moral limits of profit-related activities and organizational habits were left unexpressed. Business is a messy arena—materialistic, dog-eat-dog, pluralistic, and quite unlike the spiritual purity of conversion experiences or the emotional intensity of family life. Indeed, the anti-intellectual bias of some evangelicals supports not taking too close a second look at faith in the context of business activity.

But the tendency to deny the existence of moral conflicts in business is not isolated to evangelicals. I am reminded of one study that asked CEOs and ten of their managers how often ethical issues come up for employees.[5] The CEOs guessed about once a year. The managers said anywhere from daily to once a month. The CEOs were wrong by a factor of twelve or more. So the absence of a sense of dilemma on the part of the generalists and justifiers is not particularly surprising.

Furthermore, the moral tensions in business have not historically been a burning topic among organized religions. There is an "economics gap" in religious thought that is evident not only in the scarcity of theoretical material but also in church laity work. Many interviewees complained that their churches did not care about them *as businesspeople*, and that their pastors failed to understand their problems and successes. As Charles Olcott said:

> I believe it is God's will that the leaders of the Church, not just clergy, but all godly men and women, should study what it means to live out Christ in this day. There is not a lot of that going on in the marketplace—even with evangelicals.

Ronald Thiemann, dean of Harvard University's School of Divinity, has expressed a similar view:

> The religious community has to be able to articulate these ideas internally if it is to articulate them in conversation with businesspeople.

I am strongly persuaded from the experience of seekers such as Max De Pree and Jack Willome that dialogue and a sense of struggle are essential to the process of integrating faith and work. The generalist's confidence is thin protection against the moral temptations of business. There are many businesspeople who lie and cheat every day in their business lives and still feel good about themselves. The justifier who assumes that the complementarity of Christianity and capitalistic behavior is obvious is ignoring many signs that capitalism in the 1990s is facing a crisis of moral legitimacy similar to that of the Depression era. From the wealth gap to the leadership gap, American capitalism shows many symptoms of moral disease, and has always done so.

There is always the need for moral self-questioning by business leaders, especially today among devout people who are willing to deal with the difficult "people" questions, as were the CEOs I interviewed. Healing this system will take more than spiritual self-improvement. The evangelical must be willing to direct his or her attention to the complexity of ambiguous choices that are posed by the culture of economic life today. So far, however, the main evangelical public debate has remained doggedly restricted to issues of personal faith, family, and moral education.

I feel optimistic, however, that many aspects of the evangelical worldview make it particularly well suited to *lead* the creation of a moral dialogue about work. The leaders interviewed here have already taken the first steps by refusing to weed out a spiritual orientation from their business environment. Their self-understanding of their role as business leaders is integrated with the concept of being a person of faith. As such, they are indeed believers in business. Also, evangelicalism's strong emphasis on the small detail—its holistic integration of the minor event with the larger kingdom of God—has the potential to move the dialogue beyond meaningless generalizations.

This book invites all of us to acquaint ourselves with the particulars of faith and business. Many who were interviewed, though initially suspicious that I was on a hunting trip and shooting for bear, confessed that they enjoyed probing the particulars. Several asked to meet again. They did not, however, find it easy.

Robert Slocum, in his book *Ordinary Christians in a High-Tech World,* tells of being issued a similar invitation during a consultation with management expert Michael Maccoby. Slocum had been talking at length about the need for heart in the high-tech industry. Maccoby suddenly asked, "What difference has development of HEART made in your own work?" Reports Slocum:

> My mind went blank. I kicked myself for not anticipating that this question would come up and preparing my answer. I fumbled around and came up with something about helping people keep from becoming underemployed in a large corporation. The truth was that in some areas it had made a difference. But I was not prepared to tell my story because I found it difficult to focus on the HEART in the context of my daily work.[6]

Slocum's tongue-tied response is understandable. Reading the comments of the evangelical leaders quoted here is a good way to start loosening tongues. I remember meeting with Allen Morris and Charles Olcott in Miami to share with them my first set of findings.

We were talking about some of the difficulties I had had in eliciting concrete responses. Olcott made an important observation:

> People had a hard time answering because they'd never thought about these things quite this way before. But your questions started them thinking. I'll bet if you returned to these interviewees, they'd now have a lot more to say.

Some interviewees have begun to use the seven creative tensions as a basis for fellowship discussions. For others who are interested in doing the same, the Study Guide at the back of this book can help.

One of the most important discoveries that I made during this research was that people need an example or a metaphor to help them capture the interplay of faith and business. Some kind of shorthand image seems to be essential to keeping the dialogue productive. I suggested the image of Heraclitus's bow to capture the sense of sustained opposition that the very different phenomena of faith and business represent in the lives of seekers. For many interviewees, the creative tension model rang true. As one CEO said, "You should not assume that because you're Christian you're immune from problems." Another comment from Fred Roach is particularly expressive:

> People talk about absolute ethics, but those are principles. That's crazy in the real world. The right word is *tension.*
>
> I myself use the words *secular* and *sacred,* because they are easier for me to identify. You can't keep the two worlds separate and comfortable. The tension goes on in the person.
>
> But it's not that I have a secular responsibility to Weyerhauser and a sacred responsibility to God. I have *a* sacred responsibility in life.

Roach made this remark at a small gathering of believers who had met to discuss the seven creative tensions. The richness and promise of that discussion remain with me. This then, is the challenge of evangelicalism as evidenced in the remarks of participants in this study: to recognize the creative and integrating possibilities of faith even in the hard-nosed world of business.

It is not always easy, however, to find the mediating power of faith. The analysis presented here is offered as one resource among many for this journey. Like all explorations into the unknown, this one involves struggle and persistence. It can only be hoped that the seekers find the grace and strength to keep at it.

Study Guide

The following study guide is intended for use by evangelicals or a general audience. Some questions invite the reader to relate the thoughts in this book to his or her own journey of faith. Other questions are phrased in a more general way so that the book and study guide can be used by business seminar groups that want to discuss the ethics of business. *No part of this study guide may be reproduced, even for use within the church, without permission or purchase of the book.*

Format for a Discussion Group

The study guide is divided into separate sessions to correspond to the chapters in the book. For each session there are four sections that are a resource for discussion:

Part I: A summary of the chief points in the chapter.
Part II: A case for discussion (Chapters 4–10 only).
Part III: Questions about the chapter and case.
Part IV: A selection of Bible passages that have relevance to the issues in the chapter.

I would suggest covering one chapter within each study session, which would imply eleven sessions altogether. The discussion group members should read the chapter before each meeting, and should read a selected Bible passage from the list provided. The questions in the guide can help each person explore the main points of the chapter, but there probably will not be enough time in any one session to cover all of them in depth.

The study guide cases are a particularly good way of getting discussion started. Participants should search their own values and experiences for guidance, but the wealth of observations from the interviewees in this book can also be used as a basis for discussion.

Thoughts on the Discussion Process

As I learned from the interviews, many CEOs receive their strongest spiritual support either from peers who share the same responsibilities and problems or from their spouses. In their experience, the dialogue of faith is most easily extended among people who understand the context and pressures under which they operate.

Many evangelical CEOs voiced a disappointment that their clergy have not been very involved in such a dialogue. They felt that the clergy were unable to acknowledge the legitimacy of their roles as businesspeople or to see that the problems of business go beyond financial accountability.

This book is intended to help bridge that communication gap. I hope that its readers will be better able to understand the many practical and moral issues that evangelical business leaders face every day. The questions in this Study Guide help tease out concrete, day-to-day examples of creative tension in business that the reader (or spouse of the reader) encounters in his or her own career.

These are not just CEO problems, or even just evangelical problems. They are endemic to the business environment and are encountered by every manager. They, their clergy, their spouses, and their colleagues play an essential role in the understanding of how such events both affect and are affected by faith.

Session 1
Who Are the Evangelicals?

(Chapter 1)

Summary

Chapter 1 suggests that evangelicalism is a growing but often misunderstood religion in America. Even though evangelicals can be found in all denominations, there are four common aspects of an evangelical's faith portrait: prayerful, personal, relational, and intensifying. These aspects color the way in which evangelicals approach all of life. At times, this view contrasts sharply to the modern American culture, which tends to separate religious experience from many other parts of life.

This session is devoted to helping you understand what the evangelical viewpoint is about, and how evangelicals tend to have certain "character traits," such as calmness or seriousness of purpose. This session invites you to consider in a general way how being an evangelical (or not being an evangelical) influences your thinking and behavior.

Questions

1. Starting with the evangelical portrait described in Figure 1.1, which characteristics best describe your own spiritual outlook? Do you feel that being an evangelical makes you "different"? How?
2. What would you add to this portrait?
3. Think of one significant incident from your home life, one from your work life, and one from your church life (or other outside activity). Which area of your life is most closely aligned with the portrait in Chapter 1? Which is the least aligned? Why?
4. If you could explain yourself to people at work who are not evangelicals, what would you want to tell them? What do you think they would want to tell you about their worldview?

Selected Bible Passages: Matt. 22:37-40; Matt. 28:18-20; John 1:12; Eph. 2:8-9; Col. 1:16-17.

Session 2
What the Believers Say about Business

(Chapter 2)

Chapter 2 reviews Max Weber's classic argument that the values of early Protestantism, and especially New England Calvinism, encouraged a habit of mind and daily activities that were especially conducive to early capitalism. These habits included self-discipline, hard work, frugality, delayed gratification, soberness, and the development of rational thinking.

Most important, though worldly consumption was scorned, faith was integrally tied to activity *in this world*. Work was a calling, and was discussed at length by the clergy and laypeople alike. Today the evangelical dialogue has tended to shy away from specific explorations of the meaning of work from a spiritual standpoint. Some evangelicals even seem to feel that someone who is in business cannot be fully faithful to God. The interviewees, however, felt quite differently about this problem, and find it possible to achieve an integration of their faith and their work.

Questions

1. How do earlier descriptions of the Protestant work ethic, such as

those of Max Weber, compare with your own attitudes toward work and leisure?

2. Do you think that your work is an expression of faith? If so, in what way?
3. Is the Protestant ethic good for business? How? (Or how isn't it?)
4. Are there any spiritual or moral pitfalls in this ethic? If so, what are they?
5. What are the opportunities for Christian activity in corporations?
6. When was the last time your clergyperson spoke of a business matter? What did you feel that he or she understood best about the situation? What else would you have liked him or her to consider?

Selected Bible Passages: Eccl. 5:18-19; Matt. 6:25-27; Luke 7:41-43; 2 Thess. 3:6-12.

Session 3
Seven Creative Tensions

(Chapter 3)

Despite stereotypes that suggest that all evangelical businesspeople are sleazebags, the interviewees had many thoughtful comments on their responsibilities. Overall, they tend to adopt a revised, somewhat "softened" approach to capitalism, and their faith plays a strong mediating role in that process.

The interviewees could be described according to three basic types, based on their responses to discussions about work and faith:

1. The *generalist* is never able to move the discussion toward *concrete* examples of how faith makes a difference. He or she never indicates any discomfort with any aspect of business. To the generalist, attitude is everything. The right thing to do from a Christian standpoint is so obvious that the generalist never questions the business actions of a fellow believer. Simply saying you are "Christian" is enough.
2. The *justifier* gives concrete examples, but all of them demonstrate

the perfect fit between profitable activity and Christian values. Faith justifies success, and success justifies faith.

3. The *seeker* is aware of tremendous paradoxes in biblical values, and sees the same paradoxes when he tries to make business decisions. In other words, "reading God's handwriting" through prayer and biblical guidance does not always find an easy fit between common practice in business and the seeker's sense of what is right from an ultimate point of view.

The first two types tend to encourage denial of any struggle over maintaining a Christian attitude and ethics at work. This can invite hypocrisy or insensitivity to wildly unethical behavior. The seeker is more aware of potential conflicts in his choices, but his faith mediates the tension between biblical values and capitalism so that he can discover a creative alternative.

The chapter identifies seven of the most common tensions, and includes Jack's story as an illustration.

Questions

1. Why are businesspeople in general and evangelicals in particular so often accused of being hypocrites? Is there any validity to this charge?
2. Think of a businessperson whom you especially admire. If you were to sketch a portrait of that person's character traits, and ways of doing business, what would stand out? What would happen to your business if you were to adopt the same management philosophy?
3. Are there times that you feel you have resisted God's will for the sake of the business?
4. Jack had a dramatic change of perspective about his approach to the lawsuit after discussing the issue with his prayer group. What do you think happened in this event? Have you had a business problem similar to Jack's? How many of the seven tensions are present in your problem? How might you approach these tensions in a way that is more consistent with your religious faith?
5. Are there groups or activities in your life that would stimulate the same change of perspective?
6. The chapter suggests that there is a tension between business and Christian faith that is a creative force like a bow, with its "backward-stretching harmony." This is a very complex idea.

Discuss your own views of tension. Is it valid? Is it frightening? Is it creative? Does it even exist?

7. Did you illegally photocopy this Study Guide or paraphrase the tensions without any attribution? How would a generalist, a justifier, and a seeker each understand such business behavior in light of the eighth, ninth, and tenth Commandments?

Selected Bible Passages: Lev. 19:11-13; 2 Chron. 15:1-2; Matt. 13:1-23; Matt. 20:1-16; Mark 5:11-12; Phil. 4:12; James 1:5.

Session 4
Tension 1: The Love for God and the Pursuit of Profit
(Chapter 4)

The first creative tension rests on the biblical injunction that you cannot serve two masters. Christians and non-Christians alike are all too familiar with the phenomenon of being "owned by the business." This chapter explores the potential connection between a management career and one's "true self," especially as a Christian.

There are several ways to understand work as it relates to the higher purposes of God. Is it a curse? Is it in harmony with God's order? Is it a sign of redemption? Does a capitalistic system fit well with God's moral order for humankind, or doesn't it?

Whatever this understanding, the evangelical worldview does not tolerate servitude to the growth of the bottom line, and yet every business leader has a responsibility for the ongoing health of the organization. Where, then, does profit fit in? What is the legitimate purpose of business?

The interviewees offer several views that rest on the concept of service and stewardship. They also value other supporting concepts, such as quality.

Case: Study the case that is given in the Preface concerning the printer's contract with the gay performance group. What do you think the printer should have done?

Questions

1. Do you think the church has "looked down" on business? Why? What have been the effects of this attitude?
2. If you could "write your own ticket," what would you want to

accomplish in your career over a lifetime? How does this desire relate to your understanding of what it means to be a Christian?

3. What about your work gives you the strongest sense of pride? What about your work or the comments of the CEOs seems most in harmony with your understanding of Christian values? On the other hand, what about work makes you or your spouse most uneasy?

4. Many people say that work carries the seeds of selfishness and atheism. Do you agree? Why or why not?

5. Frequently, people adopt two personalities: a private religious identity and a career identity. How does this fit with your experience of work?

6. Would you say that your organization shares the same commitments and purposes that you hold? If not, where are the greatest tensions? How would your faith influence your perspective on these tensions?

7. Have each person in the group identify one specific area of business activity that goes against his or her understanding of biblical or ethical responsibilities of business—but one that most people accept as normal business behavior.

8. Do you believe that God offers you a choice between serving him and serving mammon?

Selected Bible Passages: Gen. 2:15-17; Prov. 16:3; Eph. 4:28; Col. 3:22-24; 2 Thess. 3:7-14.

Session 5
Tension 2: Love and the Competitive Drive

(Chapter 5)

Capitalism is traditionally defined in Darwinian terms of competition and survival of the fittest. New Testament commandments to love your neighbor, however, suggest a different approach. As Ken Wessner argued, you can either be oriented on self-interested motives or on love and service to God.

This chapter discusses how the seekers draw on their faith to redefine the parameters of the competitive environment. They report being intensely involved in performance issues and yet having a certain detachment

from the business. An attitude of service also redirects management attention toward the customer rather than toward simply "winning." This in
turn invites participative, collaborative approaches. The term *covenantal ethic*
is used to describe this business philosophy, and its four characteristics are
outlined.

Case: You are the producer of a high-quality baby food, in which all
the main ingredients are "natural." The cost of your ingredients, however,
has skyrocketed, and the business has steadily lost money over the past three
years. Yesterday, your senior vice president approached you with the
suggestion that you slightly modify some of the product formulas to use
cheaper substitute flavorings. He pointed out that none of your competitors
were using all natural ingredients, and reminded you that none of your
plans to improve the manufacturing process could be financed at the
current loss of profits. What will you do?

Questions

1. Is there any room for benevolence in the marketplace?
2. Did Jack Feldballe's story demonstrate how a Christian point of
   view makes a difference? If so, how?
3. In the case above, what values and economic issues did you consider in making your decision? How did these relate to the tension between love and competition?
4. Think of an experience you've had in which your company's approach was discovered to be *potentially* harmful (to customers, employees, the public, the neighborhood, or other businesses). How
   would a covenantal ethic define what needed to be done? What
   would an enlightened self-interest approach argue? What would be at
   stake? How would you expect your faith to mediate this problem?
5. The late Jim Beré wrote down the values that he felt were the
   most important to his management approach, which can be
   found in Chapter 5 along with ServiceMaster's four missions.
   Make a list of the basic values that form your understanding of
   business purpose. Make a second set, a mission statement, for
   your organization. If you already have a mission statement, bring
   it in to share with the group.
6. What are the chief "don'ts" for you in business? What would a
   Christian refuse to do that most businesspeople regard as normal? How have you handled a situation of going against "business as usual"?

Selected Bible Passages: Ezek. 33:31; Matt. 5:38-48; Matt. 22:37-40; Luke 6:31; Luke 3:14.

Session 6
Tension 3: People Needs and Profit Obligations

(Chapter 6)

Of all the ways in which the interviewees described the differences that their faith made at work, the people issues were the most concrete and detailed examples of an integrated faith. Many distinct aspects of employee relations are covered in this chapter, and the seekers' approaches to these issues rest on both relational and practical considerations.

The seekers held several values in common:

- the obligation to provide meaningful jobs
- the dignification of all workers
- a nonhierarchical, participative structure of decision making
- a long-term view of success

None of these values is necessarily in conflict with Christian faith, and it seems that the seekers have extended the concept of Christian stewardship to the stewardship of lives. But other typical events in the corporation put the evangelical's faith in a state of tension with the profit needs of the business. Chief among these are wages, growth, labor negotiations, and the underperforming employee.

Case: Ryan was very disturbed. He had just had a conversation with one of his best salesmen who had hinted that he knew of another salesman who was cheating on expense reports. Apparently, "everybody knew about it," and didn't think there was anything wrong with the practice "as long as it didn't get out of hand." Ryan even got the sense that the employee who had mentioned this activity admired the other salesman for his "creative accounting." "After all," said the first salesman, "everybody knows that it's hard to be in sales. If you can squeeze a little extra for yourself, you perform better in the long run."

Questions

1. Would you agree that treating your employees well is an impor-

tant test of being a good Christian? Is this true for other profes-
sions with which you are acquainted?

2. Is there a national mission for the evangelical to provide meaningful jobs where none exist or where closures have occurred?
3. Does a CEO have the "responsibility of empowerment" toward
   his or her employees? What effect does this have on business performance in your firm?
4. Take a look at the quote at the opening of the chapter. Why
   would this be so? What can you do to improve the attitude of
   other managers toward employees? Employees toward managers?
5. What have you done in your business to help align the needs of
   individual employees with the needs of the team?
6. Write down the things that give you the most joy in your employee relations. Then write down the things that raise the biggest conflict in your heart. What is the source of the difference?
   (Possible discussion topics: the breakdown of dignification, a
   nonegalitarian structure, a downturn in business, various expectations among employees, poor communication, and so on).
   Which of these factors are within your control to change? What
   would your faith tell you to do?
7. In the face of the several conflicts raised in the chapter, the interviewees frequently came up with creative solutions. Pick one
   that particularly spoke to you, and discuss what occurred, and
   how the person's faith mediated this solution.
8. With regard to the case above, what should Ryan do? How valid
   are his employee's claims? How many different responsibilities
   toward employees must he think about?

Selected Bible Passages: Ps. 78:72; Matt. 13:31-32; Matt. 18:21-35;
1 Tim. 5:18; James 5:4; 1 Peter 2:18.

Session 7
Tension 4: Humility and the Ego of Success

(Chapter 7)

In this chapter it seems that the evangelical CEO's attitude toward his
own success and ego needs is a crucial factor in his ability to carry out the
kind of employee relations that he seeks to establish and that many corpo-

rations seek today. His attitude is also the force behind his ability to deal with failure and to take risks. The tension, however, lies in the delicate balance between having a motivational self-confidence and not being deluded about one's own worth.

Christianity expresses a similar paradox in the idea of individual redemption and universal fallenness. The interviewees struggle with this paradox in a variety of ways, and both their prayer lives and fellowship groups play a strong role in that process. Bringing ego into proper perspective causes them to rework the basic definition of business success and managerial responsibility.

Case: Sue had just been offered the job of a lifetime. For the past seven years, ever since the death of her husband, she had been working as a service representative at a computer software firm. She was not very happy with the job: few raises, few benefits, and a lot of headaches.

Today, one of her biggest clients had approached her for a job. They had been so impressed with her recommendations for their business that they wanted her to join their new branch office. Since the job meant moving to the west coast, they had offered Sue a substantial "signing bonus" and promised her a chance to share in the profits as soon as they got past the start-up stage. Even better, Sue would be in charge of twenty other computer systems employees.

Sue was only hesitant about one thing: Her two children would not want to leave their high school friends. She was frank about her feelings, and mentioned them to the client at the time he offered the job. He was very understanding. "Sue," he said, "you have to make this decision for yourself. But let me tell you, you are being wasted at this firm. You are bright, intelligent, and you deserve better things. You've sacrificed a lot to raise your family. Now they should sacrifice for you."

Questions

1. Make a list of what you feel are the biggest contributions to a manager's ego. Have the inducements increased in the past decade? How does a believer become aware of and resist these inducements to pride? (See the chapter for many concrete examples, and discuss the interviewees' solutions.)

2. Read Galatians 6:3-4, quoted in the chapter. Is holding a position that is officially described as being "at the top" inherently sinful?

3. There was great controversy among the interviewees about how closely the business could be related to God's will. How do you

feel about this? Is God the chairman of your board? What does that mean?

4. What is the place of friendship in your life? Do your friends feed an egotistical attitude in you, or do they put your ego into perspective? How?

5. What would you like your fellowship group to accomplish? Can you as a group write out a spiritual manifesto stating these goals? Would any reference to business be appropriate?

6. In what areas are believers most vulnerable to ego in your experience? How do you deal with this problem?

7. Referring to Sue's case above, how would you evaluate her situation? What should she think about? What should be her first step?

Selected Bible Passages: Eccl. 4:9-10; Matt. 5:5; Matt. 20:16, 20-26; Mark 10:13-16; Luke 5:29-32; 1 Tim. 5:8; Heb. 10:24-25.

Session 8
Tension 5: Family and Work

(Chapter 8)

Evangelicalism has placed strong emphasis on family values. How does such an emphasis relate to the many antifamily pressures of the business environment?

The interviewees reported feeling this pressure very strongly. They claimed to have a strong commitment to family, however, and they stated paradoxically that their families were a source of good business performance. This chapter explores these claims and some of the pitfalls that CEOs encounter in trying to serve family needs.

Case: When young David Williams got home that afternoon, he was ecstatic. His soccer team had decided to have a special exhibition game the following week, and David had been picked to give a short speech to the parents about the youth soccer league and its victorious season. He bubbled on about the speech at the dinner table. Suddenly his father said, "Wait a minute. What day did you say that was? Wednesday? I can't go on Wednesday. I have to be in Seattle to give a presentation to a new client. There's no way I can go. Why do these coaches think they can schedule anything they want at the drop of a hat? Last week you had an extra game. This week it's a speech. I can't go to everything."

David was silent. Finally, he looked up at his father angrily. "You're *always* working," he grumbled, and stalked out of the room.

Questions

1. What are the Christian functions of family?
2. In several of the anecdotes in this chapter, other members of the family seemed to be saying, "Act less like a CEO." What would prompt this kind of response?
3. How much time do children need to spend with their fathers? What is the source of your information? Relate your opinion on this topic to the case above. What are the issues for this businessman? For his family?
4. What special gifts do you have that you would want to pass on to your children?
5. Think of a business or career decision you had to make that was profoundly influenced by concerns for your family. How did your faith contribute to the decisions you made? What were the results? What were the business results?
6. What does your company do to promote the ability of employees to live out family values? How does it hinder family values? Are there Christian opportunities here?
7. Many of the interviewees deplore the "free sex" culture of today's corporate society. They see signs of it in many activities of the corporation. Discuss these examples and your own assessment of them.
8. The author had a great deal of trouble probing certain examples of segregation by gender. What is your reading of these examples?
9. Assume for a moment that the evangelical family agenda as generally described (the intact family, the working husband, the nonworking wife whose status as mother and housewife was respected) were to be universally adopted in America. Discuss what would be the consequences on

  - Business
  - Widows with children
  - Wives whose husbands' jobs formerly expected strong involvement of the spouse

- Families with working husbands who earn a below-poverty-level income

What responsibility would the Christian businessperson have in each scenario?

Selected Bible Passages: Gen. 1:27-28; Prov. 20:7; Prov. 22:6; Eccl. 1:3-4; Eph. 6:4; 1 Tim. 5:8.

Session 9
Tension 6: Charity and Wealth

(Chapter 9)

In this chapter the Bible's own ambiguous references to wealth and poverty are reflected in the interviewees' attitudes about their own material wealth and status as CEOs. Once again the seekers tread a fine line on this issue, claiming that wealth is "nothing" and yet holding on to their own financial assets. Lifestyle choices were among the most varied attribute of this group. Attitude turned out to be a key factor in explaining this phenomenon, and many interviewees had thoughtful observations about the meaning of money and status in their lives.

But actions are also important. The CEOs saw charitable contributions in general and the tithe in particular as important responsibilities of the Christian. These contributions, however, pick up the same procapitalistic tendencies as other aspects of the evangelical ethic.

The interviewees tended to favor contributions that served the function of "seed money" either in the development of people's religious well-being or in self-improvement efforts that were expected to lead to economic development down the road.

Such activities are the most direct and concrete example of the interviewees' concern for social issues (after the provision of dignifying jobs). Evangelicals have been sharply criticized for being too lightly involved in the problems of the poor. The data given in Chapter 9 suggest a modified view.

Case: Stan Carter was having lunch with a group of business acquaintances who were members of the same country club. They were bemoaning the recent drop in the U.S. stock market, and joking with each other about having to cut back on expenses—like the club's best lunch on the menu! After sharing a story about his latest deep sea fishing expedition, Stan proposed organizing another weekend jaunt to play golf at a favorite resort in California. As they were discussing his proposal, Stan realized that Paul had not joined in the discussion. Stan started razzing him. "Hey, Paul, don't tell me you're not going with us again? What's the matter? Don't you like our company?

Paul smiled politely and replied, "You fellows go ahead. I'll beat you when you get back here. I just don't like to spend my money that way."

After Paul left, Stan turned to another executive at the table. "That Paul really gets me," he said. "What's wrong with having some fun? I work hard. I support my family and my church. I deserve a little treat for everyone's sake."

Questions

1. Why are some of the interviewees so suspicious of wealth? Are their reservations well founded?
2. In the case above, what do you think of Stan and Paul's reactions? How might Paul or Stan's attitude toward the golf outing affect their businesses? What is an appropriate response to the problems of wealth for a successful manager? Why not just give all the money away and live an ascetically simple life?
3. It was suggested that an upscale lifestyle contributes to a broken relationship with the rest of the human race. Do you believe this to be true? In what ways do you disagree?
4. How does the church understand personal wealth? Is it more Christian to take a vow of poverty?
5. Do you believe that if you have personal monetary success it is a sign of God's approval of your behavior?
6. The opportunities for giving are endless. On what basis do you decide how to distribute your charitable contributions? Do you demand any accountability about what has happened to the money? What would you most like to have happen?
7. How does the evangelical attitude toward charity look from the other side of the fence—that is, from the receivers?
8. What charity do you ask of others? Is it acceptable to coerce employees into contributing to a charitable cause?

Selected Bible Passages: Isa. 55:1-3; Matt. 19:16-22; Luke 11:9-13; Luke 12:13-21; Phil. 2:4; 1 Tim. 6:9-10.

Session 10
Tension 7: Faithful Witness in the Secular City

(Chapter 10)

Tension 7 is the tension that most distinguished the evangelical businessperson, although the problems of integrating personal religion in a pluralistic society are shared by all religious peoples. Here the problem takes on special significance in that evangelicalism demands active witnessing. What does that mean today? What are the potential conflicts between this call of faith and the call of the corporation?

The interviewees were keenly aware of the trade-offs encountered in "getting along" in the business world. They countered these tensions with various strategies, from staying as separate from the secular city as possible, to being a model of Christian behavior prepared to answer questions about their faith. The question of "disguising" religion was raised and explored in depth. It was apparent that most interviewees were concerned both about how overt they should be about their faith, and how to keep from being "contaminated" by the overwhelming cultural forces around them. Prayer groups, an active devotional life, group Bible study, and the activities of faith were all important supports in this effort. Once again the relational aspect of the faith was evident as the interviewees stressed the importance of their peers in this process.

The tendency to turn to peers has led to charges of unfair exclusivity by outsiders. These charges are discussed, and some responses are reported. While no "conspiracy of believers" was discovered, there were no absolutely "right answers" on how best to be a faithful witness or how directly the CEO's religious belief should be allowed to impact the rest of the organization.

Case: Keith was an evangelical who ran a small but successful accounting firm. Early in his career, he had decided that it was not right to try to share his religion with people at work. After a few very disappointing conversations with friends who were not believers, he also extended this rule to friendships.

But today Keith encountered a very strong urge to break his own rule. A senior manager in the firm, named Randy, had blown up at a secretary. Keith invited Randy into his office and asked what the problem was. Randy suddenly broke down. He was in deep despair over his marriage. Many years of working overtime and traveling had taken a toll on him and his wife, and she had told him she wanted a divorce. Randy turned to Keith. "I don't know what to do," he said. "I'm totally at a loss."

As Keith sat there trying to decide what to say, he was moved to talk of his religion, to introduce Randy to Jesus.

Questions

1. List the primary ways in which you carry out your personal witness. Which are the most effective from your personal standpoint?
2. How do you know when it is right to discuss your own religious belief with an employee? In the case above, what should Keith do? What are his intentions? What are the likely results? Are there any ground rules for religious conversations with employees? What is at stake?
3. Many of the interviewees drew the line on making hiring decisions based on religion. Do you believe, if the law were different, that this is absolutely wrong?
4. Do your business decisions or associations favor other believers? Is this ethical?
5. What are the most problematic aspects of the secular business culture for you as a Christian?
6. Do you believe that Christian beliefs can be "secularized" for a corporation? Do you know of any good examples?
7. Evangelicals are sometimes criticized as being exploitative when they talk about Jesus. Why are they criticized, and does it matter? How do you handle this in your own discussions of your faith?

Selected Bible Passages: Ex. 20:9; Deut. 25:13-15; Dan. 6:4; Matt. 10:5-42; Matt. 12:1-8; Luke 8:1; Acts 8:35; Rom. 10:15.

Session 11
Conclusions

(Chapter 11)

In the final chapter of the book, the main points are reviewed and the connection between the evangelical worldview and business success is again suggested. The role of creative tension is also explored again.

The main characteristics of the evangelical CEOs are reiterated, and the author suggests that the traditional Protestant work ethic as described by Weber, though relevant, is not what really distinguishes the new evangelical elite in business. Rather, their uniqueness as managers lies in their relational and holistic biases. These are particularly well suited for new calls for learning organizations and management flexibility. They are also well suited for creating a view of management that better integrates the demands of faith with economic responsibilities.

Some questions remain that the book cannot answer. Will the comfort of the interviewees with the business world "corrupt" them in their faith? Will they be co-opted by the system? Part of the answer lies in how well they maintain what amounts to a "different" set of values. This marginality may also partly explain their business success. So "being different" is both a religious and an economic must, rather than the handicap that it is normally assumed to be by outsiders.

Questions

1. How does being a Christian make you different from many of your business associates?
2. How does it make your business different?
3. Do you think that being a Christian has had economic advantages or disadvantages for you?
4. Does the metaphor of the bow make sense to you? Why or why not?
5. Are there other polarities, or tensions, between faith and business that have not been identified in the book? How would the generalist, justifier, and seeker each interpret these tensions?
6. What are the greatest challenges ahead for doing God's will on earth in the area of business leadership?
7. What are the greatest dangers to evangelicalism?
8. What is the one best thing evangelicalism could contribute to the business system as we know it today?

Selected Bible Passages: Job 5:8; Ps. 111; Ps. 118; Matt. 5:43-48; Acts 26:22; 2 Cor. 5:17, 26:22.

Notes

Acknowledgments

1. Peter L. Berger, *A Far Glory: The Quest for Faith in an Age of Incredulity* (New York: Free Press, 1992).

Preface

1. Terry Mattingly, "Prayer Gets Its Own Perspective," Scripps Howard News Service, 1990.
2. Laura L. Nash, "The Johnson & Johnson Credo," in *Corporate Ethics: A Prime Business Asset* (New York: The Business Roundtable, 1988).
3. Garry Wills, *Under God: Religion and American Politics* (New York: Simon and Schuster, 1990).

Chapter 1

1. William James, *The Varieties of Religious Experience: A Study in Human Nature* (New York: Collier Books, 1961), 267.
2. Robert Scheer, "Jimmy, We Hardly Know Y'All," reprinted in *Thinking Tuna Fish, Talking Death* (New York: Hill and Wang, 1988), 224.
3. George Gallup Jr. and Jim Castelli, *The People's Religion: American Faith in the 90's* (New York: Macmillan, 1989), 93. Fifty-seven percent of Baptists describe themselves as "born again," as compared to 14 percent of Episcopalians.
4. Ibid., 17.
5. James Davison Hunter, *Evangelicalism: The Coming Generation* (Chicago: University of Chicago Press, 1987).
6. Figures are compiled from successive volumes of *Yearbook of American and Canadian Churches* (Nashville: Abingdon Press). For a list of books on evangelical identity, see Graig M. Gay, *With Liberty and Justice for Whom? The Recent Evangelical Debate over Capitalism* (Grand Rapids: William B. Eerdmans, 1991), 8, n. 10.
7. "Religion in America," The Graduate School and University Center of the City University of New York, survey published April 1991.
   For the purposes of this study, I have concentrated on conservative Protestant evangelicalism, although some would make the case for including Catholic charismatics and evangelical Jews in the group. Three are in fact included among the interviewees. For the distinction between Catholic Charismatics and Protestant evangelicalism, see David Martin, *Tongues of Fire: The Explosion of Protestantism in Latin America* (Oxford: Basil Blackwell, 1990), 290-91.
8. Ibid., 2.
9. See George Marsden, ed., *Evangelicalism and Modern America* (Grand Rapids: Wm. B. Eerdmans, 1984), viii-x.
10. See, for example, the excellent discussion of today's Protestant work ethic in James Hunter, *Evangelicalism: The Coming Generation,* Chapter 3, 50-75.
11. Martin Marty, *Pilgrims in Their Own Land: 500 Years of Religion in America* (New York: Penguin Books, 1984), 173-74.
12. Daniel J. Boorstin, *The Americans: The Democratic Experience* (New York: Vintage Books, 1974), 560.
13. I am indebted to Gordon Redding for the phrase "seriousness about the tasks," which was

applied by Herman Kahn to the people of China. See S. Gordon Redding, *The Spirit of Chinese Capitalism* (New York: Walter de Gruyter, 1990), 69.

Chapter 2

1.   See, for example, Daniel Yankelovich, *New Rules: Searching for Self-Fulfillment in a World Turned Upside Down* (New York: Bantam Books, 1981), 5-6.
2.   Max Weber, *The Protestant Ethic and the Spirit of Capitalism,* trans. Talcott Parsons (London: Unwin Paperbacks, 1930), 44.
3.   Ibid., 54, 71.
4.   Ibid., 51.
5.   H. L. Mencken, "Sententiae," *The Vintage Mencken* (New York: Vintage Books, 1956).
6.   Simon Schama, *The Embarrassment of Riches: An Interpretation of Dutch Culture in the Golden Age* (New York: Alfred A. Knopf, 1987), for example, p. 335: "It is important to understand that so far from his [a Dutch businessman's] religion accommodating his business, it generated a great deal of moral discomfort. That discomfort was only made more tolerable by acts of conspicuous expenditure on both pious and personal objects."
7.   Hunter, *Evangelicalism,* 51.
8.   Marty, *Pilgrims in Their Own Land,* 387.
9.   Peter L. Berger, *The Sacred Canopy* (New York: Doubleday, 1969), 133.
10. Marsden, *Evangelicalism and Modern America.*
11. Ibid., 100.
12. Robert K. Greenleaf, *Servant Leadership: A Journey into the Nature of Legitimate Power and Greatness* (New York: Paulist Press, 1977), 249-90. Since this study began, several evangelical books have appeared that tackle the problems of business in greater detail. Among these are Doug Sherman and William Hendrick's *Your Work Matters to God* (Colorado Springs: NavPress, 1987) and the Navigators' new series *Christians in the Marketplace: Biblical Principles and Business: The Foundations,* ed. Richard C. Chewning (Colorado Springs: NavPress, 1989). These works are referred to in other chapters.
13. James Baker III, speaking at the National Prayer Breakfast, Washington, D.C., 11 February 1990.
14. Charles Colson, *Against the Night: Living in the New Dark Ages* (Ann Arbor: Vine Books, 1989), 9, 11.
15. Elmer W. Johnson, "Fiduciary Ethics and the Market," lecture, University of Chicago Graduate Schools of Business and Divinity, 25-26 October 1977.

Chapter 3

1.   Heraclitus, DK B51,80.
2.   This choice of topics sharply contrasts with other survey data about ethical issues. See, for example, Ron Berenbein and Laura L. Nash, "Current Practices in Corporate Ethics," Survey for The Conference Board, Spring 1991. The top three topics that executives addressed in their own ethics codes were respectively the use of proprietary information, purchasing practices, and environmental responsibility.
3.   "Reinventing the CEO," Korn/Ferry International and Columbia University Graduate School of Business (New York: Korn/Ferry, 1989), 42-43.
4.   Ibid., 42.
5.   There were, naturally, a few notable exceptions. Elmer Johnson, former executive vice president of General Motors and partner at Kirkland & Ellis, has written and spoken extensively on the larger moral issues posed in a capitalistic system. See, for example, his privately published papers: "Co-Creation and the Middle Way for Corporate Capitalism: The Problem of Bureaucracy," University of Notre Dame, 3-5 May 1982; "Shaping Our Economic Future," San Francisco, 11 December 1985; "Management and Labor: Breaking Away," DePaul University, Chicago, Spring 1988; "Ethics in Military-Industrial Contracting," for the United States Air Force Academy, John M. Oilin Lecture Series in National Security and Defense Studies, 8 November 1989; and "Corporate Leadership and Personal Values," Laity Lodge Leadership Forum, Bermuda, March 1990.
6.   Berger, *The Sacred Canopy,* 134.

Chapter 4

1. Dorothy L. Sayers, *Essays Presented to Charles Williams* (Salem, NH: Ayer Company Publishers, 1947).
2. J. Philip Wogaman, "Christian Faith and Personal Holiness," in *Biblical Principles and Business: The Foundations,* ed. Richard C. Chewning (Colorado Springs: NavPress, 1989), 47.
3. Myron Rush, *Lord of the Marketplace* (Wheaton: Victor Books, 1986), 26.
4. Johnson, "Corporate Leadership and Personal Values," address, Laity Lodge Leadership Forum, Bermuda, 31 March 1990.
5. Robert E. Slocum, *Ordinary Christians in a High-Tech World* (Waco: Word Books, 1986), 166ff.
6. Brian Griffiths, *The Creation of Wealth: A Christian's Case for Capitalism* (Downers Grove: InterVarsity Press, 1984), 68.
7. Slocum, *Ordinary Christians in a High-Tech World,* 168.
8. Doug Sherman and William Hendricks, *Your Work Matters to God* (Colorado Springs: NavPress, 1987), 14.
9. Robert Bellah, et al., *Habits of the Heart: Individualism and Commitment in American Life* (New York: Harper & Row, 1985), 67-69.
10. Ibid.
11. Wogaman, "Christian Faith and Personal Holiness," 47-48.
12. Ibid.
13. I am grateful to Michael Maccoby for the reference. See *Why Work: Motivating and Leading the New Generation* (New York: Touchstone, 1988), 75.
14. Note that this is a generalized, composite view of the group's approach. Individual CEOs differed in how often they explicitly referred to the Bible and in how literally they interpreted it. I will comment on specific theological disagreements, such as the appropriateness of debt financing, only where interviewees themselves explicitly disagreed. Because this is not primarily about theological interpretations of biblical authority and there were only a few fundamentalists in the group, I have omitted references to certain fundamentalist controversies such as the degree to which Old Testament law is relevant today.
15. For more information on the essential prescriptive role of the Old Testament in business behavior, see, for example, Walter C. Kaiser Jr., "A Single Biblical Ethic in Business," in *Biblical Principles and Business,* ed. Richard C. Chewning (Colorado Springs: NavPress, 1989), 84ff.
16. We can see a similar emphasis on quality in businesses headed by evangelical (but not necessarily Protestant) CEOs not interviewed: Eckerd's Drugstores, Wal-Mart, Potlatch Corporation, Weyerhauser, J.C. Penney, and others.

Chapter 5

1. Adam Smith, *The Wealth of Nations* (New York: Alfred A. Knopf, 1991).
2. Thomas Jefferson, *Writings,* ed. Merrill D. Peterson (New York: Library of America, 1984), 1121.
3. Amitai Etzioni, *The Moral Dimension: Toward a New Economics* (New York: The Free Press, 1988).
4. See also Laura L. Nash, *Good Intentions Aside: A Manager's Guide to Ethical Problem-Solving* (Boston: Harvard Business School Press, 1991), Chapters 3 and 4.
5. Max DePree, *Leadership Is an Art,* 13.
6. Ibid., 7.
7. Ibid., 11.
8. James L. Heskett, "Lessons from the Service Sector," *Harvard Business Review* (March-April 1987), 123ff.
9. William J. Broad, "The Patriot's Success: Because of 'Star Wars' or in Spite of It?" *The New York Times,* 10 February 1991, E5.
10. Lois Therrien, "Raytheon May Find Itself on the Defensive," Business Week (26 May 1986), 74.
11. For a very explicit discussion of this view, see George Marsden, "Evangelicals, History, and Modernity," in *Evangelicals and Modern America,* 94-102.

12.   Jack Eckerd and Charles Paul Conn, *Eckerd: Finding the Right Prescription* (Old Tappan: Revell, 1987), 189, as told by Chuck Colson.

13.   Adapted from Nash, *Good Intentions,* 60, 92.

Chapter 6

1.   Quoted in Studs Terkel, *Working* (New York: Ballantine, 1972), 262.

2.   F. J. Rothlisberger, *Man-in-Organization* (Cambridge: The Belknap Press, 1968), 122ff.

3.   William Rentschler, "The Impact of Ethics and Technology on Work: A Management Perspective," inaugural address, GTE Lectureship Series, DePaul University, Chicago, 2 December 1986.

4.   Max De Pree, *Leadership Is an Art* (New York: Doubleday, 1989), 51.

5.   Peter Senge, *The Fifth Discipline: The Art & Practice of the Learning Organization* (New York: Doubleday, 1990), 235.

6.   Peter Drucker, *Concept of the Corporation* (New York: New American Library, 1983), 252f.

7.   Rosabeth Moss Kanter, *The Change Masters: Innovation & Entrepreneurship in the American Corporation* (New York: Simon and Schuster, 1983).

8.   Michael Schrage, "Questions Remain about GE amidst Leadership Tour de Force," *The Boston Globe* (Los Angeles Times Syndicate), 9 March 1992.

9.   See Burton M. Leiser, "The Rabbinic Tradition and Corporate Morality," in *The Judeo-Christian Vision and the Modern Corporation,* eds. Oliver Williams and John Houck (Notre Dame: 1982), 151-53.

10.   Ibid., 153.

11.   John Snyder, private publication of mission statement.

12.   Joseph Blasi and Douglas Cruse, *The New Owners: A Market Analysis* (Rutgers: Rutgers University, 1991).

13.   For example, 1992 estimates of wealth distribution in the United States generally put 47 percent of the wealth in the top one-fifth of the population, while the bottom one-fifth command only 3.9 percent of the nation's wealth.

Chapter 7

1.   Donald J. Trump with Tony Schwartz, *Trump: The Art of the Deal* (New York: Random House, 1987), 15.

2.   E. R. Dodds, *Pagan and Christian in an Age of Anxiety* (Cambridge: Cambridge University Press, 1965), 134.

3.   Charles M. Kelly, *The Destructive Achiever: Power and Ethics in the American Corporation* (Reading: Addison-Wesley, 1988), is a well-researched study of how corporate cultures inspire behavior that is often insanely financially dysfunctional in order to cater to the demands of pride and ambition in exchange for power. It is only one example of a whole industry of corporate folktales about the draw of money and power in the 1980s.

4.   Connie Bruck, *The Predators' Ball* (New York: Penguin, 1988), 95.

5.   Douglas Coupland, *Generation X: Tales for an Accelerated Culture* (New York: St. Martin's Press, 1991).

6.   Berger, *The Sacred Canopy,* 153.

7.   Allan C. Emery, *A Turtle on a Fencepost* (Waco: Word Books, 1979), 14.

8.   Patrick Morley, *The Man in the Mirror: Solving the 24 Problems Men Face* (Brentwood: Wolgemuth & Hyatt, 1989), 194.

9.   Fred Smith, *You and Your Network* (Waco: Word Books, 1984), 154.

10.   Robert S. Weiss, *Staying the Course; The Emotional and Social Lives of Men Who Do Well at Work* (New York: The Free Press, 1990), 195-96.

11.   William H. Whyte, *The Organization Man* (New York: Simon and Schuster, 1956), 330ff.

Chapter 8

1.   Weiss, *Staying the Course,* 261.

2.   Hunter, *Evangelicalism,* 76.

3.   Ibid.

4.   Gallup, *The Unchurched American: 10 Years Later* (Princeton: The Princeton Religion Research Center, Princeton, 1988), 5.
5.   By one estimate, 90 percent of religious books are purchased by women.
6.   Zig Ziglar, *Top Performance* (Old Tappan: Revell, 1986), 277.
7.   Ibid.
8.   Ibid., 273.
9.   Ibid.
10. Weiss, *Staying the Course,* 262.
11. Antoine Prost, *Riddle of Identity in Modern Times* (Cambridge: Belknap Press of Harvard University, 1991).
12. Morley, *The Man in the Mirror,* 92.
13. Daniel Yankelovich, *New Rules* (New York: Bantam Books, 1982), 98-103.
14. Hunter, *Evangelicalism,* 92.
15. Ibid., 108.
16. I am told that Billy Graham made the decision early in his career to never be alone with a woman, in order to avoid being misinterpreted.
17. Morley, *The Man in the Mirror,* 101.
18. Barbara Dafoe Whitehead, "The Family in an Unfriendly Culture," *Family Affairs* 3, 1-2 (Spring-Summer 1990), 5.

Chapter 9

1.   Brian Griffiths, *The Creation of Wealth* (Downers Grove: InterVarsity Press, 1984), 61.
2.   Graef S. Crystal, "The Great CEO Pay Sweepstakes," *Fortune,* 18 June 1990, 94.
3.   Griffiths, *The Creation of Wealth,* 61.
4.   Clayton Brown, "Beyond the Bottom Line," *Action* (May/June 1988), 5.
5.   Johnson, "A Statement of Faith," Wheaton, June 1974.
6.   Marty, *Pilgrims in Their Own Land.*
7.   Charles Colson, *Against the Night: Living in the New Dark Ages* (Ann Arbor: Servant Publications, 1989), 187-191.
8.   Sherman and Hendricks, *Your Work Matters to God,* 92.

Chapter 10

1.   Berger, *The Sacred Canopy,* 135.
2.   Wills, *Under God,* 380-81.
3.   As a representative example, see the current version of the Johnson & Johnson Credo, an extremely admired document with high ethical commitments. In 1979 then-chairman James Burke, himself a devout Roman Catholic, decided that the phrase "with God's grace" should be deleted from the Credo on the grounds that it was offensive to some employees. Needless to say, the decision was extremely controversial, especially among the senior generation of officers and board members.
4.   George Marsden, *Fundamentalism and American Culture* (Oxford: Oxford University Press, 1980), 4.
5.   Dietrich Bonhoeffer, *Prisoner for God* (New York: Macmillan, 1959), 123.
6.   Smith, *You and Your Network.*
7.   Slocum, *Ordinary Christians in a High-Tech World,* 150-151.
8.   Ibid.
9.   Thomas J. Peters and Robert H. Waterman, Jr., *In Search of Excellence: Lessons from America's Best-Run Companies* (New York: Harper & Row, 1982).

Chapter 11

1.   John William Ward, "Benjamin Franklin: The Making of an American Character," in *Benjamin Franklin: A Collection of Critical Essays,* ed. Brian Barbour (Englewood Cliffs: Prentice-Hall, 1979), 61.
2.   Weber, *The Protestant Ethic and the Spirit of Capitalism,* 70: "Any relationship between religious beliefs and conduct is generally absent, and where any exists, at least in Germany, it tends to be of the negative sort. The people filled with the spirit of capitalism today tend

to be indifferent, if not hostile, to the church. See also Peter Berger, *The Sacred Canopy,* 109ff, in which Berger suggests that the modern economic process itself carries the seeds of secularization.

3.   Peter M. Senge, *The Fifth Discipline: The Art & Practice of the Learning Organization* (New York: Doubleday, 1990), 172.

4.   David Martin, *Tongues of Fire: The Explosion of Protestantism in Latin America* (London: Basil Blackwell, 1990), see especially Chapters 10 and 11.

5.   Survey, Center for Ethics, Responsibilities, and Values, College of St. Catherine, St. Paul, Minn.

6.   Slocum, *Ordinary Christians in a High-Tech World,* 154.